The Soul Also Keeps the Score

A Trauma-Informed Companion to the Spiritual Exercises of St. Ignatius

Robert W. McChesney, SJ

LITURGICAL PRESS
Collegeville, Minnesota

litpress.org

Imprimi Potest: Very Rev. Joseph M. O'Keefe, SJ, Provincial

Library of Congress Cataloging-in-Publication Data

Names: McChesney, Robert W., SJ, author.
Title: The soul also keeps the score : a trauma-informed companion to the spiritual exercises of St. Ignatius / Robert W. McChesney, SJ.
Description: Collegeville, Minnesota : Liturgical Press, [2025] | Includes bibliographical references. | Summary: "In this work, McChesney interprets the classic sixteenth-century mystical text of the Spiritual Exercises as born in violence to the body and soul of their author, the traumatized, battle-wounded-turned-saint, Ignatius of Loyola. McChesney insists that the two languages of mental health and spirituality can speak in one voice"— Provided by publisher.
Identifiers: LCCN 2024057471 (print) | LCCN 2024057472 (ebook) | ISBN 9780814689752 (trade paperback) | ISBN 9780814689769 (epub) | ISBN 9798400801990 (pdf)
Subjects: LCSH: Ignatius, of Loyola, Saint, 1491-1556. Exercitia spiritualia—Criticism, interpretation, etc. | Spiritual exercises. | Spiritual healing. | Psychic trauma—Religious aspects—Catholic Church.
Classification: LCC BX2179.L8 M298 2025 (print) | LCC BX2179.L8 (ebook) | DDC 234/.131—dc23/eng/20250203
LC record available at https://lccn.loc.gov/2024057471
LC ebook record available at https://lccn.loc.gov/2024057472

"There has been an explosion of quality research and best clinical and pastoral practices in better understanding diverse trauma experiences and how spirituality can contribute to hope and healing. Fr. McChesney provides an important contribution to this extremely important and timely topic."

—Thomas G. Plante, PhD, ABPP, professor of psychology, Santa Clara University

"Here Fr. McChesney has crafted a sturdy and engaging vessel, navigating the turbulent waters among disciplines in the service of that most Ignatian of goals: to help souls."

—Christine Marie Eberle, author of *Finding God Along the Way: Wisdom from the Ignatian Camino for Life at Home*

"*The Soul Also Keeps the Score* is must-reading for spiritual directors and pastoral ministers today, given contemporary understandings of trauma and its varied expressions. Fr. McChesney helps caregivers understand the experience of trauma survivors and offers wise counsel on how to contribute to their healing of mind, body, and spirit."

—Fr. Kevin O'Brien, SJ, vice provost and executive director, Fairfield Bellarmine, and author of *The Ignatian Adventure: Experiencing the Spiritual Exercises of Saint Ignatius in Daily Life*

"McChesney's *The Soul Also Keeps the Score* presents trauma as an experience that impacts the entire human being, emphasizing that a 'soul wound' affects all aspects of a person—physical, psychological, neural, moral, and spiritual. This text is a valuable resource for clinicians, spiritual directors, or anyone who accompanies individuals who have experienced trauma in recognizing God's presence and love for them, resulting in profound spiritual healing that cannot be obtained from traditional trauma-informed treatment alone."

—Kristin Austin, LCSW-C, CCTP, secretary for safeguarding, Jesuit Conference of Canada and the US

"Drawing upon a rich knowledge of the spirituality of healing, psychology's understanding of posttraumatic growth, and the amazing life of Ignatius of Loyola, Robert McChesney in *The Soul Also Keeps the Score* teaches us that darkness need not be the final word in life."

—Robert J. Wicks, PsyD, professor emeritus, Loyola University Maryland

"As a trauma counselor who seeks to integrate effective psychological treatment with healthy Christian spirituality in an ethical manner, I found this book to be a multidimensional gem, a rich source of wisdom, trauma-informed education, and practical guidance."

—Gerry Ken Crete, PhD, LPC, LMFT, founder, Transfiguration Counseling and Coaching; co-founder, Souls and Hearts; and author of *Litanies of the Heart: Relieving Post-Traumatic Stress and Calming Anxiety through Healing Our Parts*

"Fr. Rob McChesney's work is revealing, instructive, and immensely important. Regrettably, the number of people displaced by force from the safety of their homes by conflict or disaster, and whose cultures are savaged, increases daily. Trauma unfortunately abounds. Fr. Rob writes from extended field experience in counselling survivors, enhanced by deep research. In this groundbreaking work he generously shares his wisdom and insight."

—Mark Raper, SJ, former international director, Jesuit Refugee Service

"Fr. McChesney's book is a vivid and well-researched illustration of applied spirituality in the context of today's world. He shows how St. Ignatius of Loyola as a survivor of violence and its traumatic impact, and Ignatian spirituality with roots in that experience, can be connected to our age of trauma and new research in various fields to provide profound and effective spiritual care resources."

—Rev. Dr. Michael O'Sullivan, SJ, executive director, Spirituality Institute for Research and Education, Ireland, and past president (2023–2024), International Society for the Study of Christian Spirituality

"As an adult survivor of childhood sexual abuse who has sought healing through psychological care as well as spiritual direction, and as a Catholic theologian whose research focuses on the redemptive meaning of suffering, I am grateful for what Father Robert W. McChesney, SJ, has accomplished with this book. This book will help psychological practitioners to appreciate the role of faith in healing so they may employ approaches that work with, rather than against, patients' understanding of the divine."

—Dawn Eden Goldstein, JCL, STD, author of *Father Ed: The Story of Bill W.'s Spiritual Sponsor*

For Mary

a beautiful wildflower, eternally in bloom

and Fred

I couldn't have done it without you, bro

and my Jesuit family

ditto, brothers

and the urban refugees in Amman
as well as the hospitable people of Jordan who welcome them

you remain an inspiration

O Lord, you deceived me,
  and I allowed myself to be deceived.
You were too powerful for me,
  and you have prevailed.
All day long I am an object of ridicule;
  everyone mocks me.
Whenever I speak, I must cry out;
  my message is violence and destruction.
For the word of the Lord has caused me to endure
  reproach and derision all day long.
If I say, "I will not mention him
  or speak any longer in his name,"
within me I experience a fire burning in my heart
  and imprisoned in my bones.
I am weary holding it in,
  and I can no longer do so.

Jeremiah 20:7-9 (New Catholic Bible)

I have found that violence is strangely capable of returning my characters to reality and preparing them to accept their moment of grace.

Flannery O'Connor, *Mystery and Manners*

Contents

Foreword *by Lisa López Levers* xi

Prologue: Two Languages, One Voice xv

Part I: The Soul of Violence

Chapter One: Every Saint Has a Past: The Chivalrous Courtier 3

Just Another Loyola Boy 8

This King or That 12

Manresa Episode 16

The Forgotten Warrior by Colonel Robert Macpherson, USMC (Ret.) 20

Chapter Two: The Morally Injured Íñigo 23

Follow the Symptoms 31

Situating Moral Injury in Recent Literature 35

A Dark Hole in My Soul: Helen's Testimony 39

Chapter Three: Every Sinner Has a Future 43

A Spiritual Model of Moral Injury 45

The Case Study of Tola 46

Moral Injury and Sin 48

A Trauma-Informed Christian Spiritual Paradigm of Moral Injury? 51

Chapter Four: The Spiritually Injured Íñigo 53

Spiritual Injury 55

The Clinical Value of Spiritual Injury: A Case Study 62

Chapter Five: The Soul Also Keeps the Score 65

The Odd Couple 66

The Soul Keeps the Score 69

Has Psychology Lost Its Soul? 73

The Oskar Pfister Award and Lecture 75

Interdisciplinary Advances 78

Personal Encounter with the Living God 83

Part II: From Spiritual Injuries to Spiritual Exercises

Chapter Six: Consoling the Afflicted with Spiritual Exercises 89

The Pilgrim 91

A Person of Interest 93

Judicial Investigations 95

A Spirituality of Affliction 100

Chapter Seven: The Invisible Mugged Traveler: Encountering God as Hero or Casualty 109

"The Good Samaritan" Parable, Reconsidered 110

EverySurvivor 116

Íñigo's "Cannonball Moment," Reconsidered 119

Pamplona, Reconsidered 123

Chapter Eight: Noticing Hibakusha: A Trauma-Informed Reading of the *Incarnation Contemplation* 127

Spirituality for an Age of Trauma 129

The *Incarnation Contemplation* 130

Interdisciplinary Dialogue and Collaboration 140

Proximity to Ground Zero 144

Chapter Nine: Memory, Understanding, and Will: A Trauma-Informed Reading of the Ignatian *Suscipe* 145

Ignatius of Loyola Meets Judith Lewis Herman 147

Herman's Stage One: Overcoming Powerlessness of Will through Personal Safety and Security 148

Herman's Stage Two: Remembrance and Mourning 152

Maggie's Story 158

Herman's Stage Three: Reconciling with Oneself, Reconnecting with the Wider Community, and Exploring a Survivor Mission 160

Back to the Future 167

Epilogue: Body and Soul Keep the Score 169

Acknowledgments 173

Bibliography 175

Foreword

I was asked to speak at a national trauma symposium a couple of years ago. The invitation made sense, because I have been providing trauma counseling for over fifty years and teaching graduate trauma courses for about three decades; my trauma counseling textbook has been widely used in courses and by practitioners. After agreeing to speak, I learned that the title of the symposium was "Soul Trauma: Personal, Interpersonal, Communal." Soul trauma was conceptually new for me, and I found it intriguing, immediately recalling a number of clients, from my past clinical years, whose horrific experiences most likely would have qualified as soul trauma. Then I learned that I would be co-keynoting, both on the first evening of the symposium and the next morning, with Jesuit Father Robert W. McChesney. Full disclosure: I found this a little intimidating! All those memories of 1950/60s Catholic school immediately came cascading back into my consciousness. I wondered how I might find common cause, to speak in a way that would connect with what a man of faith, a priest no less, might say about trauma.

I decided to face my dilemma straight on, so I contacted Father McChesney right away and asked if we might schedule a Zoom meeting, well ahead of the symposium. I was hoping that we could become acquainted and begin to coordinate our keynotes. I was relieved to find that Father McChesney, who quickly became Father Rob, was down-to-earth and accessible. As he began to share his experience of accompanying those who had been traumatized and to unpack the extent of his field experience, much of it framed by St. Ignatius's *Spiritual Exercises*, I quickly discerned that we had traveled some parallel pathways on our journeys to becoming helpers. He has led retreats that follow the *Spiritual Exercises*, enabling guides and careseekers to assist others who have experienced trauma or to find healing themselves, just as I have taught masters- and doctoral-level counseling students about trauma and how to assist clients with their trauma recovery. Probably of greatest importance, I learned right away that he has *listened* to the survivors who sought his consolation. He has been on the ground for over thirty years, accompanying survivors, *listening* to their range of trauma responses, and helping them to feel safe and build resilience. During my earliest years of providing trauma counseling, in the mid-1970s, before posttraumatic stress disorder (PTSD) was even officially recognized as a diagnosis and before much appeared in the professional literature about trauma, I learned about the soul-gripping effects of trauma by *listening* to my clients' trauma stories. Remarkably, our paths were even parallel regarding our work within Indigenous cultures and with their healers, Father Rob's in the Middle East and my own throughout sub-Saharan African countries. We met by Zoom several more times and were able to choreograph mutually supportive and connected keynotes for the symposium, which were well received by the sponsors and those in attendance.

Those preparatory Zooms and keynotes sparked a rich professional collaboration surrounding issues related to trauma and recovery. Father Rob invited me to continue meeting regularly, by Zoom, to discuss trauma aspects of the book that he was writing about St. Ignatius and his spirituality. I was happy to engage and intellectually curious, but I worried that I did not know anything about the saint other than that he had founded the Jesuits, the Society of Jesus. I had no idea how much I was about to learn, and thus embarked on a journey that has deeply enriched my fuller understandings of trauma. The notion of soul trauma and its related construct of spiritual injury add multidimensional and nuanced contours to our more quotidian perspectives of psychosocial trauma.

As a Jesuit of fifty years, the author is supremely qualified to write this book, aimed at both guides and careseekers in pursuit of spiritually integrated trauma recovery strategies. The author has created a remarkable literary mosaic that illuminates the life of Ignatius of Loyola, or Íñigo, the saint's given Spanish name. Born at the end of the fifteenth century, he was, in many ways, the quintessential sixteenth-century hero-of-the-day: a rake and a swashbuckler, he was an intractable medieval paladin who took his passions into battle and was ultimately severely injured in combat. Recovering from the trauma of a cannonball to the knee, Íñigo also was simultaneously recovering from the trauma of moral and spiritual injuries imposed by lifestyle, by the insinuations of a cultural and era-driven zeitgeist. But in so many ways, his remarkable story also serves as a telling narrative for the twenty-first century; it is an exemplar for survivors who experience complex trauma, tap into their inner resilience, and are able to transcend the worst effects of trauma.

The author has constructed an intriguing interdisciplinary narrative, simultaneously weaving a tapestry of history, prose, and trauma instruction. The lived experience of Íñigo, from courtier to survivor, from behavioral excess to transcendence, serves both as a powerful metaphor and an astute lesson. The author reminds us how, in many ways, people may experience trauma like the facets of a prism; some sides show survivors of injury and mourning stuck in the shadows, while other sides pick up the sunlight of recovery and refract the resilience into gorgeous bursts of colors. Íñigo's life illuminates every aspect of trauma and recovery, from the shadows to the colors. The author is able to present this absorbing account because he is literate about the effects of trauma and is particularly knowledgeable about the adverse repercussions of soul injury. He adroitly brings together the two languages of mental health practice and spiritual endeavor into the single voice of assisting the whole person.

In *The Soul Also Keeps the Score*, the author proposes fresh, trauma-informed insights into the life of the sixteenth-century saint. More importantly, he reads the latter's *Spiritual Exercises*—born in violence—as viable healing wisdom for twenty-first-century survivors in search of soul repair. For any reader who is one of them or who is a mental health practitioner or a spiritual guide, this book is a thought-provoking read about trauma and the quest for psychospiritual resilience. As a trauma specialist of fifty years, I heartily recommend this book. It helps us to understand, in the most visceral ways, that while the body surely keeps the score, so too does the soul.

Lisa López Levers, PhD, LPCC-S, LPC, CRC, NCC
Professor Emerita (Counseling and Human Development)
Scholar in Residence (Center for Global Health Ethics)
Rev. Francis Philben, CSSp Endowed Chair in African Studies (2012–2017)
Fulbright Scholar (University of Botswana, 2003–2004)
Duquesne University

Immediate Past-President, 2024–2025
International Association for Resilience and Trauma Counseling (IARTC)

Prologue

Two Languages, One Voice

"It's very normal to leave reality to survive," said psychologist Jan Ilhan Kizilhan. "But if it becomes too frequent, it can be pathological. If you have to leave reality, the body will survive, but the soul will not." In a *New York Times Magazine* cover story,[1] Dr. Kizilhan was referring to Midya, a Yazidi girl kidnapped in 2014 by the Islamic State of Iraq and Syria from her ancestral home in Kurdistan, northern Iraq. Just five years old, she was considered a prize. Under ISIS' reign of terror, Yazidi women over forty reportedly sold for $42, but a girl under nine could fetch $173.

Fortunately, three years later Midya was rescued and returned to a Yazidi refugee camp in Kurdistan, near the border with Turkey. There she began meeting with Dr. Kizilhan, who diagnosed her with posttraumatic stress disorder (PTSD). He reported that Midya, then eight, used to faint twenty times per day. "Just to survive, she had to leave our real world," Kizilhan told a visiting reporter.

The body will survive but the soul will not. The comment haunted me. I had accompanied war refugees, military veterans, and survivors of sexual violence and child abuse—body and soul—for more than thirty years. While serving in Amman, Jordan, with the Jesuit Refugee Service, an international nongovernmental organization, I had worked with survivors from the Yazidi Community, including girls Midya's age, and visited their Kurdistan camps. I was disturbed by her experience and puzzled by the psychologist's reference to Midya's soul. What did he mean by claiming

1. Jennifer Percy, "How Does the Human Soul Survive Atrocity?," *New York Times Magazine,* November 3, 2019.

that it would not survive? I had no answers, but, as a Catholic priest, I *had* become hooked on exploring the interconnected survival of body and soul in the wake of physical violence and the related, critical intersection between mental health and spirituality in the healing of trauma.

In March of 2020, the COVID lockdown caught me on a home furlough for a family wedding in the United States, and I was unable to return to the Middle East. Unsurprisingly, the distressing refugee stories I'd absorbed abroad accompanied me home. Recurring nightmares soon drove me to seek professional help and to review the latest mental health literature. Fortunately, I had access to a university library and dove in, learning about secondary and vicarious trauma as well as other recent constructs.

In Lisa López Levers's comprehensive *Trauma Counseling*, I learned that the term "trauma" refers to "any experience that overwhelms a person's ability to cope *and* often is combined with a sense of helplessness, fear, and horror at what has happened." Levers adds that " 'Trauma,' in some ways, is defined by the one experiencing it."[2] Being in a motor vehicle accident, for example, may leave one passenger traumatized, but not another. Witnessing an innocent child's death in a school shooting may leave one classmate traumatized, but not another. A difficult event is only potentially traumatizing, according to the individual experiencing it. " 'Trauma,' then, is an overarching concept, and refers to any event that is negative, overwhelming, and has significant implications for a person's future."[3]

A survivor of incest whom I've long accompanied, with diagnosis of PTSD, recommended *The Body Keeps the Score*, a *New York Times* bestseller of four-plus years by trauma psychiatrist Bessel van der Kolk.[4] Here I found an eye-opening account of neuroscience's ability to map the human brain, and have made the book a go-to reference. The citations included in these pages reflect my esteem for this landmark text; its contributions to trauma studies and body-based therapies are inestimable.

2. Lisa López Levers, *Trauma Counseling: Theories and Interventions for Managing Trauma, Stress, Crisis, and Disaster*, 2nd ed. (New York: Springer Publishing, 2023), 429–30.

3. Levers, *Trauma Counseling*, 430.

4. Bessel van der Kolk, *The Body Keeps the Score: Brain, Mind, and Body in the Healing of Trauma* (New York: Viking, 2014).

In my research, I discovered that an increasing minority of mental health professionals and trauma counselors now acknowledge that religious belief and spiritual practice play an integral psychic role in trauma recovery. This was encouraging in light of a 2023 Pew Study. "Spirituality among Americans" noted that "83% of all U.S. adults believe people have a soul or spirit in addition to their physical body."[5] In a related vein, "70% of U.S. adults can be considered 'spiritual' in some way, because they think of themselves as spiritual people or say spirituality is very important in their lives."

None of this surprised me. Years of solidarity with those afflicted by violence had taught me that spiritually integrated trauma therapies are in demand by survivors—but also, unhappily, that mental health professionals, including most trauma counselors and social workers, generally lack the requisite training and soul-intervention skills sought by religious and spiritual careseekers.[6] It is a serious limitation, often an impediment, in the holistic healing of trauma for this demographic.

In my research, I frequently encountered the concept of "trauma-informed care," which suggests that *all* care systems—including spiritual and pastoral care—have a responsibility for identifying and responding to trauma. I learned that a diagnosis of PTSD always equals trauma, but trauma does not always equal PTSD. The relatively recent construct of "moral injury," in particular, caught my attention, because it is widely linked with spirituality. It describes a form of trauma and associated treatment, different from PTSD, that welcomes religious and spiritual assistance. Body *and* soul, mental health *and* spirituality: two languages, one voice in trauma recovery. It's time to put Humpty Dumpty together again.

I am a Jesuit priest, one of fourteen thousand members of the Society of Jesus worldwide. We are a Catholic religious community of men founded in 1540 by St. Ignatius of Loyola. The pages ahead will introduce Íñigo (his baptized name) as a morally injured, swashbuckling product of late

5. Pew Research Center, "Spirituality among Americans," December 7, 2023, https://www.pewresearch.org/religion/2023/12/07/spirituality-among-americans/.

6. The word "careseeker" is not found in most dictionaries and is typically spelled as two words: "care seeker." However, "careseeker" is regularly employed in health-care settings as a single word.

medieval European chivalry. After suffering a severe battle wound inflicted by state-of-the-art French artillery, he eventually developed traumatic symptoms that tempted him to suicide. A survivor of violence himself, he found healing of body and soul through God's mercy and translated his ordeal into the *Spiritual Exercises*. Published in 1548 and still widely practiced, this influential Christian text offers a track to personal, healing encounter with God. Like the North Star, it has guided me for fifty years.

The Ignatian Exercises are a proven, sixteenth-century pathway, accessible today, as then, to disciplined practitioners accompanied by a competent guide. In truth, they are as astonishing in their sophisticated discernment of the inner spiritual landscape as recent research that maps the impact of trauma on the brain and body. Intuitively, I recognized the latent potential of this classic resource to absorb and translate insights from recent trauma-informed literature and clinical practice. This in turn could leverage fresh insights and tools for persons of faith or God-seekers, Christian or otherwise, whose souls or spirits have been wounded by the distress of violence—endured, witnessed, or perpetrated.

However, the original Latin and Spanish texts of the Exercises, in even the best English translation,[7] read like Egyptian hieroglyphics. Without specialized preparation and guidance, the period language renders them maddeningly opaque to uninitiated modern seekers. Could key insights and meditations be reinterpreted contextually for a traumatized twenty-first-century survivor of violence? What about someone progressing through posttraumatic growth who is vicariously unsettled by the distressing events portrayed on social media or the nightly news? *The Soul Also Keeps the Score: A Trauma-Informed Companion to the Spiritual Exercises of St. Ignatius* examines these questions and invites the motivated reader to come along. The book is a selective *companion* to the Exercises themselves, not a substitute. Those without interest in the basics of Ignatian spirituality may find their attention stretched.

7. There are many editions available, a fair number inferior. Two are particularly recommended. *The Spiritual Exercises of Saint Ignatius: A Translation and Commentary* (henceforth, *SpEx*), by George E. Ganss (St. Louis: Institute of Jesuit Sources, 1992), is the most authoritative. Some may prefer to begin with David L. Fleming's popular gateway to the Exercises, *Draw Me into Your Friendship: A Literal Translation and a Contemporary Reading of the Spiritual Exercises*, 2nd ed. (Chestnut Hill, MA: Institute of Jesuit Sources, 1996). For those encountering the Exercises for the first time, Fleming's book may be the best starting point.

This terrain is not well traveled. Nevertheless, while accompanying countless survivors over the years, I had discovered that the Ignatian heritage offers various helpful applications in the treatment of trauma. Some are analogous to accepted mental health practices, including several recommended by van der Kolk. The time seemed right for a basic primer of select interdisciplinary insights and methods that could promote psychospiritual healing at the intersection of mental health and spirituality, as well as catalyze further discourse, debate, and collaboration. Groundbreaking neurobiological advances could now be complemented by examining trauma's fingerprints on the soul and spirit.

This book can be read in two ways. Most will prefer to limit themselves to the text itself. For pastors or pastoral associates, spiritual directors or companions, pastoral counselors or chaplains, it can make a timely addition to their professional libraries and toolkits. A thoughtful reading can deepen their understanding of trauma and introduce them to fresh healing insights and practices. Since chapters 2 through 4 are more theoretical, such readers may prefer to bypass their construction of an interdisciplinary trauma scaffold.

Other readers will appreciate the many foundational footnote citations and choose to dig deeper into the peer- and evidence-based research. (The fact is that because of its omnipresence in pop culture, the word "trauma" today can mean almost anything—or nothing.) Certified caregivers and academics, including faculty in seminaries, universities, and spiritual or pastoral leadership programs, may appreciate this more scholarly component.

Part 1, "The Soul of Violence," constructs an interdisciplinary, trauma-informed framework from Ignatius of Loyola's vivid early narrative, grounding accessible moral and spiritual injury trauma theory in his distressing experience, symptoms, and sins. Those who perpetrate, endure, or witness violence are wounded of *soul*—understood in the traditional Christian sense as a unifying principle inclusive of body, emotions, mind, brain, and spirit. This large population, finally, finds a welcome in spirituality.

Chapter 1, "Every Saint Has a Past: The Chivalrous Courtier," chronicles swashbuckling Íñigo in an unvarnished sketch drawn from his documented clan heritage and recent research on late medieval chivalric culture. For *both*, physical violence was a characteristic linchpin. Íñigo's severe battle wound to his leg in 1521 required holistic healing. To his nearly fatal dismay, he discovered that interior wounds could kill as easily as a live battlefield. Ignatian spirituality is born in violence perpetrated, suffered, and witnessed. Many readers today, including those who feel shell-shocked by the cruelty and crassness of the twenty-first century, may discover through Íñigo an unexpected pathway to God.

Chapter 2, "The Morally Injured Íñigo," depicts the chivalrous courtier as a survivor of moral injury trauma, understood as a severe violation of one's conscience and moral code.[8] The overlap between its symptoms and the Ignatian spiritual heritage is striking. The chapter reviews the construct of moral injury in recent professional literature.

Chapter 3, "Every Sinner Has a Future," confronts the twentieth-century distortion of spirituality by certain perspectives of Western psychology. For example, the three Abrahamic traditions, comprising billions of devotees, all rely on the category of sin. Yet many psychologists routinely dismiss it. A case study of holistic healing from violence-based trauma is presented, in which the two languages of mental health and spirituality successfully collaborate.

Chapter 4, "The Spiritually Injured Íñigo," introduces the concept of spiritual injury, understood as rupture of one's relationship with God. A significant research study on Australian military veterans is presented to highlight similarities and differences between moral and spiritual injury, illustrated by Íñigo's experience of battle and trauma recovery. This marks a shift in focus from the healing of psychological symptoms to *encounter with Divinity*. A case study of the clinical value of spiritual injury is highlighted.

Chapter 5, "The Soul Also Keeps the Score," situates "soul" within the Western Christian heritage as the principle of unity that integrates the various components of the one human person. A *soul* wound, therefore, comprises not only physical, psychological, neural, moral, or spiritual aspects of the human person, but *all of those in one*. Until recently, psychology was at risk of losing its soul—while swallowing those of religion

8. This chapter is an expanded, sharpened version of my October 2022 article in *The Way*, titled "The Morally Injured Íñigo de Loyola: New Insights for Ignatian Spiritual and Pastoral Care," *The Way* 61, no. 4 (October 2022): 51–68. Used by permission of *The Way*, www.theway.org.uk.

and spirituality as well. Two successful programs of spiritually integrated therapeutic care are highlighted.

Part 2, "From Spiritual Injury to Spiritual Exercises," aims to situate distressed casualties of violence closer to the center of Christian consciousness. In the beloved New Testament parable of the Good Samaritan, the spotlight here is trained on the battered crime victim left at roadside by violent perpetrators. Íñigo's tense confrontation with sixteenth-century heresy hunters is colorfully depicted through archival, first-person testimony. Select Ignatian spiritual exercises, insights, and practices are presented in counterpoint with critical trauma recovery principles.

Chapter 6, "Consoling the Afflicted with Spiritual Exercises," picks up Íñigo's lively narrative, featuring his 1527 confrontation with the Spanish Inquisition in Alcalá, Spain. One witness testified that Íñigo taught her how to pray with the "three faculties of the soul"—memory, intellect, and will. Íñigo's reliance on traditional Christian devotion surely helped to persuade the suspicious inquisitors of his orthodoxy. The significance of these three human characteristics, moreover, offers twenty-first-century interdisciplinary cues for trauma recovery.

Chapter 7, "The Invisible Mugged Traveler: Encountering God as Hero or Casualty," offers a close reading of the parable of the Good Samaritan. Jesus's original story (later adapted by the evangelist Luke) is more aptly titled "The Battered Traveler." Van der Kolk notes that the majority of Americans, or their loved ones, will experience a violent crime during their lifetimes. Violence may leave scars on the body, rewire neural pathways, cause severe psychological trauma, threaten a believer's relationship with God or the church—or all of the above.[9]

Chapter 8, "Noticing Hibakusha: A Trauma-Informed Reading of the *Incarnation Contemplation*," introduces a second violence-scarred Jesuit, Pedro Arrupe. His presence near Hiroshima's Ground Zero on August 6, 1945, transformed him into a "*hibakusha*"— an "explosion-affected person," as the Japanese called survivors of the atomic bomb. Today's *hibakusha* can benefit from a trauma-informed reading of the pivotal *Incarnation Contemplation* prayer from the Exercises, contextually tailored for survivors of violence- and race-based spiritual injury. The chapter

9. This chapter is an expanded, sharpened version of my January 2025 article, with the same title, "The Invisible Mugged Traveler: Encountering God as Hero or Casualty." *The Way* 64, no. 1 (January 2025). Used by permission of *The Way*, www.theway.org.uk.

features healing practices shared by van der Kolk and Ignatius, each according to his discipline.[10]

Chapter 9, "Memory, Understanding, and Will: A Trauma-Informed Reading of the Ignatian *Suscipe*," details the potentially curative counterpoint between the climax prayer of the Exercises and psychiatrist Judith Lewis Herman's seminal three stages of recovery from trauma.[11] The *Suscipe* offers a lifelong methodology of prayerful encounter with God. But the evil of trauma can *inhibit* or *erase* memory, *paralyze* the will's freedom and agency, and *obscure* the intellect's capacity for understanding and meaning. Concrete practices for trauma-informed spiritual and pastoral care are explored, yielding sustainable interdisciplinary guidance for both caregivers and careseekers.

A brief epilogue, "Body and Soul Keep the Score," brings the presentation full circle. The Christian spiritual tradition over recent centuries has understood prayer, largely, as silent, interior verbal communication of the mind, heart, and soul with God. But this has obscured another, essential part of the heritage—prayer as body language, posture, gesture, location, facial expression, and breath. Van der Kolk's emphasis on somatic healing modalities is a wake-up call to reclaim the physical dimension of spirituality as one more interdisciplinary option for recovery. Body *and* soul. Mental health *and* spirituality. Two languages, one voice.

On a topic of such sensitivity, I am aware of four reasons that may cause prospective readers to turn away. Most obviously, traumatized careseekers will rightfully ask if I have walked in their shoes. The answer is no—surely a legitimate conversation-stopper. I recall someone in my care circle, only recently, struggling with adverse childhood experiences, traumatic adolescent events, addiction, and, late in life, major depressive disorder. All my efforts to reach out and engage my loved one were respectfully—if decidedly—rebuffed. Subsequently, at a bittersweet memorial service after he took his life, I learned that during his final years he considered

10. This chapter is an expanded, sharpened version of my October 2023 article, with the same title, "Noticing *Hibakusha*: A Trauma-Informed Reading of the Incarnation Contemplation," in *The Way* 62, no. 4 (October 2023): 49–61. Used by permission of *The Way*, www.theway.org.uk.

11. Judith Herman, *Trauma and Recovery: The Aftermath of Violence—from Domestic Abuse to Political Terror* (New York: Basic Books, 1992).

Tom Petty's song "You Don't Know What It's Like to be Me" something of a personal anthem. I was not the only one present that evening to be heartbroken by the soloist's anguished rendition. I realized with regret that I had not, in fact, known what it was like to be him. My earnest desire to *fix* my friend, rather than simply to walk with and love him, had become a barrier. *Trauma Caregiving 101* lesson learned.

Second, the fact that I wear a "Roman collar" when in uniform may make some wary. Understood. Let me assure prospective readers that I have no interest in religious proselytization, only universal human flourishing. As a young Jesuit, I accompanied Guatemalan refugees in southern Mexico. There, I learned that the Spanish word "*cura*" is used for "pastor" or "priest," and that the corresponding verb "*curar*" means "to heal" or "to care for." That is my only aim. I seek to convince others of nothing, but instead to seed a wider conversation. Those raised in Roman Catholic or Protestant Christian traditions, practicing or otherwise, will find themselves welcome here. So, too, may many Jews, Muslims, and Buddhists—indeed anyone for whom the "Jesus story" is attractive despite doubt or disbelief in his divinity.

The Soul Also Keeps the Score is for persons of denominational belief, those who consider themselves active seekers of Divinity or a Higher Power, those who identify as spiritual but not religious, and those who claim no religious affiliation—sometimes designated as "nones." (Note that nones are not necessarily atheist; many say they believe in God or some sort of "universal spirit," and a significant percentage consider themselves religious.)[12] Nones—or, better, "somes" —are as welcome here as "believers" and "seekers."

Third, there is no question, today, that many women find it difficult to get past the sixteenth century patriarchal chauvinism of vocabulary and imagery in the Exercises. Ignatius's androcentric language and military metaphors can be jarring to contemporary sensibilities. Fortunately, there are well-regarded companion texts to the official *Spiritual Exercises*, authored by women, that do justice to their unique experiences and context.[13]

12. Ryan Burge, *The Nones: Where They Came From, Who They Are, and Where They Are Going*, 2nd ed. (Minneapolis: Fortress Press, 2023).

13. An excellent resource is Elizabeth Liebert and Annemarie Paulin-Campbell, *The Spiritual Exercises Reclaimed: Uncovering Liberating Possibilities for Women*, 2nd ed. (New York/Mahwah, NJ: Paulist Press, 2022).

Finally, some may be worried about stumbling across a minefield of triggers in the traumatic events mentioned here. Let me say a bit more about what to expect. In addition to briefer references, three extended first-person accounts are incorporated strategically alongside or within select chapters, examples of the "testimonial literature of witness." Survivors of trauma are proffered the dignity to speak for themselves, in their own name or anonymously, as they prefer. The compelling accounts speak an earthy, vernacular language from painful experience, and are a mirror through which readers may recognize themselves. For psychiatrist Herman, the trauma story becoming testimony constitutes an essential part of the recovery process.

But—always—prudence is recommended. Certain accounts may be triggering. Some survivors of violence, in particular, may prefer to skip the three testimonies in the shaded sections. Others may decide to read the book from the safe place of dialogue with a trusted counselor, friend, or medical professional. Readers should maintain whatever level of control they require. However, the " 'not telling' of the story" is not an option, since that would serve "as a perpetuation of its tyranny."[14] The question is when and to whom, not if. If you are a careseeker, consider the book an invitation and safe opportunity to begin.

Those wondering, still, if this book is for you, can ponder the appeal of the following verses attributed to the poet Rumi.[15] A mystic from the Sufi tradition, he has been widely translated, remains in print, and is cherished by seekers the world over.

14. Ukrainian-born Israeli American Holocaust survivor Dori Laub (1937–2018), a longtime clinical professor in Yale University's Department of Psychiatry and specialist in the area of testimony methodology; Dori Laub, "Truth and Testimony: The Process and the Struggle," *Trauma: Explorations in Memory*, ed. Cathy Caruth (Baltimore: Johns Hopkins University Press, 1995), 61–75.

15. Rumi was a thirteenth-century Islamic theologian and sage. Though the precise source is unclear, the poem reflects Rumi's broader teachings on love, pain, and suffering.

I said: what about my eyes?
He said: Keep them on the road.
I said: What about my passion?
He said: Keep it burning.
I said: What about my heart? He said: Tell me what you hold inside it.
I said: Pain and sorrow?
He said: Stay with it. The wound is the place where the Light enters you.

PART I

The Soul of Violence

"Until the age of twenty-six, he was a man given to the vanities of the world. What he enjoyed most was the exercise of arms, having a great and foolish desire to win fame.

"And when he was in a fortress that the French were attacking, all were of the view that they should surrender in order to save their lives, for they saw clearly that they could not offer resistance. But he gave so many reasons to the commander, that he actually persuaded him to resist, even though it was contrary to the opinion of all the officers, who nevertheless drew courage from his spirit and determination.

"When the day came on which they expected the bombardment, he confessed to one of those companions in arms. After the bombardment had lasted a good while, a shot struck him on one leg, shattering it completely. And because the cannon ball passed between both legs, the other one was badly injured."[1]

1. Ignatius of Loyola, *A Pilgrim's Testament: The Memoirs of Saint Ignatius of Loyola*, ed. Barton T. Geger (Chestnut Hill, MA: Institute of Jesuit Sources of Boston College, 2020), no. 1. Henceforth, *Auto.*

1

Every Saint Has a Past

The Chivalrous Courtier

Íñigo (EE-nyee-goh, hard "g") López de Oñaz y Loyola[1] (1491–1556) was a *swashbuckler* right out of late medieval Castilian central casting: a "swaggering swordsman, soldier, or adventurer; daredevil."[2] The result, seemingly inevitable in sixteenth-century Spain, was a severe wound—in his case, a blast to the leg inflicted by a French cannonball at the 1521 battle of Pamplona. Nearly fatal psychological and spiritual meltdown soon followed. Military veterans of active battlefields today, indeed any of life's scarred "adventurers," would do well to take note of this singular man. "Every saint has a past, and every sinner a future," observed playwright Oscar Wilde.[3] St. Ignatius of Loyola has a doozy of a backstory, reflective of the period violence, gender roles, and sexual mores of chivalric chauvinism. History's enduring fascination with the man surely reflects a Jekyll and Hyde narrative with which so many flawed human beings today can identify.

1. His baptized name at birth. Following the practice of biographer José Ignacio Tellechea Idígoras, I shall refer to the future saint during the first part of his life by this name. He would not Latinize his name to "Ignatius" until sometime after his dust-up with the Spanish Inquisition in 1526–27, by which time he was well into his thirties. Thus, name references roughly correspond to his biographical timeline and actual period usage. José Ignacio Tellechea Idígoras, *Ignatius of Loyola: The Pilgrim Saint*, trans. Cornelius Michael Buckley (Chicago: Loyola University Press, 1994).

2. *Collins* Online Dictionary (www.collinsdictionary.com/us).

3. Oscar Wilde, *A Woman of No Importance* (London: Methuen, 1894).

Though the saint would go on to found the Society of Jesus (Jesuits) in 1540, sinner Íñigo's eventful early years are a fascinating, illuminated window onto the ambivalence of European chivalry. The best chronicle is his own *Autobiography*.[4] Commentators on the period reference "the gap between chivalry's high ideals of the heroic life and the reality of knightly action in which 'violence [was] carried out on any scale possible to achieve any end desired.' "[5] Monastic chronicles and other historical sources expressed concern for the violent public disorder, envisioning *reform* of chivalric ideals as the solution. The conundrum, however, was that "the chivalric knight himself was the principal source of such disorder."[6] Viewing this Catholic minor nobleman within the contradictions of Castilian chivalry offers a notably fresh perspective onto the hero of Pamplona. "The Christian faith and a chivalrous sense of honor were the most precious possession of the family."[7]

Miguel de Cervantes published his literary masterpiece, *Don Quixote,* just fifty years after Ignatius's death in 1556. The fictional title character and Íñigo were cut from the same cloth, men of conscience and kindred spirits enamored of novels of chivalry. Both admired the Iberian classic *Amadis of Gaul*, a romance from the early fourteenth century. Both lived defiantly, with vain grandiosity, as if "what the world most needed was knights errant."[8] Cue Íñigo. Like Don Quixote, both hidalgos represented old-fashioned ideals such as rank, nobility of character, presentation, and achievement of glory through gallantry and bloody conquest.

Certain period interpreters speculate, improbably, that Cervantes wrote *Don Quixote* as a parody of Ignatius's earlier *Autobiography*. In

4. Ignatius of Loyola, *A Pilgrim's Testament: The Memoirs of Saint Ignatius of Loyola*, ed. Barton T. Geger (Chestnut Hill, MA: Institute of Jesuit Sources of Boston College, 2020), 4. Henceforth, *Auto.* The original manuscript had no title and is commonly referenced in English as Ignatius's "Autobiography." But "testament" or "memoirs" are both accepted titles.

5. Patricia DeMarco, review of *Chivalry and Violence in Medieval Europe*, by Richard W. Kaeuper, *Studies in the Age of Chaucer* 23 (2001): 561–63. In the citation within the broader reference, DeMarco cites Kaeuper's volume, 22.

6. DeMarco, review.

7. Paul Dudon, *St. Ignatius of Loyola*, trans. William J. Young (Milwaukee: Bruce Publishing, 1949), 18.

8. Miguel de Cervantes, *Don Quixote,* trans. with intro. and notes by John Rutherford (London: Penguin Classics, 2000), part 1, chap. 7, p. 61.

this view, the fictional hero of the brilliant farce becomes "Don Quixote de Loyola." Parallels of character, language, and the motif of chivalric ambivalence in both accounts are striking. To appreciate the milieu in which young Íñigo was shaped, one can hardly do better than to read Cervantes's masterpiece.

Though the mature Ignatius had long outgrown earthy, risk-taking frivolity, to imagine the young Jesuit founder as "Don Íñigo de Quixote" is not a lengthy stretch. In fact, it was the very code of chivalry that underlay his so-called religious "conversion." Medieval European historian Samuel Claussen notes that "violence was the linch-pin of chivalry."[9] Like a page out of Cervantes, only his bloody combat experience, even if in a losing cause, could get the swashbuckler's attention and redirect his life toward service of a heavenly Madonna and divine King.

According to the limited evidence, the chivalrous courtier enjoyed the occasional romance and bedding of women. After all, this was part and parcel of the lifestyle, and only served to increase the honor due him. A confidante of Ignatius, his secretary Polanco, was blunt: "Rather was he much addicted to gambling and dissolute in his dealings with women, contentious and keen about using his sword."[10] Another close Jesuit friend, Diego Lainez, was inclined to downplay Íñigo's personal accountability in favor of the reigning chivalric mores, asserting that his behavior was "because of bad customs."[11] But one of Spain's premier Renaissance historians, the late Father José Ignacio Tellechea Idígoras (1928–2008), a specialist in Spain's golden age and sixteenth-century Castilian church history and vocabulary, reads period sources to propose that Íñigo's exploits should be understood as "deliberate moral bankruptcy."[12] Every saint has a past.

In the end, there are serious limits to historical knowledge surrounding Íñigo, with the abundance of sources only exceeded by their fragmentary, divergent, even contradictory strands. Foundational events in the life of Ignatius and the Society of Jesus he founded five hundred years ago "are filtered through the memories and biases of a small number of individuals;

9. Samuel A. Claussen, *Chivalry and Violence in Late Medieval Castile* (Suffolk, England: Boydell & Brewer, 2020), 28. It is a point which Cervantes's fictional hero, in farcical manner, reinforces.

10. James Brodrick, *Saint Ignatius Loyola: The Pilgrim Years 1491–1538* (New York: Farrar, Straus and Cudahy, 1956), 45, citing Polanco.

11. Tellechea Idígoras, *Ignatius of Loyola*, 113, citing Diego Lainez.

12. Tellechea Idígoras, 112–13.

and this filtering cannot but reflect those individuals' concerns and agenda . . . there is an inevitable gap between these documents and the events they record—a gap for which we must allow in our reading."[13]

Chapter 1, therefore, is an exploratory meditation of informed speculative history,[14] grounded in the Ignatian tradition and subject to further interpretive, scholarly correction. The task includes available historical data, but it also explores, more fluidly and intuitively, the *contemporary resonance* of the man. For example, Ignatius himself sometimes recounted his moral transgressions publicly, in great detail, because he thought it might help other sinners to aspire to sainthood. This same constructive procedure can yield valuable insights, and spiritual growth, for sinners today.

Contemporaries of Íñigo would have been amused at the suggestion he would mature into a devout priest and mystic. He hailed from one of the twenty-four principal families of the province of Guipúzcoa in the Basque region. From age sixteen he led the good life of an *hidalgo*, a well-dressed gentleman of the minor nobility who enjoyed courtier's privileges in the household of the royal treasurer of the Kingdom of Castile. Íñigo surely learned mannerly relations with women during these years, verging on Madonna worshipful. Described as handsome and long-haired, the young man matured into a dashing and fashionable presence around the halls of power, enhanced by a dynamic temperament and charismatic leadership capacities.

By day, the elegant gentleman gracefully negotiated the dance of chaste courtly love or refined his swordplay skills. Both pursuits accentuated his chivalrous gallantry. Íñigo was evidently a proficient duelist, a period martial skill required to conquer an opponent, enhance his reputation, and, if needed, restore impugned honor. If such valor occasionally rewarded

13. Philip Endean, "Who Do You Say Ignatius Is? Jesuit Fundamentalism and Beyond," *Studies in the Spirituality of Jesuits*, 19, no. 5 (November 1987): 22.

14. Frank Palmeri, "In Praise of Speculative History," *Chronicle of Higher Education*, July 10, 2016. "Resistance to conjectural history comes from positivists and scientistic thinkers, who enshrine facts as truths. Darwin, who wrote a classic conjectural history in *The Descent of Man* (1871), understood that a theory is necessary and prior to the marshaling of facts. . . . [A]s the philosopher of science Thomas Kuhn and others have pointed out, a theory or paradigm cannot be disproved by a particular empirical finding; it can only be superseded by another theory that provides a stronger framework for understanding."

him with the nocturnal favors of a desirable lady of the court, personal and clan honor were well served. Íñigo was a natural in his world, a "man's man." Today, many women scarred by male manipulation or violence find the narrative of young Íñigo to be offensive. Ignatius, of course, was not the only saint to overcome a deplorable past. He was God's work in progress. Those who can delay throwing the first stone at an adulterous sinner, as enjoined by Jesus, may be surprised by, perhaps even drawn to, the turn Íñigo's story takes.

An underlying challenge in late medieval Castilian culture was to negotiate the uncertain tightrope walk of honor. A false step might be viewed as shameful for the individual and his clan. Wartime opponents, for example, should be allowed to surrender, and should be held safely, pending payment of a ransom. The captive, on his or her part, had a duty to cooperate respectfully with his jailers. The code of conduct was loose and the tightrope sometimes slippery, but Íñigo was deft. Well-schooled at home and court, he grasped readily that *both* bloody conquests *and* shrewdly managed amorous exploits were part of one chivalric package.

"[M]asculine honor in an honor society," notes Claussen, can be achieved "through a fistfight, through renewed vigor on the battlefield, or the sexual conquest of a woman."[15] In the age of conquistadores, "conquest" may be the operative term. On a fraught journey to manhood, virility could be established by one signature claim such as Íñigo's heroic performance at Pamplona. "Indeed, it is nearly a trope in chivalric literature and history that great heroes begin their adult lives only once they have fought (and preferably won) in battle."[16]

Today, of course, the psychological *costs* of violence perpetrated, suffered, witnessed, or shirked are much better understood. A medical diagnosis of PTSD is available, for example, with related treatment options. For far too many, violence leaves interior scars on the conscience, for example shame, guilt, or recurring nightmares, sometimes more destructive than any physical wound or existential event. For Íñigo, too, there would be a subsequent price to pay, a terrifying episode that precipitated suicidal ideation as an escape from its relentless symptoms. Fortunately for contemporary survivors of violence, out of that crucible Íñigo lived

15. Claussen, *Chivalry and Violence*, 177.

16. Claussen, 177.

to devise a healing pathway to God that offered peace of heart. Those who wonder if their very souls have been wounded by violation of their value systems can find in this man—if they are prepared to go deeper—a kindred spirit, fellow survivor, and spiritual psychologist extraordinaire.

Just Another Loyola Boy

The maternal family name "Loyola" is often explained as a derivation of the Spanish "Lobo-y-olla," meaning "wolf and kettle." That is surely a valid *Castilian* interpretation, given the image of a pair of wolves flanking and feeding at a cooking pot between them. In medieval heraldry, the wolf is often a symbol of nobility and courage. The image is carved in stone on the face of the family castle and serves as the emblem on the family shield of the Oñaz-Loyola family. It suggests a valiant, hospitable clan that prides itself on its generosity.

Tellechea Idígoras, himself Basque, explains *Loyola* less valiantly. He claims that it means "bog."[17] The name is of *Basque*, not Castilian, origin. Loyola is the Castilianized form of "Loiola," a habitational name associated with Guipúzcoa and Biscay provinces in the Basque country. *Loiola* (sometimes rendered "Loiolakoa") means something like "from a place of mud," or "from a muddy place." It is formed from the Basque *loi* ("mud") + the locative suffix *-ola* ("place of"), indicating location.[18]

There is no question that the reputational legacy of the House of Loyola was both courageous *and* sullied, itself reflecting the ambivalence of chivalry. The archives of the province of Navarre include a 1309 entry denouncing the clan as "abominable robbers, who in one of their many forays made off with 600 porkers from the Larraun Valley."[19] Other accounts are more chilling. The House is described as responsible for all sorts of violence, including assassinations and arson of inhabited homes in pursuit of plunder. According to one biographer, "fathering bastards

17. Tellechea Idígoras, *Ignatius of Loyola*, 6. The author is wary of Spaniards snatching away Íñigo's Basque identity and heritage.

18. *Dictionary of American Family Names*, ed. Patrick Hanks (New York: Oxford University Press, 2003).

19. Mary Purcell, *St. Ignatius Loyola: The First Jesuit* (Chicago: Loyola University Press, 1981), 4.

was a family pastime."[20] There was a macho swagger about the males of the House. If the clan had grown less ruthless by the time of his birth in 1491, Íñigo surely inherited the same DNA.

Any tendency to modern judgment, of course, must be tempered by period perspective. Wanton destruction of property and life, for many clans, would have been celebrated by the regnant ideology that "valorize[d] violent assertiveness as the mark of chivalrous identity."[21] To *modern* Christian eyes, such behavior marks the Loyola clan as sinners, transgressors of the fifth and sixth commandments that forbid murder and lust, respectively. However, from a *period* gaze, the view could be one of honor and prestige. Even ecclesial efforts at reform were half-hearted, demonstrating the prevailing ambivalence. The "clerical ideology of reform" was marked by "both hostile condemnation of the 'evils inherent in the knightly life' and legitimating praise of chivalric ideals."[22]

Guipúzcoa was located in the Basque region of northern Spain along the Pyrenees border with France. Íñigo's clan members were prominent landowners of the lesser nobility. "According to a local historian of the sixteenth century, Guipúzcoa means 'to terrify the enemy,' as though one should say, 'We will tear you to pieces!' "[23] The period lore surrounding the region's males is unsparing—they were belligerent and ferocious, unyielding as iron.

An anarchic, bellicose strain runs through Basque history well into the present day. From 1959 to 2018, for example, a despised separatist movement known as the ETA (Euskadi Ta Askatasuna, meaning "Basque Homeland and Liberty"), murdered close to a thousand victims and wounded many more, relying on terrorism in their failed campaign for a Basque homeland independent of Madrid. To this day, family members of ETA's victims are known to spit venomously at the very mention of the Basque region because of its association with the terrorist organization.

Such was the heritage into which Íñigo de Loyola, the youngest of thirteen, was born. He stood barely five feet and two inches tall. His seven older brothers evidently took the regional and clan reputation to heart—all but

20. Tellechea Idígoras, *Ignatius of Loyola*, 50.
21. DeMarco, review.
22. DeMarco, review, citing Kaeuper, 75.
23. Dudon, *Saint Ignatius of Loyola*, 13.

one became conquistadores overseas or men-at-arms in Spain. The other chose priesthood in the family's hometown of Azpeitia. Íñigo had but passing interest in matters religious, and instead viewed himself in the chivalric lineage of the pugnacious Loyola boys. With so many older brothers to claim the family inheritance, there was never much doubt he would have to fight his way forward in life. "Until his 26th year he was a man given to worldly vanities," he recalled in his *Memoirs*. "What he enjoyed most was the exercise of arms, having a great and foolish desire to win fame."[24]

Because time, hagiography, and pious devotion have lightened Ignatius's darker underside and obscured his immersion in chivalric contradiction, one must demythologize the tradition to notice more dispassionately his violent temperament and acknowledge there would have been victims. Today, a "boys will be boys" perspective is unacceptable, disrespectful of the women and men he liked to dominate. A sampler of citations from his contemporaries and modern biographers is unsparing. None of this is new, but it sets the stage for fresh, overdue reconsideration of the collateral damage the cocky courtier would have left in his wake.

Citations documenting the unrepentant young Loyola man include:

- "With my own eyes I saw Íñigo one day in Pamplona, when a file of men who were going along the street collided with him, flinging him against the wall. He drew sword and chased them the length of the street where, if it were not for those who held him back, he would either have killed some of them or they him."[25]
- Archival documentation describes a violent feud Íñigo had with another courtier, Francisco de Oyo, apparently over the affections of a young lady. De Oyo had previously wounded Íñigo and threatened to kill him. Uncharacteristically unnerved, Íñigo had begged royal permission to legally bear arms and hire two bodyguards. Once again leveraging royal access, he received clearance to bear arms for one year, renewable, as well as to hire one professional bodyguard.[26]

24. *Auto.*, no. 1.

25. Purcell, *St. Ignatius Loyola*, 27. Account of family member of the Duke of Najera (later bishop of Salamanca).

26. Tellechea Idígoras, *Ignatius of Loyola*, 85–86; W. W. Meissner, *Ignatius of Loyola: The Psychology of A Saint* (New Haven: Yale University Press, 1992), 24.

- "A man of the world . . . fearing no danger, with sword in hand, and with a head filled with notions of romantic chivalry and libidinous adventure . . . a libertine whose morals were questionable but whose *machismo* was never in doubt."[27]

- Trial transcripts from a court case in Loyola establish that criminal charges were brought against Íñigo and his brother Pedro, the priest, during Mardi Gras of 1515 for some sort of "nocturnal adventure" in what was obviously a serious, though unspecified, offense. Ignatius may be the only saint with a notarized police record: for nighttime brawling with an intent to inflict serious harm. One witness in the criminal case testified of the twenty-four-year-old Íñigo: "He is in the habit of going round in cuirass and coat of mail, wears his hair long to the shoulder, and walks around in a two-colored, slashed doublet with a bright cap."[28] By virtue of his noble connections at court, the code of chivalry left him above the law. Íñigo escaped conviction—and immediately, ignominiously fled town.

The colorfully attired gentleman was a volatile man, reflecting family temperament and the uncertainty of chivalry in a very Catholic country. He was a physical threat to anyone who flared his temper but was unprepared to fight. In the rare event he was cornered, opponents were vulnerable to the whim of his political connections. Short in stature, the cocksure courtier welcomed the opportunity to demonstrate his masculinity and bravado, ever alert to a (perceived) insult to his honor.

Not unlike the animal kingdom, chivalry rewarded dominant behavior and exploits. Such a male qualified to mate with an admiring female, after all. Íñigo was a belligerent risk-taker, a gambler who shrugged off accountability because of royal protection. From a prominent Catholic family, he was a man of medieval faith without morals, heedless—until battle-wounded—of sin. His religious practice seems to have been perfunctory. In sum, one can imagine Guipúzcoans back home shrugging: "just another Loyola boy."

27. Meissner, *Ignatius of Loyola*, 23.

28. Meissner, 23–24, quote attributed to von Matt and Rahner. (*Ed. Note: a cuirass is a piece of armor covering the body from neck to waist. Some had a collar to protect the throat. It might be made of iron or leather and was designed to leave the arms free for swordplay.*)

This King or That

Eventually, Íñigo's fortunes at the court of Castile faltered, forcing him to scramble for suitable new placement. Again, he parlayed noble connections, and, in 1517, arranged to enter service with the Duke of Nájera as a gentleman of the household. The duke also served as viceroy of the province of Navarre, which bordered France and was hotly contested. It was located in the Pyrenees immediately south of Guipúzcoa, a region hopelessly entangled in political and military tensions occasioned by a large French-speaking Navarrese population. The *Spanish*, in fact, were regarded as an occupying power, and formal hostilities with France loomed.

When the new king of Spain, Charles I, journeyed outside the country, the king of France pounced, and a joint Franco-Navarrese army found common cause. Íñigo led a group of volunteer reinforcements from Guipúzcoa into a garrison of perhaps a thousand Spanish regulars hunkered down in an uncompleted fortress, while the much larger, better equipped Franco-Navarrese force of over twelve thousand men advanced toward Pamplona, near the French border.[29] The Spaniards were at a hopeless disadvantage, their shabby fortress indefensible. Meeting nervously inside, the defenders voted unanimously to surrender. All but one, that is. For brave Íñigo, the honor of the House of Loyola was at stake: "Defend the citadel or die," he boldly challenged them.[30] Might Íñigo have spoken differently if he had a wife and children waiting at home? Likely not, given his overwhelming narcissism and grandiosity.

Nevertheless, such courage pricked the chivalric Spanish code of gallantry. After all, "violent self-assertion" was "the mark of noble identity."[31] The commander, Don Francis de Beaumont, agreed to fight. But the French had transversed the Pyrenees with more than a score of state-of-the-art mobile bronze cannon, easily the finest in Europe. One sixteenth-century military historian called them "more diabolical than human" because they introduced solid iron balls into medieval European war-

29. Candido de Dalmases, *Ignatius of Loyola, Founder of the Jesuits: His Life and Work*, trans. Jerome Aixala (St. Louis: Institute of Jesuit Sources, 1985), 39–40.

30. Purcell, *St. Ignatius Loyola*, 29–33.

31. DeMarco, review.

fare.[32] Lacking timely intelligence, the Spanish garrison was caught off guard by the destructiveness of the new ordnance; the ensuing, relentless French bombardment was withering.

After a six-hour siege, Íñigo was felled by a single cannonball that severely wounded both legs. The solid iron ball hit the right leg and splintered the tibia, and the left was severely gashed, likely by flying shrapnel from stone fortifications caused by the same ball. Spanish resistance immediately ceased. The leg wound was dire, according to the physician back home at the family castle. At one point, he gave up medical hope and advised the family to call their priest for the Last Rites. However, summoning fierce Guipúzkoan grit, Íñigo battled back from two primitive surgeries and, with steely resolve, made a dramatic recovery. Nevertheless, the proud man would thereafter walk with a pronounced, painful limp, a future saint carrying a permanent reminder of past dubious and sometimes sinful compromises in pursuit of chivalric honor. In today's parlance, Íñigo's body kept the score.

Facing an extended bedridden convalescence at the Loyola Castle, Íñigo asked for some "worldly books of fiction, commonly labelled chivalry."[33] But none were to be found in the house, he recounts. Instead, Íñigo recalls, "they gave him a 'Life of Christ' and a book on the lives of the saints in Castilian."[34] "They" is presumably a reference to his sister-in-law and chief caregiver, Magdalena. Renowned for her beauty,[35] she oversaw the household, and it was her side of the family that owned the few available books.

32. Phil Klay, "Can the Trauma of War Lead to Growth, Despite the Scars?," *New York Times*, July 6, 2020. An amateur military historian, Klay has researched sixteenth-century weaponry and concluded that at Pamplona the French were using a dreaded new weapon. The new generation of cannon "used solid iron balls, rather than the shot that had been previously used, which tended to shatter on impact." The upgraded ordnance was made possible by improved French smelting techniques, "ironically, developed for casting church bells!" (Private correspondence with the author, July 13, 2020.)

33. *Auto.*, no. 5.

34. *Auto.*, no. 5.

35. "Many years later, as superior general of the Society [of Jesus], Ignatius admitted to a novice that memories of her beauty sometimes distracted his prayer!" Barton T. Geger, "Six Little-Known Facts—Really—about the Society of Jesus," *Chronicles on Jesuit Higher Education*, March 1, 2022.

A former lady-in-waiting to Queen Isabella,[36] Magdalena would have known from personal experience the gendered code at court that objectified women, thereby risking *their* honor and that of *their* families. But ladies, too, had their role to play in chivalry. In the period literature, they often serve as mirrors of moral reflection for the knight. It is possible Magdalena played this role for her brother-in-law, taking the opportunity to encourage her patient to examine his behavior with the ladies of the court in light of Christian precepts. (Females of a lower class were another matter.)

To his surprise, Íñigo found himself captivated by the religious books. Over time, the pious reading resulted in what has been described as his "conversion." This is misleading, however. "There is no evidence that Íñigo was an unbeliever before his experience on his sickbed. The crucial change at that point was that he suddenly became aware of the activity of the Holy Spirit in his soul."[37] Regardless, Íñigo was still a spiritual neophyte. Worse, he was clueless that only his military combat had ceased. The more dangerous battle with evil within his soul was just beginning.

Once physically recovered, Íñigo was eager to resume his vain quest for honor and glory. Ever grandiose, he determined now to outdo all the famous saints of the Catholic heritage about whom he had been reading, men like St. Francis of Assisi. His first chivalric step, of course, must be to pay obeisance to the Blessed Virgin, the noble Lady whose intercession had protected him and called him to service. He therefore determined to make a pilgrimage to the storied eleventh-century Benedictine monastery in Montserrat, cut into sheer rock cliffs towering over Barcelona. Dressed in his best hidalgo regalia, he carried little but his prized sword and notebook. However, his inner, violent demons were far from subdued. Bad habits die hard. A frightening, interior, decisive battle with the powers of evil lay ahead.

Along the pilgrimage route Íñigo records that he fell into conversation with a "Moor," who insulted the honor of his Lady in a dispute over her lifelong purity. His blood rose. He must preserve the honor of the

36. "Magdalena de Araoz . . . the wife of the elder brother of Íñigo . . . so the story goes, had been held at the baptismal font by Queen Isabella." Dudon, *St. Ignatius of Loyola*, 19.

37. Joseph A. Munitiz, "Preliminaries to a Conversion," *The Way* 61, no. 3 (July 2022): 55.

Blessed Virgin the only way he knew how—with bloody violence. Perhaps he should murder the innocent Moor, he thought, "to stab him for what he had said."[38] Though circumstances intervened, and the Moor escaped unharmed on his way, the ambivalent impulses of Castilian culture remained strong. Well into the sixteenth century, "Conquistadores, noblemen, and explorers imagined themselves as medieval knights going forth in service of God and the lord king, augmenting and defending their honor, and pursuing violence against their enemies . . . and slaughtering non-Christians."[39]

For Íñigo, the storied encounter with the Moor was an opportunity to give glory to God, his new Liege Lord, by the highest honor possible. There was a *hierarchy of honor* to be served and sought in Castile, after all, according to the fourteenth-century French knight Geoffroi de Charny: "The man who makes war against the enemies of religion in order to support and maintain Christianity and worship of Our Lord is engaged in a war which is righteous, holy, certain, and sure, for his earthly body will be honored in a saintly fashion and his soul will, in a short space of time, be borne in holiness and without pain into paradise. . . . [O]ne can lose in [religious war] neither one's reputation in this world nor one's soul."[40]

Once arrived at the celebrated shrine of Montserrat, the hidalgo began a process of ritualized repentance for his past sins. He exchanged his fashionable attire for a rough penitential pilgrim's tunic of sackcloth. He gave away his mule to the monastery and kept only his knapsack containing his prized notebook. To cleanse his stained conscience, he presented himself for a general confession. It stretched over three days. Next was a vigil of arms—a medieval custom the night before a squire was knighted in service to his lord.

In a dramatic climax, the following day the pilgrim formally surrendered the cherished sword before the twelfth-century Black Madonna enshrined in the sanctuary. Thus, with studied, symbolic flourish, the

38. *Auto.*, no. 15.

39. Claussen, *Chivalry and Violence*, 1.

40. Richard W. Kaeuper and Elspeth Kennedy, *The Book of Chivalry of Geoffroi de Charny: Text, Context, and Translation* (Philadelphia: University of Pennsylvania Press, 1996), 85–87.

Basque hidalgo turned his back on the royal Spanish courts and the code of chivalry, their empty accoutrements of privilege, and their temptations to moral profligacy. Íñigo the sinner had begun to substitute one identity for another, a process that would eventually require a new name. He ambitioned service of a liege lord and lady who ruled a heavenly realm. But that required a showdown with the prince of darkness.

Manresa Episode

Descending Mount Montserrat, Íñigo headed fifteen miles north to Manresa, an obscure town of two thousand inhabitants. There, for eleven tumultuous months from March 1522 to February 1523, he waged spiritual battle. Historians agree that the crucible of Manresa was decisive. Still buoyed by the mountaintop experience of Montserrat, upon arrival Íñigo described "an interior state of very steady joy."[41]

It was short-lived. The traveler was carrying weighty, unresolved moral baggage that threatened to sever his newly reconciled relationship with God. The Spanish "champion" of the battle of Pamplona, for example, was responsible for entirely avoidable casualties. These included fellow warriors[42] as well as scores of bereft widows and orphans back home. Many years later, the mature Ignatius would regret Pamplona, admitting that his companions-in-arms were right, and he was wrong.[43] "Just as Cervantes describes the many mad adventures in the life of his character Don Quixote, so too are there many mad adventures in the life of Loyola—none more exquisitely mad than" what took place at Pamplona.[44] It was "the madness of honor."[45]

Though the precise content of his memories of immoral behavior and related temptations cannot be clearly ascertained, it is a matter of record that, one year before his death, the mature Ignatius did not shy away from

41. *Auto.*, no. 20.

42. Alonso de San Pedro (Pedro de Malpaso), the inspector of the fortress works, was badly wounded during the siege and remained with Iñigo in the castle some days after the cessation of hostilities. He died the following month. Tellechea Idígoras, *Ignatius of Loyola*, 106.

43. Tellechea Idígoras, 100.

44. Tellechea Idígoras, 100.

45. Tellechea Idígoras, 102.

detailing "his youthful transgressions, clearly and distinctly, with all the details."[46] He gave his account to a Portuguese Jesuit, Luis Goncalves de Camara, who immediately wrote it down so as to be faithful to the record. However, "for fear of scandalizing readers," either Ignatius or "the prudish Goncalves"[47] had second thoughts about including a detailed chapter about Íñigo's sins in his *Memoirs*.[48]

At Manresa, Íñigo continued to exhibit a touch of that same madness. Along with his tunic of sackcloth, "he went bareheaded, letting his hair and his beard grow long and unkempt. He did not trim his nails, and walked without a shoe on his left foot, while on his right, which was still unhealed and bandaged, he wore a sandal."[49] Recognizing a weaponless target of opportunity, the "enemy" (as Íñigo referred to Satan) immediately pounced. Thus commenced a frontal, relentless assault on Íñigo's soul—he mentions unnerving, seductive visions of colorful serpents; exhausting nightmares and intense, debilitating scruples; desolation, sadness, and despair; and an obsessive refusal to eat. One suspects that memories of past shameful sexual adventures were plaguing him, along with the many gambling fiascos. Harrowing voices of self-doubt and regret—occasioned by his brawling lifestyle, relish for violence, and decisive role in the Pamplona carnage—presumably underlay the horrid symptoms, as well.

Finally, Íñigo's tormented memories and conscience drove him to a local priest, obsessively and compulsively. He confessed the same sins, over and over. The pilgrim's fear of hell was so deep-seated that he found no relief from the torment. The interior shame, confusion, sorrow, and guilt were excruciating, the desolation unrelenting, and finally the proud hidalgo was overcome by persistent suicidal ideation. Neither the healing grace of the pilgrim's Pamplona "conversion," nor his noble daydreams of sanctity, nor the Montserrat vigil and reception of the sacraments had proven sustainable. His memories were toxic, his will paralyzed, his affect numb, and his understanding confused about his purpose in life.

46. Luís Gonçalves da Câmara, Memoriale, in Geger, "Six Little-Known Facts," 22.

47. Tellechea Idígoras, *Ignatius of Loyola*, 111.

48. *Auto.*, 109n5.

49. Dudon, *St. Ignatius of Loyola*, 59.

Íñigo the spiritual seeker was enduring what might be labeled an "episode" in the language of psychology. Someone dealing with a "manic episode," for example, may talk breathlessly and rapidly, sleep very little, be hyperactive, and feel invincible. Discrete periods of antisocial behavior may be labeled an episode of "acting out." An episode can be understood as a critical, typically troubled series of events, separable but integral to a longer continuous narrative, with characteristic symptoms. The duration may be short or long; symptoms may come and go. These can include altered sleep patterns or appetite, self-reproach, toxic shame or guilt, agoraphobia, or perhaps emotional numbness. In more extreme cases, recurrent thoughts of death, self-mutilation, suicidal ideation—or even attempts—manifest. Íñigo's four-month period of severely injured conscience lasted from roughly April to August 1522 and can be aptly described as his "Manresa Episode."[50] Every saint has a past.

The enemy, however, had underestimated the stubbornness of the Loyola clan as well as Basque resilience. Even as Íñigo flirted with suicide, he remained determined and resourceful. He had never met an enemy he could not defeat, and prided himself on it. He was a survivor. And he was canny. By moderating his obsessive devotional practices, pursuant to conversations with experienced men and women of God, Íñigo moved from meltdown toward spiritual enlightenment. In an abrupt notebook pivot, the former hidalgo began to record resting at more regular hours[51] and allowing himself to eat meat.[52] He decided "with great lucidity not to confess anything from the past anymore,"[53] recognizing symptoms of today's obsessive-compulsivity.

Moderation had prevailed—and likely saved his life. The terse Íñigo is disinclined to elaborate further upon what had precipitated his about-face. There is but one elliptical, precious, reference—God's mercy. "From that day forward, he remained free from these scruples, and he held it

50. "[E]veryone seems to agree that the trials that came one after another during the first four months of his stay in Manresa finally gave way to a period wreathed in light that began around the month of August." Tellechea Idígoras, *Ignatius of Loyola*, 194–95. And note Lainez's comment that "his first four months" at Manresa were a period of distress when even "his face and figure underwent a complete change." Purcell, *St. Ignatius Loyola*, 67.

51. *Auto.*, no. 26.

52. *Auto.*, no. 27.

53. *Auto.*, no. 25.

for certain that Our Lord had mercifully deigned to deliver him."[54] The frightening, four-month Manresa Episode was the occasion, historically and spiritually, for the creation of his guide to personal encounter with Divinity known as the Spiritual Exercises. Every sinner has a future.

If there is one Western painting that captures the horrendous ordeal of a Manresa Episode, it would likely be Edvard Munch's *The Scream,* created by the Norwegian artist in 1893. The *Mona Lisa* of modern art, some have called it; the artist himself referred to it as his "soul painting." Many contemporary viewers see a panic attack of an isolated human being whose "friends" are depicted with backs turned. Throughout Munch's adult life, both the artist and his sister struggled with mental illness and chronic anxiety. Eventually, she was institutionalized; Edvard dreaded the same fate.

The painting could serve as a dramatic artistic representation of someone enduring Íñigo's Manresa torments—isolated and alienated from others, from God's mercy, and from one's very self. Many a contemporary seeker of a Higher Power will see in the wraith-like figure their own bitter, perhaps traumatic existential distress. Perhaps she or he, like the artist, dreads (another) panic attack or emotional breakdown, has been diagnosed with PTSD, or fears eternal damnation.

Could it be said, five hundred years on, that Íñigo himself was suffering from PTSD? The contemporary field of trauma studies has, in fact, made it possible to understand and assess his defining symptoms through a more sophisticated lens than the rather blunt diagnosis of "posttraumatic disorder." The following chapter considers Íñigo from the perspective of the modern paradigm of "moral injury trauma." Today's traumatized survivors of violence, witnesses thereto, repentant perpetrators—indeed anyone whose conscience or values are notably unnerved by the trajectory of current events—can discover in the morally injured Íñigo and his *Spiritual Exercises* tailored guidance for healing of their own beleaguered and bewildered soul.[55]

54. *Auto.,* no. 25.

55. *Spiritual Exercises*—italicized and headed by capital letters—shall refer to the official text itself, published in Latin in 1548. "Spiritual Exercises," or, simply, "Exercises"—without italics or quotation marks and headed by capital letters—shall refer in looser form

The Forgotten Warrior

by Colonel Robert Macpherson, USMC (Ret.)[56]

The *Spiritual Exercises* saved my sanity. I call Ignatius of Loyola "the forgotten warrior." My name is Robert Macpherson. I am a U.S. Marine infantry veteran of thirty years and two tours in Vietnam, followed by Beirut, Iraq, and Somalia, and retired as a colonel. On leaving the Marines, I joined the humanitarian organization CARE. As a humanitarian aid worker, I have witnessed unspeakable violence and bloodshed in Sarajevo, Rwanda, Kosovo, Congo, the West Bank, and Iraq. Too often, my dreams returned to those memories and became nightmares.

As a Marine and a combat veteran, I turned to the Veterans Administration, and the clinical therapy I received there helped. But much of that assistance came from prescribed medicines, making me disappear into something as dangerous as complex posttraumatic stress disorder (CPTSD.) An existence without passion or emotion, a comfortable indifference. With encouragement and reassurance from a fine therapist, I gradually eliminated the chemicals.

Regardless of the therapy, fear followed me, even though I tried to convince myself that I was learning to handle it. I continued to struggle with anxiety and unhappiness. Without more help, I knew the illness would break me.

I searched for God at an eight-day Jesuit retreat, and the sanctuary was helpful. But on returning to a secular environment, I lost my intimacy with Christ. Silent meditation allowed me to realize desolation had become an established norm. Just as I recognized my hand as a part of my body, so did I perceive despair and fear as integral to my being.

---

to the comprehensive process or key dynamics of the formal text, often with reference to "making," or praying, one of the forms of an Ignatian retreat. Finally, "spiritual exercises"—without italics or quotation marks and headed by lowercase letters—are any structured forms of prayer designed to lead someone into personal encounter or relationship with God. They may be taken from the *Spiritual Exercises*, or from some other religious tradition entirely. The sense of the text will make the meaning clear, but further distinctions and elaboration will be presented when required for greater precision.

56. Robert Macpherson is the author of *Stewards of Humanity: Lighting the Darkness in Humanitarian Crisis* (Durham, NC: Torchflame Books, 2021). The above testimony is used with his permission.

As the illness got worse, I spoke with my Jesuit pastor in Charlotte, Father Jim Shea. We discussed the *Spiritual Exercises*, and he suggested I read the autobiography of St. Ignatius. Within the first pages I realized our common association as combatants—wounded in battle and spending many months enduring a painful recovery.

For a lengthy period, my eyes were bandaged. On removing the dressings, I could see with one eye, and books became an escape from the withdrawal that accompanies a long recovery. Like Ignatius, I spent hours reading about notable women and men throughout history. When reading Ignatius's request for romance novels, I smiled, recalling a hospital filled with hundreds of young Marines; I had marveled at how fast the latest *Playboy* magazine made its way through the wards. But the memory reminded me of Ignatius's description of the sense of emptiness that followed those episodes. Through his autobiography, I developed a kinship with him in our shared commonality of struggling to overcome the loss of self-worth that accompanies a severe wound or illness.

When I started reading his memoir, I sought a path to lead me out of my desolation. After finishing it, I knew I had found a fellow traveler within the grip of a posttraumatic stress disorder: an illness defined by the U.S. Veterans Administration with symptoms of negative perceptions about self, feelings of isolation, withdrawal, aggression, emotional regulation difficulties, suicidal tendencies, persistent fear, guilt, and shame.

In Ignatius I found a man I could relate to, a soldier at war with himself, fighting battles never won. His symptoms concurrently call attention to what he considers unspeakable sins and his need to redirect attention from them. He alternates between feelings of healthy detachment and reliving an event in exacting detail. PTSD is like this—it causes complex, sometimes rapid, and unexpected changes of consciousness.

Beyond Ignatius's description of his struggles is a man who understands what it is like to live with PTSD. I searched the internet for a reference about *Ignatius* and *PTSD*. Besides several short articles, there is no in-depth research associating his combat experience with a mental illness.

But how does Ignatius balance his knowledge of "the enemy," as he calls Satan, against his struggles of contemplating self-harm? While he speaks and writes about enlightenment, grace, and forgiveness, he cannot escape the suspicions of inadequacy. Ignatius knows the enemy is probing the lines of his defensive perimeter, and at times the fortifications are broken. When falling into periods of fear and desperation, he must have felt it was because he failed to embrace Christ, which resulted in increased anxiety that evil was "winning."

Ignatius had no support groups, therapists, or drugs to help mitigate his illness. However, in a remarkable achievement that was as inspired as it was reasoned, he created the sacred exercises. In doing so, he found a way not only to help moderate his illness but also, with a penetrating emotional intellect, to demonstrate that varying degrees of depression and anxiety are a natural part of living.

For Ignatius, the seeds for his growth did not occur after a single event. PTSD can result from one experience, but the illness often grows through a series of cumulative experiences building toward a single incident, "triggering" the illness. Ignatius's determinants may have included the complexities of his childhood, many armed fights and encounters, promiscuous behavior, all culminating in the battle wounds of Pamplona. Looking back over half a millennium, we will never be sure of the specific causes for his mental distress.

What happened? How did Ignatius the *soldier*, tormented with complex PTSD, become the *saint* whose *Spiritual Exercises* helped reclaim the lives of so many people over five centuries? Ignatius created a method and tools for "finding God in all things." He used his mental illness to connect with people and their pain. Pope Francis once wrote: "The danger that threatens in a crisis is never total; there's always a way out: Where the danger is also grows the saving power . . . in the threat itself; that's where the door opens." Ignatius's trauma enabled him to teach others a spiritual way out of their darkness.

2

The Morally Injured Íñigo

Scientific research, publication, and discourse around the construct of moral injury have exploded during the past generation in mental health and counseling literature. Its related integration into clinical practice has been similarly dramatic. Still largely unfamiliar outside the domain of psychology (and understood variously from within), moral injury increasingly claims recognized standing in the same conversation with PTSD, a formal designation by the American Psychiatric Association dating to 1980. The former is regarded as more values- or conscience-based, the latter more fear- or threat-based. Trauma psychiatrist William P. Nash calls moral injury "an enduring and potentially life-shattering consequence of a collision between experience and deeply held moral expectations, between what is and what we know should be."[1]

"Conclusions" in the field are essentially working hypotheses, subject to further scientific study; there is still no consensus definition of moral injury. The very term can sound awkward. Of course, so did "PTSD" when it was launched; now the word "trauma" and the diagnosis of "PTSD" are both overused and increasingly meaningless pop culture darlings. "I was traumatized when my football team lost the Super Bowl." For such reasons, this chapter relies upon research-based and peer-reviewed studies, with citations for readers who wish to dig deeper into the evidence.

1. William P. Nash, "Foreword," *Religion and Recovery from PTSD* (Philadelphia: Jessica Kingsley Publishers, 2020), 7.

Nash argues that "moral injury is proving to us that our conceptions of PTSD are all wrong."[2] He designates moral injury trauma (MIT)[3] as another *type* of trauma, which offers exciting new theoretical and clinical models. Other specialists go further, claiming that a wholesale paradigm shift is underway, and propose that the treatment of moral injury, though related to PTSD, should now be addressed as an independent field.[4]

A "one-size-fits-all" approach to trauma can no longer be assumed. PTSD is now considered one of *several* reputable trauma paradigms. Since moral injury trauma discourse in mental health routinely includes the role of "spirituality," this chapter aims to orient spiritual and pastoral caregivers to the rich interdisciplinary conversation now underway. The working assumption is that *both* domains—psychology and religion—have much to learn from each other.

A morally injured conscience is precipitated by specific violence- or distress-related events, several of which track incidents in the life of the chivalrous courtier. Íñigo's early life narrative, particularly the Pamplona and Manresa chapters, make for an illuminating case study. His value system had been shattered by innumerable grievous choices and transgressions, the outcome of which was imminent psychic and spiritual meltdown at Manresa, with symptoms consistent with military-related moral injury. In his *Memoirs*, for example, he records that his compulsive scrupulosity resulted in obsessively repeated, intrusive, and unwanted thoughts. (Today, people in twelve-step recovery programs refer colloquially to this unwelcome habit as *stinkin' thinkin'*.) "While he had these

2. William P. Nash, "A 'Stain on the Soul': Why Moral Injury Requires a Different Treatment Plan Than PTSD," *Mastering the Treatment of Trauma*, National Institute for the Clinical Application of Behavioral Medicine, Module Four, 10, https://www.nicabm.com/confirm/mastering-the-treatment-of-trauma-cwzsb/,

3. Posttraumatic (sometimes rendered post-traumatic) stress disorder is a formally recognized mental health condition, typically designated by the acronym PTSD. Though MIT lacks such validation, the same convention will be followed for the sake of parallel construction. Similarly, moral injury trauma will be written without capitals, as is post-traumatic stress disorder.

4. Joseph M. Currier, Kent D. Drescher, and Jason Nieuwsma, "Introduction to Moral Injury," *Addressing Moral Injury in Clinical Practice* (Washington, DC: American Psychological Association, 2021), 3–18.

thoughts, the temptation often came over him with great force to throw himself from a large balcony in his room . . ."[5]

Research indicates that events that can precipitate moral injury trauma, in civilian as well as military settings, include[6]:

- Violent injury or serious wound (physical, emotional, neurological), perhaps fatal, inflicted on another. (The perpetrator is morally injured.)
- Violent injury or serious wound (physical, emotional, neurological) suffered at the hands of another. (The one wounded is morally injured.)
- Violence, cruelty, or distress witnessed, either in person or vicariously through mass media. (The witness experiences moral injury.)
- Betrayal of others by a leader; or failure to protect others from harmful outcomes when the leader had some ability to do so. (The leader him- or herself experiences moral injury.)
- Betrayal by a leader, or someone in a position of responsibility, to death, injury, or severe distress, including the failure of that leader to assist or protect those who are vulnerable. (Those betrayed by the leader experience moral injury.)

Available accounts suggest that Íñigo's conscience was implicated in the first four of these five characteristic precipitating events, any one of which can result in MIT. Surely, it can be estimated today, this represents a significant factor in the severity of his Manresa Episode. In Íñigo's case, his grounding in traditional Catholic religious heritage, and specifically the "value system" of the Ten Commandments, was at stake. In the notebook he carried everywhere, which gave way to the earliest version of the Spiritual Exercises, Íñigo highlighted moral emotions and affect such as

5. Ignatius of Loyola, *A Pilgrim's Testament: The Memoirs of Saint Ignatius of Loyola*, ed. Barton T. Geger (Chestnut Hill, MA: Institute of Jesuit Sources, 2020), no. 24. Hereafter, *Auto*.

6. N. Jamieson, M. Maple, D. Ratnarajah, K. Usher, "Military Moral Injury: A Concept Analysis," *International Journal of Mental Health Nursing* 29, no. 6 (December 2020): 1049–66.

guilt, shame, sorrow, and confusion, stemming from his self-perception of countless religious sins. These included violation of the sixth commandment through sexual dalliance, and of the fifth by his relish for battle and physical harm inflicted on perceived enemies.

The outcome was the horrific four-month episode at Manresa culminating in suicidal ideation. "But after these thoughts, disgust for the life he led came over him, with impulses to give it up."[7] "The more things change the more they remain the same," as the adage goes. According to the U.S. Census Bureau, in 2019 there were an estimated eighteen million military veterans. Approximately seventeen to twenty commit suicide daily, according to a recent estimate by the U.S. Department of Veterans Affairs. Military mental health specialists are convinced that a better understanding of moral injury trauma among veterans can lower those rates substantially.

Historically, moral injury can be viewed as the latest in a long line of terms originating in particular military conflicts. To be clear, the phenomenon and symptoms of moral injury are not new. *Soldier's heart* was a common "diagnosis" during the Civil War; *nostalgia* (etymologically, *to return home in pain*) was also common.[8] *Shell shock* is associated with World War I, and *combat fatigue* with World War II. PTSD was formally introduced as a medical diagnosis in 1980 in response to the distress of Vietnam War veterans. No doubt moral injury will be considered "the signature wound of our wars in Iraq and Afghanistan."[9] Many veterans in the United States have already availed themselves of its more tailored insights, resources, and treatment programs, widely available through Veterans Administration medical facilities.

The question sometimes arises whether the future saint could have been diagnosed correctly with PTSD. If anachronistic, the question is nevertheless worthy of consideration for the sake of greater precision today. The mental health field understands PTSD as a medical determination defined by a traumatic precipitating event(s) which causes an

7. *Auto.*, no. 25.

8. Dennis McFarland, *Nostalgia* (New York: Pantheon Books, 2013). In the Civil War novel, note the surgeon's diagnosis of the wounded veteran, 93–94.

9. Robert Emmett Meagher and Douglas A. Pryer, eds., *War and Moral Injury: A Reader* (Eugene, OR: Wipf and Stock, 2018), 49.

excessively expressed reaction of fear or panic, often with accompanying physiological and neural footprints. Though PTSD and moral injury can coexist in one person, it is unlikely that Íñigo was one of them. *Fear* was, after all, foreign to his makeup, unless it came to fear of (the loss of) God and its consequences, both in this world and the next. True to his ancestral and ferocious Guipúzcoan roots, the sixteenth-century courtier was renowned, precisely, for *fearlessness*. "Very careful of his personal appearance, anxious to please the fair sex, daring in affairs of gallantry, punctilious about his honor, he feared nothing."[10]

One example, in Íñigo's own words, speaks volumes. Chapter 6 will detail the distressing investigation of the former courtier by the Spanish Inquisition, and, on more than one occasion, his related imprisonment. Once released, Íñigo determined to depart Spain for Paris. But Spain and France were still at war, and the route was so dangerous that his companions abandoned him. Íñigo himself was, characteristically, unfazed by the risk. "Many important persons urged him strongly not to go. But they could never dissuade him. On the contrary, fifteen or twenty days after leaving prison, he set out alone, riding a donkey, and taking some books. When he arrived at Barcelona, all those who knew him advised him against the journey to France, because of the fierce wars. They recounted very specific incidents, even telling him that they had put Spaniards on spits. But he never had any kind of fear."[11]

According to psychiatrist Nash, the most robust conclusions of current moral injury research challenge "conceptions that trauma is exclusively the result of fear-evoking brushes with death or sexual assault."[12] Nash prefers a "stress injury model," in which injuries lie on a continuum and moral injury is understood as "a literal wound to the mind, brain, body, and spirit inflicted by a life event that violates deeply held moral expectations of oneself and the world."[13] According to present understanding, then, Íñigo's Manresa Episode points to someone susceptible to the

10. Paul Dudon, *St. Ignatius of Loyola*, trans. William J. Young (Milwaukee: Bruce Publishing, 1949), 21.

11. *Auto.*, no. 72.

12. William P. Nash, "Commentary on the Special Issue on Moral Injury: Unpacking Two Models for Understanding Moral Injury," *Journal of Traumatic Stress* (June 2019): abstract, 465.

13. Nash, "Commentary," 468.

distress of moral injury trauma, wounded in body as well as conscience and spirit, but free of fear.

According to Lisa López Levers, former president of the International Association for Resilience and Trauma Counseling (IARTC), epidemiological research indicates that "about 70% of people, worldwide, have been exposed to at least one traumatic incident in their lives,"[14] though only about 7–8 percent qualify for a formal diagnosis of PTSD.[15] The estimate of 70 percent may appear high, but the sheer pervasiveness of trauma across the human condition can be explained by the multiple events at stake—physical abuse, domestic or intimate partner violence, war, refugee displacement, elder abuse, crime, abortion, motor vehicle accidents, bullying, school shootings, medical and health-related incidents, sexual assault, human-made or climate and natural disasters. Even viewing the news or current events on TV or social media can prove triggering for some. In 2024 the surgeon general claimed that mental health risks to young people from social media platforms are enough to justify warning labels similar to those on tobacco and alcohol products. If this is philosopher Leibnitz's "best of all possible worlds," there is little wonder so many today want no part of it.

Other studies, notes Levers, suggest that "between 30% to 70% of individuals who experience trauma also report positive change and growth emerging from the traumatic experience."[16] Thus, some mental health professionals have begun to embrace the terminology, with associated clinical practice, of "posttraumatic growth."[17] Because of measurement limitations, the field is still regarded by some psychologists and clinicians as somewhat controversial. Nevertheless, there is widespread acceptance that posttraumatic growth can reliably be considered "one possible outcome of the process of working through the aftermath of trauma."[18] With suitable guidance, then, moral injury trauma can serve as a crucial

14. Lisa López Levers, *Trauma Counseling: Theories and Interventions for Managing Trauma, Stress, Crisis, and Disaster*, 2nd ed. (New York: Springer Publishing, 2023), 19.

15. López Levers, *Trauma Counseling*, 19.

16. López Levers, 19.

17. An excellent introduction to posttraumatic growth is Mary Beth Werdel and Robert J. Wicks, *Primer on Posttraumatic Growth: An Introduction and Guide* (Hoboken, NJ: John Wiley and Sons, 2012).

18. López Levers, *Trauma Counseling*, 19.

springboard for enhanced human freedom, flourishing, and resilience. Certain types of traumas do not require a formal medical diagnosis; spiritual and pastoral caregivers and seekers can be trained to recognize MIT as a growth-edge opportunity to be probed and addressed psychospiritually. The rule of thumb is that a diagnosis of PTSD always equals trauma, but trauma does not always equal PTSD. The terms should never be used interchangeably. PTSD is a psychiatric disorder assigned to trauma survivors who meet specific criteria outlined in the *Diagnostic and Statistical Manual of Mental Disorders, Fifth Edition, Text Revision* (DSM-5-TR).[19]

The term "injury" better reflects recent neurobiological research into the effects of trauma on the brain, as well as changing clinical and patient preferences. A significant limitation to reliance on the terminology of PTSD is that usage of the word "disorder" has become increasingly fraught, since social stigma is frequently attached to it. This creates an obstacle to successful treatment for some clients, such that the alternative designation "posttraumatic stress injury" is now preferred by some clinicians and many careseekers. Notably, psychiatrists Frank Ochberg and Jonathan Shay, two scholars prominent in trauma research, led a campaign of mental health professionals to have the American Psychiatric Association formally change the terminology from PTS *disorder* to PTS *injury*. Though they failed to convince the association, many clinicians remain sympathetic to the argument and have subsequently incorporated a preference for the latter into their professional lexicon.

The identification of moral injury trauma has led to a variety of fresh healing modalities, insights, and practices. Some will be of interest to Christian spiritual and pastoral caregivers who accompany wounded veterans (such as Colonel Macpherson), refugees, casualties of sexual violence, or anyone of beleaguered, bewildered conscience. In the latter case, consider an automobile driver who is drunk, or texting—or both—and causes a fatal accident while remaining physically unscathed themselves. Evidence-based research indicates that such people are quite susceptible to moral injury trauma.

The fresh terminology is valuable because it lends itself to interdisciplinary research and clinical practice. For mental health specialists open

19. *Diagnostic and Statistical Manual of Mental Disorders*, 5th ed., Text Revision (DSM-5-TR) (New York: American Psychiatric Association Publishing, 2022).

to the numinous, such as Joseph M. Currier, Timothy D. Carroll, and Jennifer H. Wortmann, moral injury is viewed as a "thin construct."[20] Heaven and earth, as the Celtic saying goes, are only three feet apart, but in thin places that distance is even narrower. In certain rare locales, such as Stonehenge, or Mount Tabor where Jesus was transfigured, the distance between a spiritual realm and a material world collapses entirely. For certain specialists in psychology and religion, a thin place is one in which a perceived hard boundary between the two domains, upon closer inspection, is understood to be—perhaps experienced as—diffuse. The qualifier *thin* does not suggest "a lack of substance or utility"; instead, it "may compel biomedically oriented clinicians to consider the variegated role of religious faith and/or spirituality" in the suffering and healing of traumatized people.[21]

In the past generation, clinical pioneers in mental health have cracked open the door to religious consideration across disciplines, and there is no turning back. They note that survey research in the southern United States, for example, indicates "moderate to high importance of religion and spirituality in life" (70–90 percent) and a high rate of belief in the existence of God or a Higher Power (60–70 percent).[22] Such mental health pioneers await more robust engagement by spiritual theologians and practitioners.

One reputable example of trauma-informed, holistic healing practice is the creative model of Jesuit Father Charles Barnes, a Veterans Administration chaplain who applies the principles of Ignatian spirituality to spiritual and pastoral care for military personnel who have experienced traumatic events, including those negotiating PTSD, posttraumatic growth, and moral injury.[23] Many veterans lament the absence of "soul repair" as a therapeutic option, Barnes notes.[24] They understand their traumatic injuries as both psychological and spiritual, and *value* thin, interdisciplinary

20. Joseph M. Currier, Timothy D. Carroll, and Jennifer H. Wortmann, "Religious and Spiritual Issues in Moral Injury," in *Addressing Moral Injury in Clinical Practice*, ed. Joseph M. Currier, Kent D. Drescher, Jason Nieuwsma (Washington, DC: American Psychological Association, 2021), 53.

21. Currier, Carroll, and Wortmann, "Religious and Spiritual Issues," 53.

22. Currier, Carroll, and Wortmann, 54.

23. Charles Barnes, "To Stand before the Cross and Not Run Away: A Practical Guide to Directing the Spiritual Exercises for Retreatants with Post-Traumatic Stress Disorder and Moral Injury," *STUDIES in the Spirituality of Jesuits* (Summer 2021), especially section 2, "PTSD, Moral Injury, and the Soul."

24. Barnes, "To Stand before the Cross," 9.

healing modalities. For persons of faith from the Abrahamic traditions, certain injuries are viewed as "sinful," and Barnes adapts the initial exercises on sin for them.

It is notable that Barnes requires supplicants under his guidance who are praying through an Ignatian retreat to see a mental health professional on a regular basis. Christian spiritual and pastoral caregivers who work with survivors of trauma would do well to review Barnes's model, and its informative appendices, as an interdisciplinary paradigm worthy of consideration. Important NextGen resources are becoming available but, as yet, few Clinical Pastoral Education trainers or spiritual formation leaders have begun to consider more integrated perspectives. Barnes's insights can be adapted for vicarious moral injury, for example, as suffered by someone viewing difficult events or content on television, in films, or on social media. (The video of George Floyd's death was viewed 2.5 *million* times in the first twelve hours after it was posted.)

Follow the Symptoms

Íñigo presents a vivid case study of the thin construct of moral injury and its characteristic symptoms, a mirror in whom today's survivors of violence may recognize themselves. According to trauma counselor Levers, "Veterans experience emotionally painful emotions such as guilt, shame, anger, disgust, and contempt, which then must be repaired."[25] MIT research is steeped in this sort of inquiry and discourse, with particular interest in such symptoms. Íñigo's distressing Manresa Episode readily comes to mind on more than one count. Moral injury trauma theorists look to a variety of such difficult affects to identify characteristic symptoms in need of healing.

Though there is hardly consensus, specialists have proposed that certain symptoms can be distinguished from PTSD, for example, in the widely referenced and reproduced taxonomy of the Venn diagram below.[26] In this popular schema, five symptoms are *particular* to moral injury—

25. López Levers, *Trauma Counseling*, 404.

26. David Wood and John Montorio, "Moral Injury," *Resources for Moral Injury*, Dart Center for Journalism and Trauma, Columbia University Graduate School of Journalism, April 9, 2015, https://dartcenter.org/content/moral-injury (originally published in the *Huffington Post*, March 2014).

"sorrow, grief, regret, shame, alienation." They can serve as recognizable clues, signposts that point the way to posttraumatic growth. As Hansel and Gretel marked their way home with white pebbles visible in the dark forest, symptoms—when recognized—can distinguish a way to God. Such emotions and cognitions let a supplicant know that she or he may need to *seek healing from* a particular affect or thought pattern, and that the guidance of traditional spirituality is available.

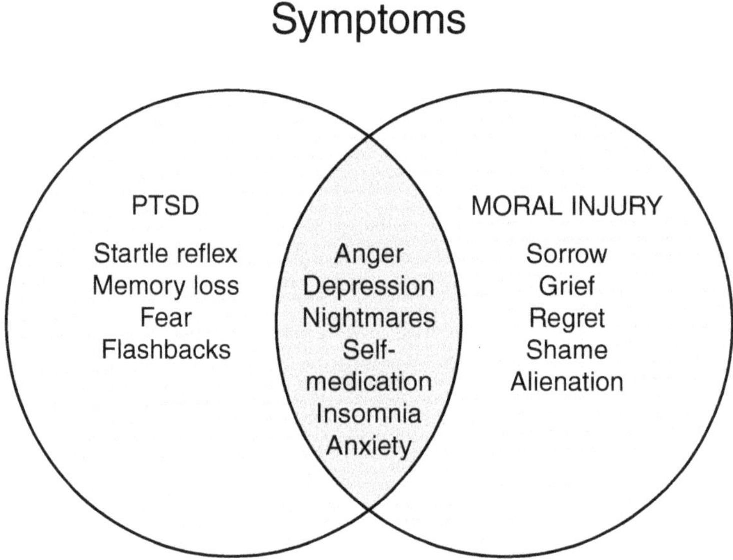

The phenomenological, often linguistic, overlap between the above moral injury symptomology, on the one hand, and Íñigo at Manresa in his *Memoirs* and Exercises, on the other, is unmistakable, and confirms the fruitful significance of a thin perspective on moral injury. "Sorrow, grief, regret, shame, alienation" all plagued Íñigo at Manresa because of his sinful choices. All are pivotal to reconciliation and reconnection—with God, others, and oneself—particularly in the "First Week" of the Exercises.[27]

27. The "Four Weeks" of the Exercises have no chronological reference and can be understood as phases of the one retreat.

It is not possible to illustrate such congruence in any depth in the format of a primer, but one striking example serves the case. In the first exercise, Íñigo invites the supplicant to petition awareness of "shame and confusion about myself" as a grace that mediates God's merciful love.[28] In the second exercise, again for spiritual healing purposes, the seeker desires personal awareness of "growing and intense sorrow and tears for my sins."[29] Íñigo is obviously working within a sixteenth-century religious/spiritual domain. But the "symptoms" he identifies—shame and sorrow—correspond closely to those of moral injury, pointing to the porous boundary between Ignatian spirituality and moral injury trauma.[30] There is profound interdisciplinary resonance, as well, with "regret," "alienation," and "grief."

Remarkably, what certain moral injury trauma theorists identify as "symptoms" appear within the Ignatian heritage as *spiritual* affect inviting God's compassionate intervention through grace and mercy.[31] In other words, symptoms offer a recognized way to God in the Christian tradition. Optimal intervention regimens for those enduring moral injury trauma should, in principle, be considered interdisciplinary. Trauma specialists Currier, Carroll, and Wortmann note that "a growing number of studies reveal diverse ways in which R/S (religion and spirituality) can influence rates and severity of commonly diagnosed mental health conditions."[32]

The distressing symptoms described by Íñigo at Manresa and incorporated into his *Spiritual Exercises* more than five hundred years ago are readily on view within contemporary trauma theory. References and insights in his *Autobiography* and *Spiritual Exercises* resonate with military

28. George E. Ganss, *The Spiritual Exercises of Saint Ignatius: A Translation and Commentary* (St. Louis: Institute of Jesuit Sources, 1992), no. 48. Henceforth, *SpEx*.

29. *SpEx*, no. 55.

30. DSM 5, moreover, for the first time considers such painful moral emotions and cognitions as reflective of the symptom criteria for PTSD.

31. The online dictionary of the American Psychological Association defines "affect" as "any experience of feeling or emotion, ranging from suffering to elation, from the simplest to the most complex sensations of feeling, and from the most normal to the most pathological emotional reactions. Often described in terms of positive affect or negative affect both mood and emotion are considered affective states."

32. Currier, Carroll, and Wortmann, "Religious and Spiritual Issues," 53.

moral injury research. With astute, timely guidance, these emotions and related values-related cognitions can be constructively adaptive for personal healing, and for reconciliation with self, others, and one's Higher Power.

Íñigo's distressing Manresa Episode, for example, demonstrates spiritual confusion and psychological alienation grounded in documented, extreme scrupulosity. According to the International Obsessive Compulsive Disorder (OCD) Foundation, scrupulosity can be regarded as "a subtype of obsessive-compulsive disorder," characteristic of persons who "are overly concerned that something they thought or did might be a sin or other violation of religious or moral doctrine."[33] This surely describes Íñigo's recorded experience and underlines the high stakes for one's understanding of sin. "He persevered in his seven [daily] hours of prayer on his knees, getting up regularly at midnight, and in all the other exercises mentioned earlier. But in none of them did he find any cure for his scruples. They were tormenting him for many months."[34]

Íñigo's first-person account can be read in an exclusively therapeutic sense, certainly, apart from any interest in reconciliation and relationship with God. But seekers of a Higher Power hunger for something more, and Íñigo's "shame and confusion" clearly manifested his *spiritual* distress. At Manresa, he devised a meditation exercise for those symptoms, a tool available to God-seekers today. The supplicant petitions to recognize his or her spiritual confusion and psychological alienation through *God's* merciful eyes, and thereby to be healed of their destructive effects.[35]

One imagines such a thin modality to be of interest to the estimated 2 percent of the U.S. population who will be diagnosed with OCD during their lifetime. Many experience their symptoms as diffuse across psychology and religion/spirituality, and look for biomedically oriented clinicians willing and able to consider their suffering and healing from trauma accordingly. Spiritual and pastoral caregivers, as well as those seeking reconnection with their Higher Power, also find here a fruitful

33. International OCD Foundation, "What is OCD & Scrupulosity?," https://iocdf.org/faith-ocd/what-is-ocd-scrupulosity/.

34. *Auto.,* no. 23.

35. *SpEx* no. 50: ". . . so that by seeking to recall and to comprehend the whole matter I may feel all the more shame and confusion . . ."

interdisciplinary lens. The following review of recent moral injury literature provides timely context and contours for a balanced consideration of the contributions of *both* the mental health *and* the pastoral theological communities. Clearly, the dialogue is well underway.

Situating Moral Injury in Recent Literature

Georgetown University philosopher and Kennedy Institute of Ethics fellow Nancy Sherman qualifies the term "moral injury" as "at least as old as the preaching of Bishop Joseph Butler in early 18th century England."[36] But, she notes, it is presently enjoying a revival in clinical circles, beginning with the military behavioral health arena. It has found vibrant resonance within the study of war and the impact of war upon surviving, returning veterans. "War . . . kills not only those it buries in the ground. It can just as surely kill the souls of warriors who, having marched off to war and Moral Injury, return home, where, standing tall while the music plays and their hometowns cheer, feel inside that they are forever lost."[37]

For Sherman, the term "moral injury" describes "experiences of serious inner conflict arising from what one takes to be grievous moral transgressions that can overwhelm one's sense of goodness and humanity."[38] She has coined the evocative noun "afterwar" in a plea for all sectors of U.S. society to take responsibility for the "moral healing" of the 2.6 million veterans of the recent "Forever Wars" (notably in Iraq and Afghanistan) upon their return.

Moral injury finds its academic home in clinical psychology and mental health studies, Sherman notes. But wider references in the literature of philosophy, mainstream Protestant theology, medicine, health care, Scripture scholarship,[39] and pastoral psychology are increasingly common. Based on research training in psychoanalysis, Sherman works clinically with veterans returning from active battlefields. Her practice confirms

36. Nancy Sherman, *AFTERWAR: Healing the Moral Wounds of Our Soldiers* (New York: Oxford University Press, 2015), 8.

37. Meagher and Prior, *War and Moral Injury*, 6.

38. Sherman, *AFTERWAR*, 8.

39. Joseph McDonald, ed., *Exploring Moral Injury in Sacred Texts* (Philadelphia: Jessica Kingsley, 2017). A collection of sacred texts is considered from the perspective of moral injury by scholars from a variety of interfaith traditions.

what has been shown to be the case with Íñigo—shooting wars leave an enduring mark on the consciences of countless military personnel scarred by violence.

Within the broader literature, moral injury is sometimes referenced not as a "construct" but as a "syndrome." Posttraumatic growth theorists, though, would be leery of the latter term. They would argue that it is unfairly pejorative, implying disorder or abnormality. Influenced by the positive psychological movement, they would counter that moral injury should be normalized as part of an adaptive healing process because it serves as an "engine of transformation."[40] In so doing, they offset the temptation of some traumatologists to pathologize moral injury up front, a tension that runs through the literature.

The definition of moral injury most widely referenced in the past generation dates to 2009 and is associated with Boston clinical psychologist Brett Litz. His work ignited the explosion of moral injury literature and practice into what has now become something of a cottage industry of publications.

> [W]e offer the following working definition of potentially morally injurious experiences: perpetrating, failing to prevent, bearing witness to, or learning about acts that transgress deeply held moral beliefs and expectations. This may entail participating in or witnessing inhumane or cruel actions, failing to prevent the immoral acts of others. . . . The individual also must be (or become) aware of the discrepancy between his or her morals and the experience (i.e., moral violation), causing dissonance and inner conflict.[41]

Note that the conventional understanding of events leading to moral injury considers them *potentially* morally injurious, reflecting the freedom and uniqueness of persons. The conclusion is widely accepted.

For example, cruel violence committed against or in the presence of a seven-year-old child will likely result in moral injury, whereas the same action committed against or in the presence of a mature adult may not.

40. Stephen Joseph, *What Doesn't Kill Us: The New Psychology of Posttraumatic Growth*, illustrated ed. (New York: Basic Books, 2013).

41. Brett T. Litz, Nathan Stein, Eileen Delaney, Leslie Lebowitz, William P. Nash, Caroline Silva, and Shira Maguen, "Moral Injury and Moral Repair in War Veterans: A Preliminary Model and Intervention Strategy," *Clinical Psychology Review* 29 (2009): 695–706.

Psychologists note that "[A]cts that involve violations of one's moral beliefs and expectations are called Potentially Morally Injurious Events (PMIEs) because events, no matter how egregious, are only potentially damaging."[42] As psychologists are aware, a variety of factors must be considered. (This is to say nothing of the estimated 1–4 percent of the population who are psychopaths or sociopaths, given to violence but, *without conscience*, incapable of empathy, guilt, or shame, and therefore beyond present consideration.)

Brad E. Kelle is a professor of Old Testament and Hebrew, one of an increasing number of theologians, the majority Protestant, who have enthusiastically taken moral injury as a research focus. His scholarship and publications actively promote the interdisciplinary dialogue required of a thin construct. They engage Scripture scholars, pastoral theologians, chaplains, doctoral students of theology, and ordained ministers, among others, to think critically about the role of moral injury from a religious/spiritual perspective. In an outstanding primer, Kelle himself broadly defines moral injury as "a multidimensional, nonphysical wound that results from the violation (directly or indirectly, by oneself, others, or outside forces) of a person's core moral beliefs about themselves and the world."[43]

Litz and Kelle are bookends who exemplify the extraordinary interest in moral injury on the part of psychologists and clinicians, on the one hand, and theologians and the broader religion/spirituality cohort, on the other. However, the conversation remains overly siloed, particularly in the area of spirituality, which has the unfortunate practical impact in real time of limiting optimal holistic treatment and care of survivors of violence and the beleaguered and bewildered of conscience. Regrettably, both domains remain largely locked into unidimensional solutions for what—in the case of people of faith and seekers—are thin, *multidimensional* healing needs. This is obviously a matter of some urgency for the large population who request some form of "soul repair," as well as those who accompany them.

42. Alanna Coady, Jessica R. Carney, Sheila Frankfurt, and Brett T. Litz, "The Emergence and Development of the Concept of Moral Injury," in *Moral Injury: A Guidebook for Understanding and Engagement*, ed. Brad E. Kelle (Lanham, MD: Rowman and Littlefield, 2020), 21.

43. Brad E. Kelle, ed., "Introduction," in Kelle, *Moral Injury*, 1.

Zachary Moon—an experienced (former) chaplain in the U.S. Navy Reserve, ordained minister, and seminary professor—is one reputable religion/spirituality contributor who operates multidimensionally. Moon situates moral injury on "a spectrum of suffering, with moral injury at the pole of most radical suffering."[44] This readily correlates with Litz's concept of potentially morally injurious events, in which some wounded survivors, perpetrators, or witnesses of violence present no distinctive symptoms. Íñigo, presumably, was near the pole of radical suffering, if his documented suicidal ideation can be taken as an indicator. In any case, Moon's location of moral injury *on a spectrum*, though lacking measurement specificity, is a significant contribution to clinical practice and spiritual guidance. There is surely room for further research in this area.

Army veteran, ordained pastor, and theologian Michael Yandell calls moral injury "despair of the world and oneself—an internalized scream: This should not have happened. I should not have been a part of this."[45] A memorable example is captured in the iconic 1970 photo of the anguished fourteen-year-old Mary Ann Vecchio on the campus of Kent State University. Kneeling on one knee above a fallen, bloodied student with whom she had only moments before struck up a conversation, her mouth is agape in a scream of despair right off Munch's canvas. The photo, referenced popularly as the "Kent State Pieta," was taken on the tragic day when panicked National Guard soldiers at an antiwar campus protest gunned down four innocent students. It reinforces the truth that *observers* of violence can be subject to moral injury, which Vecchio explicitly acknowledged many years later. Professional caregivers, as well as the broader care circle, must be attuned to this possibility and prepared to address it directly, particularly in the era of pervasive social media. Sensationalism and cruelty sell, unfortunately, and the prospect of adding artificial intelligence to the mix is alarming.

Ordained minister and emeritus pastoral care theologian Larry Kent Graham, finally, distinguishes between "agential moral injury brought

44. Zachary Moon, "Moral Injury and the Role of Chaplains," in Kelle, *Moral Injury*, 68.

45. Michael Yandell, "Do Not Torment Me: The Morally Injured Gerasene Demoniac," in Kelle, *Moral Injury*, 79. He has been active on the steering committee for the "Moral Injury and Recovery in Religion, Society, and Culture" Group of the American Academy of Religion.

upon ourselves by our own agency, and receptive moral injury caused to us by the agency of others."[46] Íñigo's extreme distress may be explained because he was *both*. The distinction is important because it places moral injury within "the context of everyday moral living."[47] No one escapes it, surely in such polarized, violent times. It is in the oxygen we take for granted. The many millions of social media viewers of the clip of George Floyd's heinous murder in 2020, hearing him cry out for his "mama," are susceptible to receptive moral injury trauma. The category may well be of particular interest to the countless innocent, wounded survivors of sexual violence, few of whom had any agency in crimes of assault, abuse, incest, intimate partner violence, and so on.

One caveat: the religion/spirituality cohort, sooner or later, must confront the adequacy of the term "moral." Choice of language is important, as astute caregivers realize. Severely traumatized people can be triggered by the wrong word, even a *perceived* hint of criticism. For *receptive* survivors of sexual violence, for example, the category of *moral* injury can immediately invoke internalized guilt, shame, and/or self-blame, all typically misplaced. Are *they* morally implicated? Are they guilty of *sin*? The following chapter offers theological nuance regarding the matter of moral injury and sin.

A Dark Hole in My Soul: Helen's Testimony

Helen was raised in a devout Roman Catholic family on the west coast of the United States. As a young woman, she treasured her faith and close relationship with God, and considered becoming a nun. Before making a lifelong commitment, however, she decided at twenty four to work abroad as a Catholic lay missionary with a congregation of priests and brothers.

Helen was sent to a jungle setting in a South American country where guerilla military groups and less organized gangs were active. Local clergy told her coordinator, a priest in Chicago, that the placement "was not a good idea." However, he disregarded their advice.

46. Larry Kent Graham, *Moral Injury: Restoring Wounded Souls* (Nashville: Abingdon Press, 2017), 13.

47. Graham, *Moral Injury*, 78.

Helen worked successfully in Young Adult Ministry and taught at the local school. But she was forced to fend off physical and verbal abuse from intoxicated men, as well as inappropriate behavior and verbal abuse from a "trusted" religious brother from the same religious congregation. She witnessed a murder and machete attack at close range.

Helen continued to express her concerns to the Catholic provincial, and he continued to ignore her. Feeling abandoned by the church, she finally quit her job. She returned to her home in a condition that her military father described as "shell shock."

For the next ten years, she suffered silently from the effects of her experience without seeking any help. Eventually, she sought out a therapist who diagnosed and treated her for posttraumatic stress disorder. But it took another fifteen years to address the wounds to her soul.

Today, Helen is in her fifties, happily married with two grown children. She enjoys her work in an academic setting. The following testimony is used with her permission.

After my return to the States, it took years for me to seek help for the symptoms that plagued me: panic attacks, chronic nightmares, flashbacks, obsessive compulsive disorder, hypervigilance, hopelessness, shame, and grief. There was a gnawing feeling deep within my soul, dragging me deeper and deeper into a dark hole. Eventually, I was able to manage my PTSD symptoms enough to create a good life with my family, but therapy never seemed to touch my deeper misery, especially the hopelessness, shame, and grief that came from my missionary experience.

The experience completely severed my relationship with God, and my faith had become an abyss of emptiness. When I quit my job as a Catholic lay missionary after fourteen months and left my placement site, I clearly remember feeling a deep-seated anger and saying to myself, "I'm so glad I don't have to deal with priests, God, or religion anymore." However, that was easier said than done. Simply overhearing a spiritual discussion, having to sit in church for an event with my Catholic family, or just walking or driving past a church could produce distressing symptoms; but one of the most difficult triggers was seeing a priest.

After years of living with the hidden rift with God, I tried to pray, but as soon as I touched the surface of that frightening, gnawing nerve, I instantly withdrew from the pain. My therapist encouraged me to find help within the Catholic Church to reconnect with my faith, but I didn't know where to go. Finally, I found an experienced Catholic priest for a spiritual director who introduced me to the concept of "moral injury trauma."

I began to understand that my trust, faith, and love for God had been morally and spiritually injured, and that it needed to be addressed by recognizing the deep dark hole within my soul, created by the chaos of the missionary experience. It was an "aha moment" describing the wound that I had felt for years, but I could never articulate it. I felt relieved that someone compassionately understood the abyss of the gnawing feeling and could help me clarify the deep-seated grief and agony.

I learned how moral injury refers to "perpetrating, failing to prevent, or bearing witness to acts that transgress deeply held moral beliefs and expectations." In other words, I had witnessed so many unbearable acts, unable to intervene—and some of the acts were even done to me. These experiences shattered my soul.

I learned that moral injury could be of a religious or spiritual nature in which a believer experiences distress in relationship with their church or higher power. In truth, I was a young, inexperienced missionary, and the institutional church had abandoned me in a place that was for more experienced male missionaries. Feeling dismissed by the higher-ups and maltreated by the trusted religious brother in my village, I can only describe the betrayal as soul murder.

Reading literature about moral injury, I was able to name my own questions—"Am I a good person? Did I do the right thing?" By meditating on these questions, I realized how much shame and guilt I had because of my missionary experience, and I sobbed cries of anguish for months while my spiritual director helped me to recognize God was there in the tears. God was working slowly to reveal the source of my distress while being by my side the whole time. It is a long journey, but now I know I am on the right path.

I am not fully recovered, but I am so content to finally understand that God has always been by my side through these years. I was just too fearful of the pain of entering that dark hole, but now that I have begun to recover my religious and spiritual life, I feel the immense energy of God's love and mercy transforming that hole.

It deeply saddens me inside to know that there are many traumatized people who may never understand their pain as symptoms of moral or spiritual injury, and that therapy for PTSD may not be enough. I am not going to lie and say that going through the pain has been an easy task, but it has been extremely positive and worthwhile physically, emotionally, mentally, and spiritually. After twenty-five years, I am grateful that I finally found the right resources. Understanding the different types of wounds due to traumas is so needed in the healing process for the many people in situations like mine.

3

Every Sinner Has a Future

> A veteran strongly believes that having killed an enemy combatant, despite being justifiable in the context of war and done at the command of a superior, is a sin. He engages in a variety of self-destructive behaviors, including drinking excessively and driving recklessly, stating that he does not care if he dies. The psychologist, eager to help mitigate the potential harm of these behaviors, conceptualizes the thought as a stuck point and encourages the veteran to write it in his stuck point log. The veteran does so, and they return to it frequently but make no discernable progress towards changing it, much to the chagrin of the concerned psychologist. In fact, the veteran becomes increasingly irritated that they keep having the same discussion. His behaviors do not change, and eventually, he stops attending the sessions.[1]

This hypothetical case study is presented by a team of clinical psychologists, Veterans Administration (variously called "Veterans Affairs") chaplains, and trauma researchers in a recent textbook on moral injury published for clinicians by the American Psychological Association. They share a concern for clients suffering from MIT that some may withdraw from treatment if religious and spiritual variables are not incorporated

1. Jason Nieuwsma et al., "Collaboration with Chaplaincy and Ministry Professionals in Addressing Moral Injury," *Addressing Moral Injury in Clinical Practice*, ed. Joseph M. Currier, Kent D. Drescher, and Jason Nieuwsma (Washington, DC: American Psychological Association, 2021), 251.

concurrently with more evidence-based clinical care. Survey research, they note, indicates that "many persons seeking treatment for mental disorders are more likely to turn to clergy than to psychiatrists or general medical doctors."[2] They are also concerned that not all spiritual and pastoral caregivers have the necessary tools to successfully intervene with such clients, and therefore urge greater collaborative efforts to ensure optimal healing outcomes. The case demonstrates the existential impact on one human life, presenting the limits of unidimensional care for people exposed to violence.

This chapter follows directly upon its predecessor, presenting additional theological nuance to the moral injury discourse about sin. The above case study makes the issue painfully obvious. The three Abrahamic traditions, comprising billions of devotees, all rely on the category of sin. According to the *Routledge Encyclopedia of Philosophy*, "the concept of sin is the concept of a human fault that offends a good God and brings with it human guilt. Its natural home is in the major theistic religions of Judaism, Christianity, and Islam. These religious traditions share the idea that actual or personal sins are individual actions contrary to the will of God."[3] How can caregivers and careseekers make sense of the current discourse on moral injury in its relation to sin?

Outside the Abrahamic traditions, parenthetically, Ignatian practitioner and Zen roshi Ruben L. F. Habito believes sin can play a constructive role in Buddhist enlightenment. The First Week of the Exercises, he suggests, offers valuable meditations that highlight in straightforward fashion the problematic aspects of the contemporary human condition, "spelling out the features of that harmful karma in great detail. . . . The Exercises thus call our attention to a dimension that many of our contemporaries tend to overlook or set aside rather than confront and address. We might take a hint from the fact that the word 'sin' in English is 'die Sünde' in German, related to 'asunder,' 'separated,' or 'broken apart.' . . . Our global community is separated, ruptured, wounded, broken."[4]

2. P. S. Wang, P. A. Berglund, and R. C. Kessler, "Patterns and Correlates of Contacting Clergy for Mental Disorders in the United States," *Health Services Research*, 38, no. 2 (April 2003): 647–73.

3. Philip L. Quinn, "Sin," *Routledge Encyclopedia of Philosophy Online* (Taylor and Francis, 1998), https://www.rep.routledge.com/articles/thematic/sin/v-1.

4. Ruben L. F. Habito, *Zen and the Spiritual Exercises* (Maryknoll, NY: Orbis Books, 2013), 55.

A Spiritual Model of Moral Injury

As Brett Litz's groundbreaking work suggests, a conscience potentially informed by violations of one's moral code is the fulcrum that determines moral injury. In the Abrahamic traditions, that fulcrum is associated with sin. A serious challenge for spiritual and pastoral caregivers seeking to grow interdisciplinary insights and tools is that the fine research and related clinical practice remain *driven* by the field of psychology. Historically, mental health in the twentieth century too often reductively excluded or obscured fundamental religious categories such as sin.

Litz and his colleagues deserve recognition because they continue to refine the broader construct of moral injury in their clinical practice and research, and now distinguish different models. Given insufficient empirical research to date, Litz notes that "clinicians and laypersons working from different perspectives and backgrounds may gravitate to different understandings," one of which he calls the "spiritual model."[5] Viewed through this lens, moral injury "stems from the loss of spiritual beliefs or a ruptured relationship with God, or difficulty in making meaning out of morally transgressive experiences."[6] It is, seemingly, Litz's tip of the hat to moral injury as a thin construct.

Certainly, a spiritual model more adequately corresponds to Íñigo's experience at Manresa. Recall the severity of his symptoms of devastating shame, sorrow, and scrupulous distress. He testifies that it was only when divine mercy broke through in his soul that his relationship with God was repaired. The sixteenth-century courtier's symptoms exemplify how sin painfully ruptures a person's relationship with their Higher Power and points to the importance for persons of faith and seekers of a more "integral" healing model. Such a model would incorporate interdisciplinary spiritual tools, including the utilization of sacred texts according to a particular religious tradition, or specific rituals such as the sacrament of confession in the mainstream Christian heritage. It would also include sensitivity to the damage the *perception* of sinfulness can wreak upon innocent, traumatized souls.

5. Alanna Coady, Jessica R. Carney, Sheila Frankfurt, and Brett T. Litz, "The Emergence and Development of the Concept of Moral Injury," in Kelle, *Moral Injury*, 27.

6. Coady, Carney, Frankfurt and Litz, "Emergence and Development," 26.

Litz's "spiritual model of moral injury" is a significant step in the right direction, if still liable to reductive interpretation. An actual case study illuminates the subtle multidimensional dynamics at play for one deeply religious person.

The Case Study of Tola

Clinical psychologist Fernando Ona, a mental health scholar and practitioner with ministerial training, fluidly integrates the role of "spiritual guide" into his clinical practice. He and his colleagues relate the case of Tola (a pseudonym), a devout young African woman of traditional Christian piety who, for political reasons, had been tortured and repeatedly raped. Eventually, Tola escaped and found her way safely to the United States, where she received political asylum. Ona diagnosed her with both PTSD and moral injury, noting that her conservative Christian conscience was shattered by the degradation of her purity in depraved sexual violence. Tola's shame was informed by the sixth commandment's requirement of virginity before marriage; as a trained chaplain, Ona understood that the moral injury lay in Tola's believing *herself* to be sinful. He notes: "For many refugees and asylum seekers, the struggle to reconcile the evil that has happened to them with their identity as people of faith or their faith in the goodness of the world becomes deeply overwhelming to them."[7]

Ona's point recalls the perspective of psychiatrist Frank Ochberg on moral injury, which the latter believes runs deeper than the fear-based trauma of any physical or psychological wound. "[W]hen what you believe in has been dirtied and damaged and insulted, the result isn't post-traumatic stress injury. It's something else that's even more profound. It's a loss of a sense of meaning. It's beyond a physical or a psychological wound. It's worse than that because it destroys what you're all about."[8] For Tola, her very identity, inclusive of her Christian dignity, was at risk.

7. Linda Piwowarczyk, Kathleen Flinton, and Fernando Ona, "Refugee Resilience and Spirituality: Harnessing Social and Cultural Coping Strategies," in *Refugees and Asylum Seekers: Interdisciplinary and Comparative Perspectives*, ed. S. Megan Berthold and Kathryn R. Libal (Santa Barbara, CA: Praeger, 2019), 171. Ona is a former clinical associate professor of public health and community medicine in the Tufts University School of Medicine and holds an MDiv from the Boston University School of Theology.

8. "Art, Trauma, and PTSI: An Interview with Dr. Frank Ochberg," *Journal of Military and Veteran's Health* 28, no. 3 (July 2020).

"How can you not love mercy?" asks Anne Lamott. "Here's how: We're so often rattled by lingering effects of trauma and paralyzing fear."[9]

Therapist Ona, recognizing the threat to Tola's self-identity, notes that "these faith struggles may exacerbate and amplify existing trauma-related symptomology."[10] He is convinced that, for such clients, the therapist must be prepared to serve as a "spiritual witness" or refer them to someone else who can assist knowledgeably in that regard. However, this may be a stretch for mental health clinicians or trauma counselors who confess to discomfort in the religious/spiritual domain. According to the *Journal of Traumatic Stress*, "Over the last 30 years, the mental health field has made significant strides in recognizing the importance of religion/spirituality and its association with positive health outcomes, yet many providers avoid discussions of spirituality or religion for fear of stepping outside their scope."[11] Such caregivers should consider the following.

A pivotal interdisciplinary healing moment for Tola came during a session when she removed her Bible from the handbag she always carried and asked Ona about his interpretation of Mark 4:35-41, a scriptural text in which Jesus miraculously calms a storm on the sea. A storm was raging inside her, she explained to her therapist, within her shattered religious consciousness. "I'm waiting for Jesus to still the storm." Ona was indeed familiar with the text and asked her an astute, scripturally savvy healing question: " 'In this passage you mention, is the storm in the disciples or was it around them?' Her eyes got big, and she looked at her therapist with astonishment."[12] They went on to discuss the fact that, actually, "her storm was around her"—*not within*—such that she immediately relaxed and readily moved onto a path toward inner peace and reconciliation with God. The external chaos perdured, but the biblical intervention from a revered text sacred to her Christian tradition proved pivotal for Tola's eventual recovery.

Ona's approach to Tola's case can be read as one in which a gifted mental health care provider incorporated Litz's spiritual model of moral injury into a clinical diagnosis of PTSD. His successful treatment indicates

9. Anne Lamott, *Hallelujah Anyway: Rediscovering Mercy* (New York: Riverhead Books, 2017), 5.

10. Piwowarczyk, Flinton, and Ona, "Refugee Resilience and Spirituality," 172.

11. Brandon J. Griffin et al., "Moral Injury: An Integrative Review," *Journal of Traumatic Stress* 32, no. 3, *Special Issue on Moral Injury* (June 2019): 350.

12. Piwowarczyk, Flinton, and Ona, 169.

a method for clinicians to address constructively the challenge of theodicy in clients of faith. Here is a fine example of spiritually informed clinical care, a methodology that responds to special, contextual needs of morally injured people of ruptured faith or spiritual doubt. It may be pivotal for holistic healing to explicitly address one's self-awareness as a sinner or God's identity as good. It was, of course, the *absence* of such multimodal care that forced the veteran in the fictional case study to walk away. How might Tola have fared without a caregiver versed in interdisciplinary care, unwilling to consult as needed?

Moral Injury and Sin

Despite the enormous contribution Litz has made by introducing a spiritual model of moral injury, the framework remains theologically precarious. For spiritual and pastoral caregivers, two fundamental questions remain. Most obviously, one wonders what percentage of counselors or mental health specialists have the required multidimensional training and skills exhibited by Ona, the desire to learn them, or the willingness to credit such a methodology? Mental health pre-service training is typically far too unidimensional, and many gatekeepers are disinterested in change. How many understand moral injury as a thin construct or credit Litz's spiritual model? How many are able to work constructively with clients who understand—or falsely believe—that they have sinned? Thomas Plante, former editor of the American Psychological Association journal *Spirituality in Clinical Practice*, notes that "secularized versions of spiritual practices such as mindfulness and yoga are popular, but faith tradition–based approaches are often ignored. We have much work to do to be sure that spirituality and religion is treated with respect."[13]

Second, Litz's schema is exposed to problematic terminological and theological issues. It will be imperative to sort them out in the generation ahead. What, exactly, is the significance of the word "moral" in moral injury? More than fifty years ago, world-renowned psychiatrist Karl Menninger asked, "Whatever Became of Sin?" in his bestseller of the same name.[14] The question remains outstanding in present moral

13. Thomas Plante, online interview, https://www.apa.org/pubs/highlights/editor-spotlight/scp-plante.

14. Karl Meninger, *Whatever Became of Sin?* (Portland, OR: Hawthorn Press, 1973).

injury discourse. Multimodal caregivers such as Ona understand that all three Abrahamic religions incorporate a theological concept of sin and related ethical code (though understood differently in each). Use of the word "moral"—popularly associated with morality—can be quite fraught spiritually and pastorally for certain clients grounded in any of these traditions. Did Tola's symptoms of shame, confusion, and sorrow indicate that she had sinned? Did she believe herself to be morally or spiritually compromised because of being forcibly subjected to rape, an act to which she had not consented? Sorting such questions out in a knowledgeable religious and spiritual fashion is critical to client well-being.

Spiritual and pastoral caregivers will appreciate the dilemma in ways most mental health caregivers will not. Most psychologists speak of *moral* injury with a seeming lack of awareness of its quite distinct philosophical and theological usage, as well as its spiritual implications for reconciliation. Duke University theologian and psychiatrist Warren Kinghorn notes: "Unlike the clinical disciplines, Christians can name the moral trauma of war not simply as psychological dissonance but as a tragic and perhaps even sinful reminder that the peace of God is still not yet a fully present reality."[15]

The challenge must now be addressed head-on. Various religious/spiritual commentators decry the failure to establish a cogent theological foundation to moral injury discourse and trauma intervention. Australian Anglican bishop Tom Frame, for example, a fifteen-year veteran of the Royal Australian Navy and a proponent of moral injury trauma theory, is wary of how it has evolved. In his priestly and pastoral ministry with wounded servicemembers and other survivors of violence, he has concluded that the field "has plainly been 'colonized' by psychology."[16] Perhaps this is inevitable at such an early stage of multimodal collaboration, and given the disproportionate interest, to date, on the part of the domain of psychology. In any case, the result is a Tower of *psychoBabel* in research and publication, and subsequent misapplication across or even within disciplines. Consequently, it is time for the religious/spiritual domain

15. Warren Kinghorn, "Combat Trauma and Moral Fragmentation: A Theological Account of Moral Injury," *Journal of the Society of Christian Ethics* 32, no. 2 (Fall/Winter 2012): 70.

16. Tom Frame, "Moral Injury and the Influence of Christian Religious Conviction," in *War and Moral Injury: A Reader*, ed. Robert Emmet Meagher and Douglas A. Pryer (Eugene, OR: Cascade Books, 2018), 195.

to be clearer about its disciplinary constraints, identity, heritage, and prerogatives.

One qualified specialist who clearly recognizes the significance of the challenge is Colonel Timothy Mallard, a career U.S. Army Chaplain with a PhD in Christian ethics. As a veteran of five combat and operational deployments overseas, he values highly the construct of moral injury. But he notes that the standard definition "borrows a manifestly theological concept such as transgression—which in Christian theology is tied to the antecedent concept of sin and the descendent concept of forgiveness—without any linkage between the three."[17]

Psychiatrist Jonathan Shay was among the first to introduce the construct of moral injury. Based on extensive work with Vietnam veterans, Shay was convinced that it should be considered a separate syndrome from PTSD, though the two can occur together. In his many books he recommended various treatment strategies for moral injury, understood as a wound to the soul. His reputation is such that the nonprofit Volunteers of America established the Shay Moral Injury Center in his honor, offering training and recovery services.[18]

Notably, Shay is familiar with and respectful of the Jewish and Christian heritages. He incorporates the language of sin and weaves it effectively into his writing and clinical practice. Shay notes that he would tell his patients—often majority Roman Catholic—that Catholic ideas about sin, if they "are about anything, they're about the real stuff. What the Church offers is about cruelty, violence, murder—not just the sins you confessed in parochial school."[19]

Terminological conversations can be tedious, at best, but the point is crucial at this stage of interdisciplinary discourse and practice. The categories and vocabulary of "sin" are utilized by enormous numbers of careseekers who understand and internalize certain regrettable choices, or "transgressions," as "sinful." To thoughtfully comprehend the signifi-

17. Timothy S. Mallard, "The (Twin) Wounds of War," *Providence Magazine*, February 17, 2017.

18. The Shay Moral Injuries Center, Volunteers of America, https://www.voa.org/services/shay-moral-injury-center-services/.

19. Jonathan Shay, *Odysseus in America: Combat Trauma and the Trials of Homecoming* (repr.; New York: Scribner, 2003), 153.

cance of the thin construct of moral injury, therefore, it may be that mental health professionals require more specialized pre-service training, as well as openness to multimodal professional collaboration with their colleagues.

Finally, because of the significant comorbidity between those scarred by trauma and substance use disorder, caregivers and careseekers can find it helpful to recall a twelve-step perspective on sin. That tradition considers sin a state of "falling short of perfection," or "defects of character," or "shortcomings."[20] "There is no *failure* here, for spirituality, as the ancients noted over and over again, involved a continual falling down and getting back up again. . . . [Sin is] a never-ending adventure of coming to know ourselves. . . . The great need is for *balance*—when we are down, we need to get up; and when we are up, we need to remember that we have been, and certainly will be again, 'down.' "[21] Experienced caregivers will be able to assist careseekers in this regard, aware that neuroscientists today believe there may be a biological cycle at work in which symptoms of trauma exacerbate addiction, and vice versa.

A Trauma-Informed Christian Spiritual Paradigm of Moral Injury?

One fears for the well-being of the fictitious client of record cited at chapter's outset, evidently a devout adherent of an Abrahamic religion. The outcome is all the more distressing because it is unnecessary. The past generation has witnessed the development of thoughtful "spiritually informed," or "spiritually integrated," clinical programs. The clinician of record in the above hypothetical case study has homework to do. A major generational challenge lies ahead, but there is no necessity to reinvent the wheel.

What *is* required is for the domains of psychology and religion/spirituality to listen, respectfully, to each other and be prepared to step up their holistic games for certain clients. *Follow the symptoms*, as the previous chapter highlighted. But psychiatrist and theologian Kinghorn notes that

20. Ernest Kurtz and Katherine Ketcham, *The Spirituality of Imperfection* (New York: Bantam Books, 2002 Bantam Reissue), 193.

21. Kurtz and Ketcham, *Spirituality of Imperfection*, 193.

the reduction and healing of symptoms—so that someone should "feel better"—is not the ultimate goal of spiritual and pastoral care.[22] At root it is so that sins may be forgiven and that this person "is reconciled to God."[23] For those in search of it, such as the military veteran in the case study above, psychology cannot promise the requisite divine mercy.

Part 2 will identify fresh scriptural insights, as well as reputable applications of trauma-informed, interdisciplinary insights and methods. But first, the next two chapters will document significant interdisciplinary steps forward in research and best practices that enable more tailored, trauma-informed care for persons of faith and seekers. Therapeutic regimens such as "spiritually informed clinical practice" already display a successful track record and specifically incorporate a mainstream Christian perspective on sin, mercy, and the sacrament of confession. Increasingly sophisticated frameworks, principles, and concrete multimodal regimens for MIT, reflective of traditional belief systems, are presently available. Interested spiritual and pastoral caregivers, as well as mental health clinicians and trauma counselors, may have homework to do.

22. Kinghorn, "Combat Trauma and Moral Fragmentation," 70.

23. Kinghorn, "Combat Trauma and Moral Fragmentation," 70.

4

The Spiritually Injured Íñigo

Brashly courageous Íñigo de Loyola emerged into history at the battle of Pamplona as a fearless, charismatic hero, rallying his outgunned, outnumbered, fainthearted comrades in arms, all of whom are reported to have voted to surrender to the French army. Evidently, they were not quite so fearless—or perhaps they just had better sense. (In sixteenth-century Castile during the age of chivalry, can those thousand-plus men all have been cowards?) Regardless, once Íñigo went down, the Spaniards immediately capitulated.

Íñigo seemed very much at home in period culture. Violence, warfare, and civil strife defined the chaotic reign of the House of Trastámara (1369–1516), the dynasty of record in Castile for a century and a half, well into the duration of the royal courtier's service. Queen Isabella I, who ruled over Castile from 1474 to 1504 and would eventually help unify Spain through her politically opportunistic marriage to Ferdinand II of Aragon, was of the Trastámara lineage. The imposing King Ferdinand extended the reign of "Los Reyes Catolicos" until 1516, not least by the expulsion of Jews and Muslims to "purify" the blood of the "one true Church." Likewise, Ferdinand established the Spanish Inquisition, with whom Íñigo had a fateful date.

Late medieval chivalry was a social code of honor that encouraged knights to defend the weak and innocent and to punish wrongdoers. In ideology and practice, however, it was often less noble. Recent research suggests that chivalry often motivated knights to avenge themselves violently upon their neighbors, pursue zealous holy war against Islam, and tear at the social fabric of society.[1] Masculinity arose "out of physical strength, audacity, the ability to make good on one's promises, and an aggressive and jealous sexuality."[2] Many refined courtiers doubled as fierce warriors. Family clans might commit wanton crimes in defense and promotion of their personal honor, their bloodlines, and the prosperity of their lineages.

Publicly, such violence could be sanctioned as "part of a divine plan,"[3] certainly if the clan was well connected at court. Brutality could be viewed, not as evil or immoral but, instead, pleasing to God. These were the values—and contradictions, for period Catholicism—which shaped the course of late medieval Castile and the family into which Íñigo was born. Superimposed upon the violent reality lay "a pleasant cultural veneer."[4] Inevitably during this period, many knights defined their role as defenders of the Christian faith and were expected to exhibit piety and reverence for God. Period Catholicism, for an hidalgo like Íñigo, would have required some concern for one's sins as an obstacle to relationship with God. The religious quest was not easily separated from the quest for honor.

Íñigo was faced with discerning genuine good from evil off a confusing menu of values—the authentic presence of God from its illusory manifestations in popular culture and social mores. There is no reason to doubt his good intentions. The Loyola clan presumably believed, if without much reflection, that their chivalric lifestyle was conducive to divine glory. What really mattered, though, was that their youngest, Íñigo, had achieved the vaunted status of battle hero for which he had long lusted, and which reflected enormous prestige on the lineage.

He was now free to consider alternative service—to a heavenly Lord. This is not to suggest that his vanity and pursuit of glory had diminished; rather, it was redirected. Íñigo's sins of pride and envy remained front and center. "Saint Dominic did this, so I have to do it. Saint Francis did this, so I have to do it."[5] The pilgrim had departed Loyola Castle on the road

1. Samuel A. Claussen, *Chivalry and Violence in Late Medieval Castile* (Suffolk, England: Boydell & Brewer, 2020), 3–12.

2. Claussen, *Chivalry and Violence*, 176.

3. Claussen, *Chivalry and Violence*, 7.

4. Claussen, *Chivalry and Violence*, 8.

5. Ignatius of Loyola, *A Pilgrim's Testament: The Memoirs of Saint Ignatius of Loyola*, ed. Barton T. Geger (Chestnut Hill, MA: Institute of Jesuit Sources, 2020), no. 7. Hereafter, *Auto*.

to Montserrat, seeking to outdo all previous saints in achieving honor for God. But the distressing episode at Manresa liberated his benighted consciousness to realize that the more challenging code of the Ten Commandments, and the God who revealed it, was the authentic path to the renown he sought. The quest for one's Higher Power today is similarly long and winding, not without frustrating detours, and requiring fraught decisions. A compassionate guide who has already taken many wrong turns—himself a sinner—can make an enormous difference.

Chapter 4 introduces Íñigo de Loyola as a man who presents with symptoms of both moral and *spiritual* injury (sometimes called "spiritual distress" in the literature of spirituality and mental health). Scarred survivors of violence and those of distressed conscience today—as well as caregivers from both mental health and religious/spiritual perspectives—may find in this thin distinction a compelling source of healing insight. Like its predecessors, the chapter aims to be an accessible resource to them. For those who wish to dig deeper, ample citations from peer-reviewed sources are provided.

Spiritual Injury

During the past generation, it has become routine to speak of "spirituality" in moral injury discourse. This is a remarkable development in and of itself, although the concept lacks specificity. The National Center for PTSD, for example, notes that moral injury "typically has an impact on an individual's spirituality. For example, an individual with moral injury may have difficulty understanding how one's beliefs and relationship with God can be true given the horrific event the person experienced, leading to uncertainty about previously held spiritual beliefs."[6]

Because the inclusion of spiritual and even religious dynamics into MIT studies has relied so heavily on psychological definition, and because moral injury discourse itself originates within the domain of psychology, greater terminological differentiation is illuminating. Because, the argument goes, psychology has historically undermined religion and spirituality

6. Sonya B. Norman and Shira Maguen, "Moral Injury," U.S. Department of Veterans Affairs: National Center for PTSD, https://www.ptsd.va.gov/professional/treat/cooccurring/moral_injury.asp.

in health care, perhaps a more discrete approach would make it possible for spiritual injury and distress to carve out their own footprint. Informed interdisciplinary caregiving, some specialists believe, may well benefit from a specifically *spiritual* health assessment as part of any *mental* health assessment. A related, critical advantage might be to enable more precise measurement of moral versus spiritual injury.[7]

The domain of religion and spirituality can never again allow itself to be subsumed into a narrowly psychological model, cognizant that "[s]pirituality has been psychology's clearest taboo, an enormous blind spot in the realm of human experience."[8] Psychologists William R. Miller and Harold D. Delaney detail how, over the course of the twentieth century, psychology remained *divorced* from the realm of the soul, including sin, religion, and spirituality. It was a wholesale embrace of the scientific method. "The modal response of psychologists to religion in research, practice, and training . . . became one of silence and neglect."[9] It was not benign. According to clinical psychologist David H. Rosmarin of Harvard Medical School, the silence and neglect could be hostile, largely attributable to "Sigmund Freud's characterization of religion as a 'mass-delusion' nearly 100 years ago."[10]

Nor can spirituality ever again surrender to a reductive medical model. Moral injury represents an important trauma treatment option going forward, but "it is essential to keep exploring moral injury as a spiritual suffering."[11] *Spiritual* injury is a construct unambiguously open to the

7. Murray Davies, "Assessing Spiritual Wounds and Injuries," *Journal of Military and Veterans' Health*, forthcoming. Davies provides a valuable appendix listing available "Moral and Spiritual Injury Assessment Tools," and proposes his own original tool.

8. William R. Miller and Harold D. Delaney, *Judeo-Christian Perspectives on Psychology: Human Nature, Motivation, and Change* (Washington, DC: American Psychological Association, 2005), 14.

9. Miller and Delaney, *Judeo-Christian Perspectives on Psychology*, 4.

10. David H. Rosmarin, "Psychiatry Needs to Get Right with God," *Scientific American*, June 15, 2021. With a multidisciplinary team of mental health clinicians, researchers, and chaplains, Rosmarin has created a flexible, spiritually integrated form of cognitive behavioral therapy he calls "SPIRIT"—Spiritual Psychotherapy for Inpatient, Residential and Intensive Treatment.

11. "Moral Injury and Its Causes, Symptoms, and Responses," Gabriella Lettini, in *Moral Injury: A Guidebook for Understanding and Engagement*, ed. Brad E. Kelle (Lanham, MD: Rowman and Littlefield, 2020), 40.

numinous, and shifts the focus to divine encounter. For spiritual and pastoral caregivers, the terminology and model may offer the most trustworthy path to respectful interdisciplinary discourse and collaboration.

In this regard, one rare mental health research study deserves wider attention. In a notable article titled "Spiritual Injuries—An Australian Defence Force Experience," lead researcher and author Murray Davies examines the experience of the Australian Defence Force (ADF) in the wake of two decades of international military deployments on battlefields as diverse as East Timor, Afghanistan, and Iraq.[12] Research data indicates that approximately 8–13 percent of ADF personnel who deploy to active battlefield areas are likely, upon return home, to suffer from some form of service-related mental illness. To better engage the complex *status questionis*, Davies astutely utilizes a methodology *correlated with* but not *subsumed by* moral injury. Spiritual injury is respectful of moral injury and draws from the latter's deep well of insights and resources, in this paradigm, but it also enforces working boundaries against the historic tendency of psychology to colonize religion and spirituality.

A retired officer from the Australian army, Davies wholeheartedly welcomes moral injury as a useful category in mental health care, distinguishable from PTSD, for service members and military veterans. But, he worries, "[w]hat is not being discussed, is not widely understood, or has any form of treatment regime are spiritual injuries."[13] The area is not being addressed by the Australian Department of Veterans Affairs, churches, theologians, or faith-based organizations, such that veterans mustering out of the ADF enter a " 'spiritual grey zone' or an area in which there is little to no guidance and specific help in spiritual or faith issues."[14] It sounds like the lament of countless veterans and other survivors of trauma in the West, who prefer to seek healing with religious, spiritual, and pastoral caregivers. A large percentage of this population has lost much or all sense of divine presence and goodness, Davies relates, with associated diminishment of faith, meaning, and purpose in their lives. A primary reason is the lack of suitable trauma-informed resources adapted for those

12. Murray James Davies, "Spiritual Injuries—An Australian Defense Force Experience," *Journal of Veterans Studies* 6, no. 1 (May 18, 2020).

13. Davies, "Spiritual Injuries," 160.

14. Davies, "Spiritual Injuries," 160.

mustering out, and Davies' research aims to identify and promote more contextually tailored, *spiritual* treatment regimens, insights, and tools. If Davies is wary of moral injury, it is simply because of his devout interest in promoting better spiritual and pastoral care for his beloved vets. It is a task part 2 will address head-on.

Yes, there is overlap between moral and spiritual injury, Davies understands. But he is more interested in exploring the *differences*, in particular "the nature of the injury, the way it presents and its effects and treatment."[15] "Spirituality" is defined by Davies, generically if valuably in interfaith terms, as "the belief in the relationship between the human spirit and the divine spirit," which includes "how a person appropriates beliefs about a God in the world in a journey for self-transcendence and meaning."[16] "Morality" is a construct "used descriptively to refer to certain codes of conduct put forward by a group and accepted by an individual for their own behavior."[17] Spirituality is distinct from morality in that the former is determined "by a personal and individual relationship with a God concept."[18] The symptoms of moral injury, in other words, do not *necessarily* point to a spiritual injury, nor do they point in any way to religious belief. Shame, confusion, and sorrow may or may not have any reference to *God*, according to the individual's belief system. Here Davies offers a valuable clarification compatible with the understanding of moral injury as a thin construct. Access to the numinous domain may require a measure of faith.

A spiritual injury is an outcome that derives from a "catalytic event"[19] that raises the God-question or related doubts about the ultimate meaning of life. Perhaps a person comes to believe, through costly battlefield experience, that he or she has failed or betrayed God by not acting in a way that warrants God's love or mercy. Perhaps another person believes that an omnipotent, omniscient, omnibenevolent God *has chosen to betray her*, or even the troubled course of human events, by divine indifference to military casualties. "Was God taking the day off?"

15. Davies, "Spiritual Injuries," 159.
16. Davies, "Spiritual Injuries," 160.
17. Davies, "Spiritual Injuries," 160.
18. Davies, "Spiritual Injuries," 160.
19. Davies, "Spiritual Injuries," 162.

A spiritual injury can be understood as the potentially deleterious effect that fractured faith may have on some facet(s) of holistic well-being for certain individuals. Toxic shame, loss of belief in life's meaning, addictions, eating disorders, or treatment-resistant depression, for example, may be behavioral indicators that point to potential spiritual injury somewhere along the dimensional spectrum of severity, for persons of faith and seekers. Íñigo's suicidality, presumably, perhaps even his extreme fasting, can in this sense be understood as potentially serious spiritual injuries.

Spiritual injury, therefore, may involve mental health repercussions. Optimal treatment modalities may well be interdisciplinary. The case study of Tola in the previous chapter is an excellent example, requiring a trained therapist intimately familiar with Christian sacred texts. Such trauma may manifest as anger *at*, cynicism *about*, or a sense of rejection *by* God; alienation from or anger at clergy and church personnel; withdrawal from church participation; or a strong sense of existential confusion or meaninglessness. Today, one thinks of clerical sexual abuse of minors as an example of a catalytic event that potentially results in the victim-survivor's severe spiritual distress.

At a given point in time, a soldier or other survivor of violence may display severe, mild, or no spiritual injury, given human freedom and individual temperament. This outcome may lead, therefore, to *suicidal despair* of God, of life, and/or of themselves; it may *diminish* one's trust in Divinity and/or undermine one's religious or spiritual practice; or it may have *little or no impact* at all. With proper guidance, tools, and disciplined practice, a supplicant's recognition that there *is*, in fact, a spiritual component to a particular injurious outcome can lead to posttraumatic growth; perhaps he or she may even invoke God's healing presence and divine reconciliation. Spiritual wounds, in this sense, can benefit from meditation and various forms of spiritual exercises, whether of the Ignatian school or otherwise.[20] In the Jewish and Christian traditions, the

20. Gerry Ken Crete presents healing exercises based in traditional Catholic "litany" in *Litanies of the Heart: Relieving Post-traumatic Stress and Calming Anxiety through Healing Our Parts* (Manchester, NH: Sophia Institute Press, 2023). Litanies are a form of prayer in which the supplicant gives thanks to God or cries out for divine assistance with a repeated refrain. Psalm 13, for example: "*How long*, O Lord? Will you forget me forever? *How long* will you hide your face from me? *How long* must I bear pain in my soul and have sorrow in my heart all day long?"

psalms and prophetic literature of lament come to mind. Spiritual injuries benefit from spiritual exercises adapted for a special needs population such as Davies's ADF veterans.

Spiritual injury might even be designated as the outcome of one more form of trauma—"*spiritual injury trauma*." This form of trauma would be considered fundamentally *different* than moral injury trauma, in Davies's framework, in that the former outcome occurs when an incident, event, or series of events ruptures the *relationship* between an individual and the God of their understanding. "God died on the battlefield," some veterans put it. "Spiritual injury occurs in the context of a personal relationship" with the Divine.[21] This variable distinguishes spiritual from moral injury. Those *without* relationship with or belief in God are best understood as suffering from *moral* injury manifest in symptoms identified in chapter 2 (sorrow, grief, regret, shame, or alienation) *apart from* any reference to a Higher Power or the discipline of spirituality. Though the symptoms of moral and spiritual injury can and do overlap, the point is that specifically *religious* and *spiritual* healing prayer exercises, including use of sacred texts and/or ritual practices, are typically recommended for people of faith and seekers. A pressing, trauma-informed task at hand is the identification of designated treatment paradigms, insights, and practices suitable for the special needs population of survivors of violence.

Davies incorporates a brief reference to sin, defined as "an act of transgression against God, the divine law or the Commandments of a particular faith."[22] It can be viewed "as any thought or action that endangers the ideal relationship between an individual and God."[23] Davies shows no particular interest in describing the significance of sin more fully, though he clearly recognizes that it must be addressed in any thoughtful consideration of spiritual injury. In light of Christian tradition, the area of sin and related distressed conscience remains undeveloped in moral and spiritual injury discourse.

A key indicator of spiritual injury, for Davies, is the *choice of language* on the part of the distressed individual. A spiritual injury can be distinguished from moral injury, and identified as such, when "God, in some

21. Davies, "Spiritual Injuries," 161.
22. Davies, "Spiritual Injuries," 162.
23. Davies, "Spiritual Injuries," 162.

form (Father, Lord, Allah, etc.) is named and identified as the principal source or focus of the injury."[24] Íñigo's Manresa Episode comes to mind. Following months of obsessive-compulsive scrupulosity, enslaved and tormented by toxic memories, he desperately "shouted aloud to God, saying 'Help me, Lord, for I find no remedy in people, nor in any creature. Yet, if I thought I could find it, no labor would be too hard for me. Yourself, Lord, show me where I may find it.'"[25] His distressed *cri de coeur to God* identifies the (morally injured) Íñigo as, more precisely, *spiritually* injured.

Simultaneous to these divine invocations, "the temptation often came over him with great force to throw himself from a large balcony in his room, next to the place where he was praying."[26] His extreme symptoms, including scrupulosity, sorrow, shame, and confusion, had become life-threatening. "But realizing that it was a sin to kill oneself, he shouted again, 'Lord, I will do nothing that offends you.'"[27] Again, Íñigo's choice of language and divine address is significant. His toxic shame placed his very relationship with Divinity at risk, terrifying the God-seeking courtier. Many conscientious practitioners of one of the three Abrahamic religions have been there. But, with sin as with spiritual injury, forgiveness is always available and makes possible reconciliation with one's Higher Power. This, in turn, points to the possibility of posttraumatic growth "[i]n the same way that muscle is torn during strength and resistance training and becomes thicker and stronger."[28] For practitioners of the Abrahamic religions, *healing* can be considered, virtually by definition, as *forgiveness of sin* and renewed personal encounter with God.

The Davies study makes a significant contribution to violence-related trauma studies discourse and merits further attention. His insistence on "fundamentally different"[29] care remedies for spiritual injury is a critical contribution. The point is that more tailored religious and spiritual insights and practices will be to the healing benefit of a significant number of survivors of violence like those mustering out of the Australian Defence

24. Davies, "Spiritual Injuries," 164.
25. *Auto.*, no. 23.
26. *Auto.*, no. 24.
27. *Auto.*, no. 24.
28. Davies, "Spiritual Injuries," 164.
29. Davies, "Spiritual Injuries," 159.

Forces. The foundational significance of bloody Pamplona and haunted Manresa as incubators of the Spiritual Exercises gains contemporary traction within this framework.

The Clinical Value of Spiritual Injury: A Case Study

Margaret (not her real name) was a devout young Roman Catholic woman from a practicing Catholic family.[30] She was engaged to be married and, along with her fiancé, visited a mental health professional for premarital counseling. Because of significant differences between the partners on the matter of virginity before marriage, they wished to delve deeper into their personal narratives and the conflictive dynamics that threatened their engagement. Each proceeded to develop a growth-oriented plan with the counselor, based on mutually agreed-upon needs and variables.

Margaret held strong, traditional beliefs about "waiting until marriage," maintaining her virginity until after she celebrated a sacramental Catholic union. But her fiancé was unconvinced. The counselor herself was not a woman of active religious orientation or spiritual practice, though she was professionally respectful of Margaret's piety and views.

Before the marriage took place, a stranger broke into Margaret's apartment and sexually assaulted her. Having professionally assisted many rape survivors, the counselor worked hard to help Margaret process and recover from the severe disorientation and distress of the traumatic violence. She noted that Margaret had been *forcibly* violated and bore no responsibility for the matter. But nothing that had worked with previous clients seemed to help Margaret.

The young woman was inconsolable and unable to overcome the sense of impurity that had shattered her world. Margaret believed she was now unworthy of a sacramental marriage, ashamed to speak to her priest, convinced she could never be forgiven. The counselor met with the agency's consulting psychiatrist to ensure that they did not need to identify any underlying psychiatric disorder, and this was ruled out.

At the time, recalled the counselor, the closest she could come to understanding Margaret's impasse was as an "existential crisis," though

30. The actual case study, dating back more than twenty years, was recounted to the author in a February 2023 conversation with a seasoned trauma therapist.

she could see that, for the young woman, it was so much deeper. The counselor tried every intervention available at that time, but Margaret did not respond. She and her fiancé found no common ground, grew emotionally weary of the process, and eventually discontinued therapy. Sadly, they called off the wedding as well.

When, many years later, the same counselor was apprised of the construct of *spiritual injury*, she described herself as "stunned." She immediately recalled Margaret—"It was like a lightbulb flashing in my brain." The case had long perplexed her, and she surmised that she had let Margaret down because she lacked the insight for addressing her traumatic injury. Now, the more experienced counselor could connect dots that she simply could not see all those years ago.

"I did not know about spiritual injury and how this was the profound missing link for this client." As a result, the counselor explained, she could reframe her understanding of such client narratives. "I can almost imagine Margaret's sense of restored dignity in the face of her shame, if only she had just heard those words—*spiritual injury*. Probably her relationship with God was threatened. Perhaps I should have consulted with a Catholic priest. Perhaps the marriage could have been saved. In any case, I am professionally grateful to know that, moving forward, counselors who are not active religiously or spiritually can use this construct to assist trauma-beleaguered survivors who are."

5

The Soul Also Keeps the Score

In the short history of dialogue between psychology and religion, there is surely neither relationship nor correspondence as remarkable as that between loyal friends Sigmund Freud (1856–1939) and Oskar Pfister (1873–1956). Chapter 5 is grounded in the constructive substance and spirit of that extraordinary conversation.[1] After a review of the interdisciplinary significance of their letters, with particular interest in Pfister's view that "psychoanalytic therapy is a secularized and scientifically based cure of souls,"[2] this chapter will look backward to situate the concept of "soul" in the early Western Christian tradition. The seminal figure central to this discourse is the fourth-century philosopher Augustine of Hippo, born in today's Algeria.

Going forward, the view from antiquity finds resonance in a robust example of current collaboration between the fields of psychology and religion: two models of twenty-first-century "spiritually informed trauma therapy." These evidence-based practices vividly demonstrate the possibilities of multimodal recovery regimens and point ahead to an exciting generation of enhanced interdisciplinary collaboration. In sum, the current chapter aims to illustrate how, and in what sense, the soul keeps the score at the intersection of mental health and spirituality.

1. Carlos Dominguez-Morano, *Sigmund Freud and Oskar Pfister on Religion: The Beginning of an Endless Dialogue*, trans, Francisco Javier Montero (New York: Routledge, 2024).

2. Oskar Pfister, *New Testament Cure of Souls and Psychoanalytic Therapy*, cited in Dominguez-Morano, *Sigmund Freud and Oskar Pfister*, 35.

The Odd Couple

Recognized as the father of psychoanalysis, Sigmund Freud obviously needs no introduction. Oskar Pfister was a Swiss Lutheran minister with a Reformed Congregation in Zurich. Freud was sixteen at the time of Pfister's birth, just beginning medical school. The pastor studied theology, philosophy, and psychology at the University of Zurich, and, through his work with troubled children at his parish school, developed an early interest in Freud's theories. In 1919, Pfister founded the Swiss Society for Psychoanalysis, which welcomed "lay psychoanalysts" like the minister himself. Though it was controversial, Freud himself strongly supported this school of practice in which a medical degree was not required. Somewhat uniquely, Pfister was both an ordained pastor and a practicing psychoanalyst. The men established a lifelong friendship, highlighted by a stimulating correspondence, over the last twenty years of Freud's life.[3]

The odd couple agreed on most matters psychological, and were enormously respectful of, even deferential to, each other professionally. Pastor Pfister was an occasional visitor to Freud's home in Vienna, and his infectious joy is said to have charmed Freud's children. Though Pfister dressed as a cleric, the family welcomed him as a Pied Piper who enlivened the household. The personal relationship made for quick-witted correspondence, befitting two frank intellectuals for whom no topic was verboten. Pfister was soon initiated into Freud's inner professional circle.

Religion, Scripture, theology, and pastoral care were different topics entirely. Here they disagreed intensely, even though Pfister's reformed Christianity downplayed dogma and ecclesial authority. The genial pastor made friends easily, one of whom was Carl Jung, the son of a fellow Swiss minister.[4] This might have become a sore point because of Jung's competing views on psychiatry and psychoanalysis, but Pfister considered himself Freud's loyal disciple and never wavered.

3. Sigmund Freud, *Psychoanalysis and Faith: The Letters of Sigmund Freud and Oskar Pfister*, Classic Reprint Series (London: Forgotten Books, 2018). Many of Pfister's letters to Freud were destroyed, at the former's request. But he left his remaining correspondence to Freud's daughter Anna, whom he called "the daughter of his great benefactor."

4. Jung wrote to Freud: "Pfister is a splendid fellow . . . a champion of our cause. . . . Oddly enough, I find this mixture of medicine and theology to my liking." Cited in Dominguez-Morano, *Sigmund Freud and Oskar Pfister*, 4.

The strange bedfellows can be considered the historic *patrons* of what today is the specialized field of psychiatry and religion. Pfister spoke of Freud in quasi-religious terms—"whether [you want] it talked about or not, [you are] a true servant of God according to Protestant standards."[5] (The word "Protestant" may be the operative term—Pfister and Freud found common cause in their antipathy for what they saw as Catholic sexual repression.) Pfister emphasized the analogies between the "cure of souls" and psychoanalysis, downplaying notable differences.

Intellectual historians are certain that the 1927 publication of Freud's *The Future of an Illusion* was in part a response to Pfister.[6] It presents Freud's critique of religion as a counterweight to the views of both Pfister and Jung. Freud could be combative in his letters, speaking as the consummate rationalist for whom science and progress provide all necessary answers and methodology. For Freud, God was a fantasy, and religious beliefs, illusions. Dogma, doctrine, and ritual were authoritarian means of control and repression. Freud was convinced that religion and Scripture hindered intellectual inquiry and critical thinking, and was fascinated that his friend demonstrated those very qualities while remaining a believer.

Within a year, Pfister answered *The Future of an Illusion* with a brilliant riposte, *The Illusion of a Future: A Friendly Disagreement with Prof. Sigmund Freud.*[7] Freud had invited his colleague to respond, and even published the letter in his own journal, *Imago*. With Pfister, he could be tolerant. Upon close reading, *The Illusion of a Future* is a model of

5. Oskar Pfister, "The Illusion of a Future: A Friendly Disagreement with Prof. Sigmund Freud," *International Journal for Psychoanalysis* 74, no. 557 (1993). First published in Freud's journal, *Imago*, in Vienna (1928)

6. "On 16th October 1927, Freud announced to pastor O. Pfister the publication of *The Future of an Illusion:* 'In the next few weeks a pamphlet of mine will be appearing which has a great deal to do with you. I had been wanting to write it for a long time, and postponed it out of regard for you, but the impulse became too strong. The subject-matter—as you will easily guess—is my completely negative attitude to religion, in any form and however attenuated, and, though there can be nothing new to you in this, I feared, and still fear, that such a public profession of my attitude will be painful to you. When you have read it you must let me know what measure of tolerance and understanding you are able to preserve for the hopeless pagan.'" Dominguez-Morano, *Sigmund Freud and Oskar Pfister*, 69.

7. Pfister, "Illusion of a Future."

intellectual honesty and more than a hint of evangelical fervor. None of this would have surprised Freud.

"And yet, I turn decisively against you," wrote Pfister.[8] On the matter of religion, the friends pulled no punches, relishing the intellectual and professional exchange. "Regarding the meaning and value of religion, the interlocutors were brutally candid. Pfister answered Freud's *Future of an Illusion* with a resounding statement of faith."[9] For the pastor, religious beliefs and practices, and his firm belief in God, served as psychological mechanisms offering reassurance about ultimate questions of meaning and purpose. Spiritual practices such as prayer provided entrée to encounter with God. If for Freud religion was an illusion, for Pfister, Freud's unbounded faith in science was the illusion. Nevertheless, the pastor was convinced that psychoanalysis made an immense contribution to the scientific care of souls. "And he who through the creation of psychoanalysis has provided the instrument which freed suffering souls from their chains and opened the gates of their prisons, so that they could hasten into the sunny land of a life-giving faith, is not far from the kingdom of God."[10]

Pfister's "potent rebuttal to Freud's reductionist views offered a cogent model for a new level of dialogue between religion and psychiatry."[11] He writes as an ally who is also, and unabashedly, a prominent Christian pastor and evangelist. "But I too fight on your side, for nothing else is closer to your heart, as to mine, as the overcoming of illusion through truth. Whether you with your *Future of an Illusion*, or I with my 'Illusion of a Future' comes closer to the ideal, a higher tribunal will decide."[12]

Pfister's affectionate tone with Freud is coupled with robust, substantive disagreement. Their collaborative regard sets an aspirational model for future discourse in mental health and spirituality. Pfister was a passionate practitioner of both religion *and* clinical mental health, whose greatest desire was to forge some sort of alliance for the good of humanity. His

8. Pfister, "Illusion of a Future."

9. Clark S. Aist, "The Recovery of Religious and Spiritual Significance in American Psychiatry," *Journal of Religion and Health* 51, no. 3 (September 2012): 617.

10. Pfister, "Illusion of a Future."

11. Aist, "Recovery of Religious," 617–18.

12. Pfister, "Illusion of a Future."

"cure of souls" (German *seelsorge*) today is understood as pastoral and spiritual care, a "search for [his] parishioners' spiritual, psychic, and human good."[13] His interest in psychoanalysis was in service of the broader priority of deepening his ministerial insights and skills for the benefit of his clients and sharing them with fellow spiritual and pastoral caregivers (German *seelsorger*). Pfister is remembered as an early, prominent proponent of a synthesis of psychiatry and religion, an offshoot of which is today's discourse between mental health and spirituality.

Throughout his life, Pfister wrote extensively on topics related to psychology, psychotherapy, Scripture, and religion, with interest in a holistic approach that acknowledges the interconnectedness of the mind, body, and spirit in the one human person. "[D]espite the fundamental differences between New Testament pastoral care of souls and psychoanalytic therapy . . . they present such strong affinities that they should not fight each other as adversaries (as has happened until now) but rather see each other as allies."[14] The following section explains how Pfister's consistent commitment to soul care is grounded in both Jewish and Christian sacred texts and situated squarely in the mainstream Christian tradition.

The Soul Keeps the Score

The word "soul" is rooted in the Hebrew religious and scriptural traditions as the English translation of "*nephesh*," though no one English word can capture the holistic perspective of the Hebrew.[15] It is used 756 times in the Old Testament to denote the *whole* human person and does not admit of segregating out individual components. For example, Genesis 2:7 reads: "[T]he Lord God formed man from the dust of the ground and breathed into his nostrils the breath of life, and the man became a living being"[16] (living being = literally soul, *nephesh*). Unlike the Greek

13. Dominguez-Morano, *Sigmund Freud and Oskar Pfister*, 33.

14. Citation in Dominguez-Morano, *Sigmund Freud and Oskar Pfister*, 34.

15. J. L. McKenzie, *Dictionary of the Bible* (London and Dublin: Geoffrey Chapman, 1965), 838.

16. All English-language quotations of Scripture, unless noted otherwise, have been taken from the *New Revised Standard Version Updated Edition* (Grand Rapids, MI: Zondervan, 2022). Scripture citations appear hereafter in parentheses in the body of the chapter.

word *psyche*, which favors an anthropological understanding separating body and soul, *nephesh* does not admit of disembodied entity and existence. People do not *have* a *nephesh*, scripturally, they *are* a *nephesh*. In the Shema prayer, Israelites pray: "Hear O Israel: The LORD is our God, the LORD alone. You shall love the LORD your God with all your heart and with all your soul [*nephesh*] and with all your might" (Deut 6:4-5).

The New Testament soul is "the totality of the self as a living and conscious subject."[17] A pious Jew, Jesus quotes the same Israelite confession of faith in response to a question from one of the scribes about which Torah commandment is primary. (According to later rabbinic interpretation, there were 613 in all.) Jesus answers: "'Hear O Israel: The Lord our God, the Lord is one; you shall love the Lord your God with all your heart and with all your soul and with all your mind and with all your strength'" (Mark 12:29-30). One Scripture scholar, referencing the original Greek of the New Testament, comments: "The soul (*psyche*) is our whole self as a living being."[18]

Philosophic discourse about soul begins in antiquity with Plato (428/7–348/7 BCE) and Aristotle (384–322 BCE), who both believed that soul gives life to the body. Subsequently, from early to medieval to modern to present times, the conversation goes through Augustine (354–430). One of the Latin fathers of the church, his distinctive theological work shaped Christianity to a degree arguably surpassed only by Scripture. He "devoted much time and thought to the soul, and some of the most significant points he makes on the subject will reappear, over a thousand years later, in the work of Rene Descartes."[19] For Augustine, the soul is the basis of life, a substance in its own right, and the unifying principle of human interconnectedness. Without soul, as Genesis suggests, there is no life. It animates all components of the body. The human person is "a soul endowed with reason, which is joined to its physical body."[20]

To the soul Augustine assigns three fundamental "powers" (*facultates animae*)—memory, intelligence, and will. Soul underlies and integrates them, enabling them to work together toward its ultimate purpose of seek-

17. McKenzie, *Dictionary of the Bible*, 839.

18. Mary Healey, *The Gospel of Mark* (Ada, MI: Baker Academic, 2008), 246.

19. Stewart Goetz and Charles Taliaferro, *A Brief History of the Soul* (Hoboken, NJ: Wiley-Blackwell, 2011), 32.

20. Goetz and Taliaferro, *Brief History of the Soul*, 33.

ing and finding God. More broadly, soul can be understood as "multiple essential psychological powers and/or capacities (e.g., the power to think, the power to remember, the power to choose, the capacity to experience pleasure, the capacity to desire, the capacity to fear)."[21] The parallels with twenty-first century trauma dynamics are striking—the decisive role of memory, fear, and freedom of volition (agency), for example. Such powers cannot be separated from nor exist independently from the soul.

Of course, by the time of Pfister, Humpty Dumpty's unity was well on its way to being fractured by the scientific method, cracked and desperate for repair. Freud was partially responsible. But, in the area of mental health and spirituality, happily, it is not too late to put Humpty Dumpty back together again.[22] The following chapter will describe Íñigo's defense of his Christian orthodoxy before a suspicious Spanish Inquisition by situating his Exercises quite explicitly in this Augustinian heritage of the three powers of soul.

In his short work *On the Immortality of the Soul*, Augustine noted that

> the soul is present as a whole not only in the entire mass of a body, but also in every least part of the body at the same time. For the soul senses the suffering of a part of the body as a whole, and yet not in the whole body. For when there is a pain in the foot the eye turns, the tongue speaks, the hand moves forward. This would not happen unless the soul which senses in these parts, also senses in the foot, nor could it while absent sense what was happening there. . . . The whole soul, therefore, is present simultaneously in each part, and simultaneously senses in each.[23]

One might imagine the soul as an intricate tapestry woven with threads of various hues and textures, each representing different aspects of the human being—thoughts, desires, fears, affect, imagination, and aspirations. Augustine's point was that, just as every thread contributes to the

21. Goetz and Taliaferro, *Brief History of the Soul*, 38.

22. The *Catechism of the Catholic Church* (365) presents a current, succinct formulation of the tradition, referencing the profound "unity of soul and body," such that "spirit and matter . . . are not two natures united, but rather their union forms a single nature" (2nd ed. [United States Catholic Conference—Libreria Editrice Vaticana, 1997]).

23. Augustine, *On the Immortality of the Soul*, trans. George G. Leckie (New York: D. Appleton-Century, 1938), 83–84. Augustine also examines the soul in his *Confessions*, *On the Trinity*, and *City of God*.

overall pattern and singular charm of a particular tapestry, each facet of the person reflects the unity of the soul. Despite the diverse, multifaceted nature of these threads, they are each woven together into a harmonious *whole*, reflecting the divine craftsmanship of the Creator. Individual misplaced threads—or damaged powers of soul—impact the tapestry of the human person as a whole. A similar analogy could be made with a mosaic artwork, composed of countless intricately shaped tiles of varied colors.

A *nephesh*, as a human being, is a whole organized by and into various innate capabilities or powers associated with the three fundamental faculties of memory, intelligence, and will. Health caregivers from any field need to understand that a "soul wound," therefore, affects not only physical, psychological, neural, moral, or spiritual aspects of the human person, but all of those in one. (This might be called a "faculty perspective" on heath care.) No single power or capacity may be isolated from the others without risk to the living, breathing organism.

This is of decisive significance regarding spirituality and mental health. Human attributes are permeable in their interconnectivity. One's spiritual capacities are the direct nexus to God, but not exclusive of the other faculties. Injuries to mind, body, brain, *or* spirit can affect the integral depth of a human sense of identity, dignity, and well-being. Mental health practitioners and trauma counselors reliant on scientific materialism, like Freud, will no doubt be unpersuaded. But they are locked into a diagnostic model that obscures a holistic collaborative alliance, as Pfister lamented.

The word "wound" comes from the Greek word for "trauma." Thus, trauma can be understood as a soul wound in an integral Hebraic sense—not only physical, psychological, moral, neural, *or* spiritual but the integral composite. Trauma affects the full spectrum of what constitutes the human person. Symptoms are thin and permeable among brain, mind, and body, as van der Kolk convincingly demonstrates, with trauma stored in somatic memories. *The Body Keeps the Score* persuasively demonstrates the interconnectedness of these human components in a variety of successful body-oriented therapies and mind/body practices. He is silent, however, about the spiritual component of the human person, an essential faculty for Augustine and Pfister.[24] True to that fuller holistic heritage,

24. In *The Body Keeps the* Score, van der Kolk does make isolated references to the soul and the spirit. "Silence about trauma also leads to death—the death of the soul."

and grounded in Jewish and Christian sacred texts, additional *spiritual* insights and tools are available to those enduring violence-based trauma. A more integral, "bio-psycho-neural-spiritual" healing framework is on the horizon, including evidence-based research into spirituality. The soul *also* keeps the score.

Has Psychology Lost Its Soul?

One wonders if William James (1842–1910) would recognize the discipline he is credited with founding. In the decades following Freud, psychology was at risk of losing its soul—an essential construct for James—while swallowing those of religion and spirituality as well. So much for the etymology of the very word "psychology," rooted in "psyche," the Greek word for "soul." As psychologists Miller and Delaney note, "[O]ver the course of the 20th century, psyche . . . came to be more narrowly defined, first as mind and then as behavior or even neural activity."[25] But whatever happened to the spiritual faculty?

Given this history, the Christian philosophical and theological traditions can be of constructive service in putting Humpty Dumpty back together, a tremendous contribution to the large number of careseekers enduring moral or spiritual injury trauma. Psychology, religion, and spirituality are, in principle, "allies," to recall a favorite concept of Pfister. Psychiatrist Nash notes that Erich Fromm had warned of the blind spots of mental health science as far back as 1950: "Psychology thus became a science lacking its main subject matter, the soul."[26] If, for a time, psychology had lost its soul, the coming generation is poised to benefit from increased substantive collaboration among religion, spirituality, psychology, and neuroscience. Moral injury trauma, for example, is inclusive of

. . . "being met by silence and incomprehension kills the spirit" (232). "It is one thing to process memories of trauma, but it is an entirely different matter to confront the inner void—the holes in the soul . . . " (296). The rare references are neither defined nor systematically explored.

25. William R. Miller and Harold D. Delaney, *Judeo-Christian Perspectives on Psychology: Human Nature, Motivation, and Change* (Washington, DC: American Psychological Association, 2005), 3.

26. William P. Nash, "Foreword," *Religion and Recovery from PTSD* (Philadelphia: Jessica Kingsley Publishers, 2020), 8, quoting Fromm from *Psychoanalysis and Religion.*

spirituality. This is a development that would have been unimaginable until the twenty-first century, for until then the "therapeutic culture of self-absorption" was ascendant.[27]

The field of violence-based trauma therapy has now begun to converse in a fully holistic[28] framework. Perhaps the word "begun" should be emphasized. In the next generation, one anticipates that personal and professional caregiving can more comfortably draw from the wells of *all* disciplines at stake, collaboratively when indicated, pursuant to qualified training and supervision. In a typical example: for survivors of incest, it is often difficult to distinguish spiritual or religious rage at and alienation from God (the Father) from childhood rage at or psychological dissociation from one's biological father. Traumatized survivors of incest may, as well, manifest a numbing of bodily sensation that neuroscience can detect and address through one of the several body-oriented therapies recommended by van der Kolk. Some interdisciplinary skills and insights can be taught, learned, and mentored; others will require specialized collaboration.

The point is to resist the tendency to dissect individual careseekers, and their recovery, according to siloed human attributes that discriminate against one or the other healing modality. While religion and psychology must insist upon their disciplinary prerogatives, each should inform—but never be allowed to poach—the other. Many people of faith and seekers will welcome the inclusion of sound, integrated spiritual insights and tools on the caregiving menu.

A formidable challenge to productive interdisciplinary discourse and collaboration is that *soul* has meant different things to different people and different disciplines and different religious traditions over different epochs. One must thoughtfully choose and define terms and context, lest productive conversation and collaboration falter in interdisciplinary *psychoBabel.* For this reason, it has been important to highlight in some detail the Augustinian perspective on soul as a guiding North Star.

27. Philip Rieff, *The Triumph of the Therapeutic: Uses of Faith after Freud* (Wilmington, DE: Intercollegiate Studies Institute, 2006).

28. "Holistic" is derived from the Greek *holos*, meaning whole. It is used to describe an all-embracing approach or focus on the whole rather than isolated entities or parts. In this sense it recapitulates Augustine's philosophy of soul.

Today, the traditional health-care model of biopsychosocial, and associated clinical practice, is witnessing a slow paradigm shift to a more integral schema of the human person. Occasional mental health specialists, open to the numinous, refer to a holistic "biopsychosocial-spiritual (BPSS) framework."[29] Back to the future. The continuity with the Western heritage seems promising, surely a step in the right direction. From the perspective of religion and spirituality, psychology may be recovering its *soul*—and discovering the benefits for human well-being of the alliance promoted by Pastor Pfister. Many, many direct casualties of violence, as well as those demoralized by widespread signs of cruelty and disregard for life on Planet Earth, yearn for such holistic soul recovery. It would be cruel to turn a deaf ear. Body, mind, neuroscience, and spirit *all* deserve a seat at the healing table. The soul also keeps the score.

The Oskar Pfister Award and Lecture

The extraordinary German correspondence between Freud and Pfister had been relatively unknown in the United States (apart from specialists) until the establishment in 1980 of the annual Oskar Pfister Award and Lecture. It is a joint presentation of the Caucus on Spirituality, Religion, and Psychiatry of the American Psychiatric Association and today's Association of Professional Chaplains. The annual award recognizes outstanding contributions in the field of psychiatry and religion. The Pfister Lecture catalogue has become a treasure trove for historic consideration of dialogue and collaboration between mental health and spirituality. Honorees include luminaries such as Viktor Frankl, Hans Kung, Robert Lifton, Robert Coles, James Fowler, and Paul Ricoeur.

In his 2011 Pfister Lecture, mental health chaplain and Protestant minister Clark S. Aist summarized that conversation brilliantly, noting the "broad consensus today that a recovery of religion and spiritual significance has occurred in American psychiatry."[30] (Of course, just *how*

29. Natalie M. Richardson and Angela L. Lamson, "Understanding Moral Injury: Military-Related Injuries of the Mind, Body, and Soul," *Spirituality in Clinical Practice* 9, no. 3 (September 2022), 147.

30. Aist, "Recovery of Religious," 615. This section is indebted to Aist's 2011 Pfister lecture.

broad remains debatable.) To demonstrate his point, Aist singles out five foundational ideas "that have fostered a reintegration of spiritual and religious issues into the practice of psychiatry." Each denotes an area of intersectionality between psychology and religion that, from the historical perspective of Freud and Pfister's discourse during the interwar years in Europe, can only be described as breathtaking. What might be the implications for trauma-informed spiritual and pastoral care? Each of the five seminal trends suggests a rich vein to mine further for its depth of interdisciplinary recovery implications.

The first foundational idea described by Aist is "the significance of culture in human healing." He refers to studies dating to the 1990s in race, ethnicity, and cultural identity. These have become major themes throughout all domains of society, "including the field of health care." The increased emphasis on intercultural competence has raised the boat of religious beliefs and spiritual practices, because they are often "inextricably linked." This was the case with Tola, the refugee from Africa, in chapter 3.

Caregivers who accompany war refugees from less modernized rural regions such as Darfur in western Sudan, for example, will benefit from some familiarity with so-called traditional cultures in which religion and spirituality are organically interwoven into the indigenous cosmology. Trust between caregiver and careseeker may be generated by the former's relative comfort with the latter's home customs, including respect for Allah and even openness to pray interreligiously with a devout, majority Muslim population.

Aist's second intersectional theme is "the creative power of ritualized dependence." Freud had understood ritual behaviors within a framework of neurosis, but, subsequently, cultural anthropologists came to view ritual quite positively. Erik Erikson discovered in ritual a "numinous element," a "sense of a hallowed presence." Aist comments that "a growing awareness of the creative and integrative dynamic of ritualization and its transformative power has been a salient factor in contemporary psychiatry's more positive disposition toward religion and spirituality," and offers examples from Judaism (Passover), Hinduism (Diwali), and Christianity (Eucharist).

A third "pivotal development that should be considered as authenticating the significance of spirituality and religion in psychiatry today is the growing field of research into the biology of the brain in relation to faith driven experiences." Select researchers detail an evidence-based neurobiological foundation for religious faith and spirituality. This marks a return to William James's intense interest in the empirical study of religious consciousness. Trauma psychiatrist van der Kolk, of course, deserves recognition for bringing neuroscience into the mainstream of popular attention. But he does not address the neuroscience of spirituality. Others, happily, are doing so. "Science is showing that a spiritual experience leaves fingerprints, evidence that a spiritual transaction has occurred . . . an indelible mark on the brain."[31] Pfister's search for more scientific study of the cure of souls has found a twenty-first-century way forward through neuroscience.

The fourth major development that explains the recent rapprochement between religion and psychiatry is "the relevance of first-person recovery narratives." Stories told by trauma survivors, for example, play an increasingly important role in "how we assess the significance of religious and spiritual factors in the process of recovery." The value of this tool reflects the recent "recognition of the importance of 'narrative' in structuring human identity." This new genre of autobiographical literature has been greeted by an "unprecedented level of respect . . . from mental health planners and professionals." These first-person narratives can provide "primary data for discovering recovery paradigms," including "prominent themes" such as the importance of religious and spiritual practice for certain clients.

Finally, Aist notes that in the past generation there has been "a new appraisal of the psychic function of belief." Until recently, religious faith had been regarded with suspicion in reductionist, unimodal scientific models such as Freud's psychoanalysis. But *believing* is increasingly considered a legitimate, even primary activity of the psyche.[32] Belief cannot be considered derivative, and is an innate, intrapsychic action from the beginning of life—for example, the infant's preverbal instinct that "I am loveable and wanted."

31. Barbara Bradley Hagerty, *Fingerprints of God: The Search for the Science of Spirituality* (New York: Riverhead Books, 2009), 276. Hagerty's journalistic account is somewhat dated but a valuable introductory account.

32. Ana-Maria Rizzuto, "Belief as a Psychic Function," 1997 Pfister Lecture. Cf. A-M Rizzuto, "Psychoanalytic Considerations About Spiritually Oriented Psychotherapy," in *Spiritually Oriented Psychotherapy*, ed. Len Sperry and Edward P. Shafranske (Washington, DC: American Psychological Association, 2004).

Authentic religiosity and spirituality "partake in every respect in the human complexities of the believing function." To dismiss a client's spirituality and religious beliefs a priori, therefore, compromises their human identity and dignity. Spiritually informed therapy, even psychoanalysis, "does not privilege spirituality or religion; instead, it makes them a natural part of the exploration of beliefs, fantasies, God as an object, and other dimensions of transcendent life such as purpose in life, destiny, salvation, and the relationships with others and the world of nature."[33] This is the foundational intersectional idea that underlies recent interdisciplinary advances in clinical treatment as well as mental health training programs. The following section illustrates two notable models of evidence-based collaboration among the areas of spirituality, pastoral care, mental health, and trauma counseling.

Interdisciplinary Advances

Treatment Programs

In the American Psychological Association journal *Spirituality in Clinical Practice*, scholar and therapist Thomas Plante has noted that most people consider themselves religious, spiritual, or both. (This is particularly evident outside the modernized West and globalized world capitals.) They intuitively understand faith and spiritual practice as integral components of their identity, and therefore contributors to full human flourishing. In therapeutic settings, Plante comments, people "want to be treated holistically taking these concerns into consideration." But mental health professionals, "as a rule, don't have much, if any training or experience working with these concerns."[34] True enough. Nevertheless, select interdisciplinary advances have been evident since the turn of the century, as Aist notes. Though the term "spiritual injury" itself remains an

33. Ana-Maria Rizzuto, "Psychoanalytic Considerations."

34. "Editor Spotlight Interview," *Spirituality in Clinical Practice*, 2021. Thomas Plante is an endowed professor of psychology and religious studies at the Jesuit-sponsored Santa Clara University in Silicon Valley, as well as director of the Applied Spirituality Institute; he also serves as an adjunct professor of psychiatry and behavioral sciences at the Stanford University School of Medicine. https://www.apa.org/pubs/highlights/editor-spotlight/scp-plante.

outlier in psychology and religion, what is called spiritually "informed," "integrated," or "distressed" clinical care has found a respected place in trauma literature and practice. Spiritual exercises are now welcome in such programs, including the sacrament of confession and sacred texts thematizing divine mercy from a variety of religious traditions.

Two therapeutic interventions provide a distinctive flavor of the emerging options for improved holistic care; both rely on an understanding of moral injury as a thin construct. Building Spiritual Strength (BSS) is an eight-week group therapy trauma intervention designed for faith-based settings, drawing upon James Fowler's respected stage model of faith development.[35] The intervention was designed for active-duty and military veterans but has since been adapted and expanded for other groups experiencing moral injury. Many of this population report seeking BSS services rather than conventional mental health or trauma counseling care. They prefer chaplaincy-led or -informed services that they find less stigmatizing and more attuned to soul care. Echoes of Augustine and Pfister are unmistakable.

Building Spiritual Strength directly addresses challenges raised by theodicy and relies on the terminology of "spiritual distress." Potentially morally injurious events are understood, thinly, as transgressions of the sacred, including reference to beliefs and relationship concerns with a Higher Power. To ameliorate posttraumatic stress injury and its negative symptoms, BSS utilizes interdisciplinary tools such as cognitive therapy, prayer, and meditation to restore a disrupted relationship with one's Higher Power.

Strikingly, Building Spiritual Strength is designed to be led either by mental health providers trained and supervised in "spiritually integrated care" or chaplains/clergy/pastoral counselors with specialized mental health training or a strong Clinical Pastoral Education background.[36] The therapeutic intervention affirms the sacrament of confession for mainstream Christians and welcomes spiritual and pastoral caregivers

35. Alanna Coady et al., "Trauma, Spirituality, and Moral Injury: Assessing and Addressing Moral Injury in the Context of PTSD Treatment," *Current Treatment Options in Psychiatry* 8 (December 2021).

36. An excellent summary of research into the success of BSS can be found in J. Irene Harris and Timothy Usset et al., "Spiritually Integrated Care for PTSD: A Randomized Controlled Trial of 'Building Spiritual Strength,'" *Psychiatry Research* 267 (September 2018): 420–28.

from various religious traditions to participate on leadership teams. A key feature of the program manual includes two sessions addressing forgiveness, inviting clients to enter into a threefold process of reconciliation: with themselves; with others who have hurt them; and with God or their Higher Power. "In these sessions, forgiveness is considered a means of freeing oneself from distressing feelings."[37]

The Building Spiritual Strength treatment regimen has matured to the point that its model and outcomes are now being researched in second-generation scientific literature. Spiritual and pastoral caregivers should consider it a viable option for referral. Reputable facilitator training videos and further information for BSS are readily available online and are far superior to popular New Age–flavored multimodal interventions.

A second notable example of interdisciplinary treatment is called Spiritually Integrated Cognitive Processing Therapy (SI-CPT or SICPT). It is a twelve-session individual therapy regimen that incorporates sacred texts, hymnody, and supplemental materials, including appendices, according to the client's unique religious/spiritual self-identification.[38] The model provides the kinds of spiritual resources to inform treatment that Davies, in the preceding chapter, laments are so difficult to find for Australian veterans. Michelle Pearce at the University of Maryland has developed this novel treatment with a team that includes a Veterans Administration chaplain, physicians, licensed social workers, and other qualified specialists.[39] They aim to normalize "spiritual struggle,"[40] such as ruptures in one's relationship with God or loss of faith. "Specifically, SICPT uses the spiritual concepts and rituals of compassion, grace, guided imagery, repentance, confession, forgiveness, atonement, blessing, restitution, and making amends."[41]

37. Crystal L. Park et al., *Trauma, Meaning, and Spirituality: Translating Research into Clinical Practice* (Washington, DC: American Psychological Association, 2017), 180.

38. M. Pearce et al., "Spiritually Integrated Cognitive Processing Therapy: A New Treatment for Post-traumatic Stress Disorder That Targets Moral Injury," *Global Advances in Health and Medicine* 7 (February 20, 2018).

39. Pearce is a clinical psychologist and professor in the Graduate School at the University of Maryland. She completed a postdoctoral fellowship in spirituality and health through the Duke University Center for Spirituality, Theology, and Health, which provides regular trainings on spiritually integrated health care.

40. Pearce et al., "Spiritually Integrated Cognitive Processing Therapy."

41. Pearce et al.

To address symptoms of moral injury or PTSD for clients who so wish, Pearce has taken the remarkable step of creating a treatment manual that includes separate sections, featuring therapist guidance, according to five major religious/spiritual heritages. Available options include "the spiritual version (applicable for those of any religion and those who do not identify as religious)" and "five religion-specific manuals (Christianity, Judaism, Islam, Buddhism, and Hinduism) for clients who desire a more religion-specific approach."[42]

The goals are twofold: both to educate the therapist about various religious traditions, and to take advantage of a client's particular heritage. Recommended sacred texts, prayers, and motifs are suggested according to particular belief systems. For example, on the Jewish calendar, Yom Kippur (the Day of Atonement) is the highest holy day. It offers people of faith and seekers ritualized forgiveness, restored purity, and renewed covenant relationship with God. Yom Kippur can serve as a powerful religious motif available to caregivers who accompany Jews spiritually distressed by the guilt or shame due to sexual assault or other forms of violence.

Pearce and her colleagues offer a rather sophisticated interdisciplinary therapeutic model from which spiritual and pastoral caregivers can benefit.[43] The manuals and appendices of the *Spiritually Integrated Cognitive Processing Therapy* regimen are currently undergoing empirical testing. One thinks of the advantages to hospital chaplains attending patients outside their own faith traditions, and, more concretely, beyond their spiritual, ritual, sacred textual repertoire of skills.

Like the Building Spiritual Strength group intervention, Pearce's model encourages clergy-therapist conversation, with the consent of the client. When spiritual symptoms are of sufficient intensity, the therapist is encouraged to consult with a religious leader. This is precisely the methodological tool that many trauma counselors lack, unaware that a client's spiritual distress could be the primary unaddressed barrier to recovery

42. M. J. Pearce et al., *Spiritually Integrated Cognitive Processing Therapy (SICPT) Veteran/Military Version: Therapist Manual*, with appendices for Christian, Jewish, Muslim, Hindu, and Buddhist SICPT (Durham, NC: Duke University Center for Spirituality, Theology and Health, 2017), michelle.pearce@umaryland.edu.

43. Cf. Harold G. Koenig, Donna Ames, and Michelle Pearce, *Religion and Recovery from PTSD* (Philadelphia: Jessica Kingsley Publishers, 2020).

from trauma, and that religious/spiritual professionals are available to collaborate across disciplines. According to the best practices of *Spiritually Integrated Cognitive Processing Therapy*, theological issues outside the purview of mental health care, such as theodicy—why bad things happen to good people—should be referred for care to a vetted pastor, chaplain, or spiritual guide approved by the client. Protocols are spelled out in thorough manuals.

Education and Training

In addition to therapeutic program advances, there are encouraging indicators of interdisciplinary progress in the training and education of mental health clinicians and trauma counselors. Two examples must suffice. First, clinical psychologist Cassandra Vieten and her colleagues have developed training modules in religion and spirituality, as well as coaching and consulting services, based on survey research and focus groups. In a frequently cited article, they focus on three specific "areas of competence" (attitudes, knowledge, skills) and sixteen specific "competencies" that they propose should be required for licensing.[44] Pastoral counselor and spiritual direction supervisors—as well as faculty in seminary, Clinical Pastoral Education, and formation programs—might be surprised at how highly their skills are valued and should consider the professional implications. The last of the sixteen competencies, for example, states: "Psychologists recognize the limits of their qualifications and competence in the spiritual and/or religious domains, including any responses to clients' spirituality and/or religion that may interfere with clinical practice, so that they (a) seek consultation from and collaborate with other qualified clinicians or spiritual/religious sources (e.g., priests, pastors, rabbis, imams, spiritual teachers, etc.), (b) seek further training and education, and/or (c) refer appropriate clients to more qualified individuals and resources."[45]

Also notable is a publication, by the American Psychological Association itself, of a comprehensive textbook treatment of the interrelationship among trauma, meaning, and spirituality in mental health research and

44. Cassandra Vieten et al., "Spiritual and Religious Competencies for Psychologists," *Psychology of Religion and Spirituality* 5, no. 3 (2013): 129–44.

45. Vieten et al., "Spiritual and Religious Competencies."

clinical practice.[46] It is designed as a resource for clinicians, researchers, graduate students, and educators. The core assumption is that, for many people, religion/spirituality serves as the foundation of meaning-making systems that underpin human identity, core beliefs, and values. How might clients who present themselves for care be knowledgeably assessed in the area of religion and spirituality? The authors suggest that clinicians "should examine seven aspects of spirituality to develop a comprehensive approach to spiritually sensitive assessment practices."[47] These are: beliefs and meanings; vocation and obligations; experiences and emotions; courage and growth; rituals and practice; community; and authority and guidance in spiritual functioning. Specific examples of current assessment tools are presented in extensive appendices.

The book's authors are leading theorists, clinical practitioners, and trauma counselors, including psychologists of religion, who span the three Abrahamic traditions. They also include agnostic, Buddhist, and yogic spiritualities. The authors share a conviction "that attending to the conjoint influences of spirituality and trauma is essential to a full understanding of human behavior."[48] Here the authors affirm the innate psychic function of belief. Their decision to collaborate began in a shared lament about "the lack of scientific literature necessary to effectively address spiritual concerns in trauma survivors."[49] Pfister's quest for a "scientifically based cure of souls" has found resonance, one hundred years later, among an increasing number of mental health specialists.

Personal Encounter with the Living God

The hunger for trauma-informed spiritual insights and practices is palpable and widespread among careseekers. Happily, clinical practice in the area of spirituality and mental health is beginning to respond. References in the literature to constructs such as "spiritual injury," "spiritual distress," "soul wound," and "spiritual struggle" are no longer unusual, both in the area of MIT, posttraumatic growth, and, to lesser extent,

46. Park et al., *Trauma, Meaning, and Spirituality.*
47. Park et al., 101.
48. Park et al., 4.
49. Park et al., 5.

PTSD. This represents a sea change since the turn of the century. Roughly speaking, the terms all point to a similar affliction—disruption of one's *relationship* with a Higher Power.

The popular formula for a restaurant's success is *location, location, location.* A student of the human soul, Íñigo understood viscerally what authentic faith practitioners and seekers hunger for—*relationship, relationship, relationship.* It was never enough for the wounded courtier and combatant to learn *about* Jesus Christ. Church attendance, homilies, catechetics, books, and academic degrees all point to the divine, living *presence* encountered directly in religious experience. A wounded man of action, Íñigo first *experienced* the action of God in his own soul, only after which he began to record and translate those experiences into replicable exercises.

This is his pedigree, not an academic degree. He was a practitioner taught by God, as pretentious—or even blasphemous—as that can sound. In Manresa he experienced several mystical visions. In the last of these, he recorded sitting near his hermit's cave, overlooking the Cardoner River, suddenly finding his eyes open to spiritual enlightenment. Afterward, he felt himself transformed.[50] The experience can be likened to that of Siddhartha Gautama under the Bodhi tree. One imagines Íñigo limping rapidly to his cave, snatching up notebook and pen, and feverishly scribbling the divine communication.

Approaching God primarily as a study topic, or series of propositions, misses the core of religion and spirituality entirely. Authentic God-seekers may be excused from yawning. William James may well have. Contrast the intellectualist approach with these impassioned words from *The Varieties of Religious Experience*: "The perfect stillness of the night was thrilled by a more solemn silence. The darkness held a presence that was all the more felt because it was not seen. I could not any more have doubted that HE was there than that I was. Indeed, I felt myself to be, if possible, the less real of the two."[51]

50. Ignatius of Loyola, *A Pilgrim's Testament: The Memoirs of Saint Ignatius of Loyola*, ed. Barton T. Geger (Chestnut Hill, MA: Institute of Jesuit Sources, 2020), no. 30. Hereafter *Auto*.

51. William James, *The Varieties of Religious Experience* (1902; reissue, Oxford: Oxford University Press, 2012), 58.

Íñigo is a spiritual master, temporarily afflicted by some period variant of today's moral injury trauma, who will not be displaced by psychology, neurology, or any other valid discipline. Like Pastor Pfister, Íñigo insists, respectfully and collaboratively, on his seat at the healing table as an ally. The soul also keeps the score in traditional Christian anthropology, eagerly welcoming evidence-based advances such as van der Kolk's neurobiology of trauma. "Since body and soul are united in life, the soul shares in all the brain functions that make us human."[52] Such flexibility and demonstrated openness to science likely explains the sustainability and popularity of Ignatian spirituality over half a millennium.

The Ignatian Exercises are one proven model from the Christian tradition for personal encounter with God, available in pliable format adaptable to different needs and times. The saint was always "very attentive to the world in which he lived, which was animated by various crosscurrents of culture: the discoveries of science, the adventurous spirit of the age of exploration and the intellectual vibrancy of the Reformation and Renaissance."[53] Given the sheer scale of evil characteristic of twentieth- and twenty-first-century violence, Ignatian spirituality must surely recognize the crushing power of trauma's impact on human lives, indeed on Planet Earth itself. The pilgrim would have welcomed efforts to contextualize his insights and methods for this population. Part 2 aspires to meet this need for specialized, trauma-informed care, which can bridge the best of psychology, religion, and spirituality.

No less a luminary than Pfister's friend Carl Jung encountered the living God, personally and profoundly, through certain of Ignatius's prayer exercises. Between 1933 and 1941, he delivered a series of public lectures at the Swiss Federal Institute of Technology in Zurich. They were intended for a general audience and addressed a broad range of topics. During the winter of 1939–1940, he offered sixteen lectures on the Ignatian Exercises, with particular interest in the formation and application of the faculty of imagination. Many years later, Jung narrated the following mystical encounter:

52. Joseph Lee, "The Brain and the Soul," *The Way* 53, no. 1 (January 2014): 48.

53. Kevin O'Brien, "How Can We Adapt the Spiritual Exercises in Our Times?," interview with Sean Salai, *America*, July 20, 2016.

> When I was engrossed with psychology and alchemy—no, to be more precise it was when I was giving the seminar on Ignatius of Loyola—once, in the night, I had a vision of Christ. One night I awoke and there at the foot of the bed, I saw a crucifix. Not quite life-sized. It was very clear and couched in a bright light. In this light, Christ was hanging on the cross and then I saw that it was as if his entire body were made of gold, as if of green gold. It looked wonderful. I was scared to death by it. Just then I was particularly engrossed by the "Anima Christi" [prayer]. There is a very beautiful meditation by Ignatius on it.
>
> C. G. Jung, 27th June, 1957[54]

54. Martin Liebscher, ed., *Jung on Ignatius of Loyola's Spiritual Exercises* (Princeton, NJ: Princeton University Press, 2023), cited on page xlvii. Jung demonstrates granular familiarity with the Exercises, including precise attention to "the exercise of the three powers of soul," 42.

PART II

From Spiritual Injuries to Spiritual Exercises

"She then related back to the Inquisitors what she knew from her relatives:
'they told him the afflictions they had, and he consoled them.'"

—Former prostitute María de la Flor, referring to Íñigo, from the Spanish Inquisition court transcript of May 10, 1527

"By the term Spiritual Exercises we mean every method of examination of conscience, meditation, contemplation, vocal or mental prayer, and other spiritual activities, such as will be mentioned later. For, just as taking a walk, traveling on foot, and running are physical exercises, so is the name of spiritual exercises given to any means of preparing and disposing our soul . . ."

—George E. Ganss, *The Spiritual Exercises of Saint Ignatius: A Translation and Commentary*, 21, First Preliminary Note

"The Spiritual Exercises should be adapted to the disposition of the persons who desire to make them, that is, to their age, education, and ability."

—Ganss, 26–27, Eighteenth Preliminary Note

6

Consoling the Afflicted with Spiritual Exercises

On March 6, 1527, Mencía de Benavente sat alertly in the dock of a court hearing brought by the Spanish Inquisition in Alcalá, Spain, a short distance northeast of Madrid. Presumably, it was not how she preferred to spend her Ash Wednesday. But the widow, her daughter Ana, and friend Leonor de Mena had little choice, having been summoned by church authorities to give testimony in an investigation of Íñigo de Loyola.

It had come to inquisitors' attention that the odd outsider with no theological training, who went about town barefoot and in sackcloth, was giving various spiritual exercises to many townspeople—yet his meditations and related instructions had never been reviewed for orthodoxy by ecclesial officials. Most of those drawn to Íñigo, and whom he frequently called upon in private at home, were local women such as Benavente. Few were versed in Christian doctrine. All they knew was that he was a saintly, upright man, willing to comfort and guide them spiritually at no charge. But this was sixteenth-century Catholic Europe, where Martin Luther had been excommunicated just five years earlier. An unfavorable verdict would short-circuit Íñigo's mission to share the Exercises composed at Manresa.[1]

1. It was during the 1522 Manresa Episode that Íñigo "began to compose a little book which became a landmark in the history of Christian spirituality." He would continue tinkering with the Spanish text until its completion in 1541, but "the key ideas or core of the booklet were clearly in his notes when he left Manresa." William V. Bangert, *A History of the Society of Jesus* (St. Louis: Institute of Jesuit Sources, 1972), 8–9.

Chapter 6 begins with Íñigo's departure from Manresa, spiritual notebook secure in his knapsack, and follows his odyssey through a pivotal year as a person of interest to the Inquisition in Alcalá and Salamanca in 1526–27. It was twelve months under the microscope, suspected of heresy, resulting in several short prison terms as well as house arrest.

But there was a silver lining. Precious witness testimonies were preserved in local archives; they demonstrate, in some detail, both the population drawn to what Íñigo designated as the "light" (Latin *leves*) version of the Exercises, and one key prayer method of particular significance for a contemporary, trauma-informed reading. Australian Jesuit Michael Hansen designates the light modality, focused on the First Week, as the "First Spiritual Exercises."[2] They were the first form of the Exercises to be given by Íñigo. This adaptation "can be given immediately to everyone"[3] over the course of a month within the context of their daily routine, and, claims Hansen, are "a complete form of the *Spiritual Exercises* in their own right."[4]

The documentary evidence regarding Benavente and her niece, former prostitute María de la Flor, confirms that Íñigo was consoling a large number of afflicted people who sought his spiritual wisdom and guidance. The waiting list sometimes approached twenty. Afflictions manifested in distressing symptoms, including shame, sorrow, and confusion, familiar to Íñigo from his Manresa Episode. He taught the supplicants particular prayer tools designed to heal such symptoms, by God's mercy, including an instructional exercise utilizing Augustine's three powers of the soul. At this perilous moment of the sinner's pilgrimage toward sainthood, Íñigo's clear embrace of the Christian heritage demonstrated his orthodoxy to the inquisitors and other, self-appointed heresy hunters.

The narrative of this critical period is significant for three reasons. First, it further credentials Íñigo in facing and overcoming distressing events of his own, including those of institutional religious nature. Those who have endured any sort of trauma at the hands of their churches—for example, victim-survivors of clerical sexual abuse—may find inspiration

2. Michael Hansen, *The First Spiritual Exercises: Four Guided Retreats* (Notre Dame, IN: Ave Maria Press, 2013).

3. Hansen, *First Spiritual Exercises*, 15.

4. Hansen, 15. It was these First Spiritual Exercises for which Íñigo was under investigation in Alcalá.

and guidance in the backstory.[5] Second, the influential religious order Ignatius later founded, the Society of Jesus, risked being stillborn as a result of this sixteenth-century skirmish with church officials. The origin story easily could have ended here. Most importantly, the requisite church approval of the Exercises depended upon a satisfactory outcome to the series of investigations.

Through it all, Íñigo was characteristically upbeat, refusing several offers of pro bono legal assistance. He perceived God at work, though his circle of supporters was fretful about the personal risks he faced.

The Pilgrim

Íñigo's transformation from chivalrous courtier to St. Ignatius was underway as he limped away from Manresa, if he could but negotiate sixteenth-century European religious intolerance. History teaches the fine line between authentic God-seekers and unbalanced fanatics; in Íñigo's case, Spanish religious authorities believed the jury was still out. Though his precise vocation in life remained uncertain, all that mattered to the zealous mystic was that he was on fire with God's love and mercy and wished to accompany other seekers as mentor and guide to transformative spiritual experience. Having overcome life-threatening soul wounds at Manresa, he was eager to share his practice.

As Moses had been called to free the Israelite slaves, Íñigo felt a divine commission to liberate human souls from spiritual oppression. In addition to his seven hours of daily prayer at Manresa, he had "busied himself helping certain souls who came there looking for him, with regard to spiritual matters."[6] Today, "the help of souls" remains the signature of the

5. Authoritarian fundamentalist religion is on the rise in the United States and beyond, manifest in each of the Abrahamic traditions. In 2011, therapist Marlene Winnell identified religious trauma syndrome as a recognizable set of symptoms, though it is not a formal medical or psychiatric diagnosis. "Religious Trauma Syndrome" (series of three articles), *Cognitive Behavioural Therapy Today* 39, no. 2 (May 2011); 39, no. 3 (September 2011); 39, no. 4 (November 2011), British Association of Behavioural and Cognitive Therapies, London.

6. Ignatius of Loyola, *A Pilgrim's Testament: The Memoirs of Saint Ignatius of Loyola*, ed. Barton T. Geger (Chestnut Hill, MA: Institute of Jesuit Sources, 2020), no. 26. Hereafter, *Auto*.

Society of Jesus—*ayudar a los almas*, or, used interchangeably, *ayudar a las animas*. It is considered the very charter of the Jesuit religious order.

Leaving Manresa, Íñigo set his heart on a pilgrimage to Jerusalem, the Holy City of Judaism and Christianity also revered by Islam. Though it was considerably dangerous, it went without saying—according to his piety—that first he must walk in the very footsteps of his Lord, Jesus Christ. Perhaps he was meant to spend his life there converting Muslims, he thought, maybe even blessed to die as a martyr. But the visit was ill-advised from the start. Lacking any filters, Íñigo was incorrigible in violating all safety and security procedures in the Muslim-administered city, such that horrified local Franciscans, charged with overseeing Christian pilgrims and maintaining interreligious harmony, hastily put him on a ship back to Europe.

At this point in his autobiography, Íñigo begins to refer to himself in the third person as "the pilgrim." He strongly identified with the perilous sea voyages of the heroic St. Paul, not without a touch of grandiosity. On one occasion, he had to be restrained for his own safety from castigating the sailors on deck for their sexual indulgences. To his credit, the future saint had also developed a disciplined practice of regular prayer and participation in the sacraments, overcome his belligerence and lust, embraced the Ten Commandments, and humbly confessed his sins and shortcomings. He unceasingly implored divine guidance for greater clarity on the future, and there are indications that his decision to surrender his life to God as a priest was made on board the return ship.

Once safely ashore in Europe, years of maturation and academic preparation lay ahead. From 1524 to 1527 in Barcelona, Alcalá, and Salamanca, Íñigo divided his time among begging, street preaching, private spiritual guidance, and study. The oddball sported a disheveled look, befitting a poor man who gave away most of what he successfully begged. During two trying years in Barcelona, he studied Latin grammar, required for priesthood candidates. He was old beyond his thirty-one years, and his fellow students, youths half his age, took impish delight in mocking him. "He was eager to learn and perfectly docile, but his faculties no longer had the plasticity of youth."[7] Though an adequate student, his attention some-

7. Paul Dudon, *Saint Ignatius of Loyola*, trans. William J. Young (Milwaukee: Bruce Publishing, 1949), 95.

times drifted to the sounds of the busy street outside the classroom, or to his upcoming appointments for spiritual conversation. The Barcelona years gave him time to moderate his more extreme personal tendencies, to mature in his religious and spiritual practice, and to tinker with the unfinished exercises in his notebook.

A Person of Interest

In May of 1526, at the recommendation of his Latin grammar teacher, Íñigo relocated to Alcalá for approximately one year. The plan was to study at the internationally renowned University of Alcalá, a newly founded center of Renaissance learning. Now thirty-four years of age, Íñigo seems to have accepted the fact that his goal of priesthood required more serious academic commitment. Nevertheless, the battlefield hero was still a work in progress. He again gravitated toward street preaching, and "[w]hile at Alcalá, he was engaged in giving spiritual exercises and teaching Christian doctrine."[8]

Before long, the charismatic pilgrim attracted four young male disciples whom he would mentor as companions in mission; the locals derisively labeled them "Íñiguistas" for their devotion to him, or "sack-wearers" because of their loose, coarse wool beggarly attire. The outfit gave the impression that the pious wannabes were some sort of canonically approved religious congregation like the Franciscans or Dominicans, but they had no church sanction whatsoever. Íñigo continued to style himself after the legendary St. Francis of Assisi—with whom he was still competing—shoeless and shabbily dressed, preaching God's goodness and mercy at all hours to any who would listen. If regarded as a fool, he was honored; so too had been his Lord and the great saints.

In an intolerant country and epoch on hyperalert for charismatic religious freelancers and reformist sects without sanction of the Catholic hierarchy, Íñigo and his *Íñiguistas* represented a very risky proposition in late medieval Castile. The University of Alcalá was a Protestant hotbed. Far from his clan roots in Guipuzcoa and having broken with royal connections, the pilgrim was a vulnerable outsider on a collision course with the forbidding Spanish Inquisition. " 'Who,' it was asked, 'is this Íñigo, this

8. *Auto.*, no. 57.

Caceres, this Calisto, this Juan, who dress like hermits, and who, though they are not priests, work like apostles, and draw great crowds here and there?' Running from mouth to mouth, the rumor grew and was soon distorted. By the time it reached Toledo, the Inquisitors were disturbed."[9]

It was hardly a surprise that Íñigo aroused suspicion. In the context of tightly proscribed gender relations in late medieval Castile, first of all, his prudence was questionable. Íñigo himself describes the cause of one investigation. "I believe this was another factor, that a married woman of rank had special regard for the pilgrim. In order not to be noticed, she came to the hospice at dawn, wearing a veil, as is the custom in Alcalá de Henares. On entering, she removed her veil and went into the pilgrim's room."[10] One commentator notes that "Ignatius showed poor judgement by speaking to a married woman alone in his bedroom. He learned from this and many other similar mistakes."[11]

But it was two steps forward and one back. One of those "other mistakes" resulted in Íñigo's imprisonment in Alcalá from May 1 to May 18, 1527: seventeen days without being charged or even told why. Three pious but naïve townswomen had gone missing—a mother, her daughter, and their servant—after which a suspicious university professor turned community watchdog filed a complaint against the ragged pilgrim. The missing women were among his devotees, and suspicion immediately fell upon the mysterious outsider. When Alcalá's vicar general Don Juan Rodríguez de Figueroa got around to visiting him in prison to discuss the matter, without hesitation Íñigo calmly affirmed that he did indeed know the women, that in spiritual conversation they had consulted him about their intention to make an overland pilgrimage on foot to a religious shrine in another Spanish city, and that he had advised *against* it for safety's sake because "the daughter was very young and attractive."[12]

Local authorities were unpersuaded, however, and Íñigo was required to remain in custody until, several days later, the three women returned safely from their risky pilgrimage and verified his account. Copycat re-

9. Dudon, *St. Ignatius of Loyola*, 109.

10. *Auto.*, no. 59.

11. *Auto.*, no. 59n19, 143.

12. José Ignacio Tellechea Idígoras, *Ignatius of Loyola: The Pilgrim Saint*, trans. Cornelius Michael Buckley (Chicago: Loyola University Press, 1994), 261.

ports, spicy rumors, and endless gossip about other such "incidents" were common—and false. Concern for the purity of wives and daughters in a closed, patriarchal society was to be expected. Íñigo was, after all, both exotic and charismatic.

A further cause for concern was that Íñigo believed that God was teaching him directly through the Holy Spirit—"God's schoolboy," he once called himself—and that this qualified him to catechize others. But certain of his views were dangerously similar to those of heretical sects such as the "Alumbrados,"[13] and the Inquisition scented a whiff of Martin Luther's new teachings. In the wake of Luther's recent excommunication, religious intolerance and violence raged throughout Europe, between Christians as well as in Ferdinand and Isabella's Reconquista persecution of Jews and Muslims. At the outset of the Protestant Reformation, in a European Roman Catholic state fearful of sects without sanction of the hierarchy, Íñigo and his *Íñiguistas* were a bridge too far.

Judicial Investigations

Testimony of María de la Flor

The "Tribunal of the Holy Office of the Inquisition" was charged by the Vatican to investigate matters such as scandalous public immorality and theological heresy, ensuring compliance with official Roman Catholic Church doctrine and practice. Íñigo, seemingly unconcerned, faced several rounds (or "processes") of investigation during 1526–27. When the Third Process opened in 1527, a former prostitute by the name of María de la Flor emerged as an important witness. She acknowledged that she "went around with many of the enrolled students, and was lost."[14] (One

13. The "Alumbrados" ("enlightened ones" in English) were a mystical movement in Spain during the sixteenth and seventeenth centuries whose adherents claimed that the human soul had attained a certain degree of perfection, was permitted a vision of the divine, and entered into direct communication with the Holy Spirit. Participation in the liturgy, pursuing good works, following the Ten Commandments, and observance of the exterior forms of religious life were unnecessary for those who had received the inner "light." The Inquisition issued edicts condemning them on three occasions. Cf. "Alumbrado," *Encyclopedia Britannica*, April 23, 2020, https://www.britannica.com/event/Alumbrado.

14. Tellechea Idígoras, *Ignatius of Loyola*, 253.

can imagine former clients' anxiety about what she might reveal to the tribunal.) The inquisitors were concerned about both rumors of sexual license and the orthodoxy of the preaching and spiritual teaching of the undereducated, unkempt, unsanctioned *Íñiguistas.*

On May 10, 1527, Flor was asked by the inquisitors if she knew the person of interest, and she responded that she had indeed seen Íñigo "many times" visit the house of her aunt, Mencía de Benavente, and her aunt's daughter. Those three spoke often "in secret,"[15] Flor added. The inquisitors' antennae rose. What transpired on these visits? She then related what she knew from her relatives: "they told him the afflictions they had, and he consoled them." ("*e le decian las poenas que tenian, e las consolaua*").[16] Had de la Flor herself spoken to Íñigo? Yes, briefly; she too had asked to meet with him. "Íñigo told her that he would have to talk with her over a period of a month" in order to complete his light Exercises.[17]

Other, more reputable witnesses went on to describe the unending stream of unchaperoned visitors to Íñigo's quarters in a local hospital, or his visits to any number of private residences. The practice was questionable, surely, yet no one had anything negative to say, under oath, about him. The court consistently heard that those who knew Íñigo were unanimous in their admiration of his personal rectitude; further, witnesses routinely testified to his orthodox religious beliefs, teaching, and spiritual practices. For his part, Íñigo was coming to realize that "a certain reserve in dealing with women"[18] would be more prudent.[19]

15. Judicial Processes of Íñigo Loyola, Third Process, Declaration of Maria de la Flor, X.3, *Archivum historicum Societatis Iesu* (Rome: Institutum Scriptorum de Historia S.I., 1932). MI Fontes Docum, 334, unpublished translation of S. Bermudez-Goldman.

16. Judicial Processes of Íñigo Loyola, X, 3. Manuel Serrano y Sanz offers an alternate rendering: "e decian las penas que tenia e les consolaua," in *San Ignacio de Loyola en Alcala de Henares: Estudio Histórico* (Madrid: Imprenta de Juan Iglesia, Calle de Pelayo, 1895), 38–39.

17. Judicial Processes of Íñigo Loyola, X, 4.

18. Tellechea Idígoras, *Ignatius of Loyola*, 269.

19. W. W. Meissner, a Jesuit priest and Freudian psychoanalyst, situates Íñigo's maturation in sexuality within the larger psychological development process, one that "took place in stages." At this relatively early point in his transformation from sinner to saint, "his mind was still in conflict over these contending ideals—the romantic-heroic and the spiritual—along with their corresponding values, beliefs, and codes of conduct." Meissner speculates on the psychological growth process at work, from repression to sublimation,

Testimony of Mencía de Benavente

More treasure is to be found in the Inquisition transcripts—historical detail that specifies select *content* and *method*, in skeletal form, of different exercises.[20] According to Benavente Íñigo taught the Ten Commandments, regular practice of the sacraments, the gospels, the nature of sin, daily examination of conscience, rules for discerning good from evil in the soul, and how to pray with traditional Christian faculties or powers of the soul—memory, will, and understanding—in one's devotional life. ("The first exercise is a meditation by using the three powers of the soul.")[21] Her documentary testimony suggests that Íñigo was giving her the lighter version of the Exercises. The inquisitors would have noted with approval Íñigo's orthodox Christian teaching and practices, very different from that of the *Alumbrados* sect. His firm roots in the tradition were surely a reason for the ultimate, favorable verdict.[22]

Íñigo guided supplicants through the content and flow of the month-long conversational Exercises with characteristic flexibility, according to their personal temperament, desires, capacities, and limits. They would meet privately and daily to debrief the seeker's spiritual progress toward renewed personal relationship with God, often enough brokered through a profound experience of divine mercy and forgiveness. (Íñigo typically advised those whom he accompanied that they should be prepared to shed copious tears, often a gift from God.) Always, Íñigo respected and deferred to the action of the Holy Spirit within the seeker's soul. This was

---

the latter suggesting acknowledgment of the creative power of unconscious dynamics and learning how to integrate them. It was a process of "incremental synthesis" that culminated in "the emergence of Ignatius the saint and religious leader." Meissner, *Ignatius of Loyola: The Psychology of a Saint* (New Haven: Yale University Press, 1992), 59–60.

20. Declaration of Mencía de Benavente, First Ordinary Process, March 6, 1527, Ash Wednesday, VII, 3.

21. George E. Ganss, *The Spiritual Exercises of Saint Ignatius: A Translation and Commentary* (St. Louis: Institute of Jesuit Sources, 1992), no. 45. Henceforth, *SpEx*.

22. Citing Augustine in chapter 10 of *De Trinitate*, Saint Thomas Aquinas (1225–74) offers an influential account of the powers of the soul in his masterwork, the *Summa Theologica*. Aquinas understood Augustine to hold that memory, understanding, and will constitute the one essence of the soul, not three separate powers. "Ignatius, however, seems to take memory, understanding or intellect and will as at least three distinct, albeit not separated, powers." Gerald O'Collins, "Memory in the Spiritual Exercises and John 21," *The Way* 59, no. 3 (July 2020): 67–76, footnote 8.

nonnegotiable. God was in charge, and that was sacred. The pilgrim was but a midwife on behalf of the supplicant's spiritual rebirth. The goal of the Exercises was growth in interior freedom from the psychospiritual slavery of evil. Distorted or haunted memory banks, confused understanding, loss of existential meaning or purpose, and paralyzed will could all undermine one's peace of soul and even sever relationship with God.

Identifying the Afflicted Devotees of the First Spiritual Exercises

Who was the population drawn to the First Spiritual Exercises? Tribunal transcripts provide precious, real-time details. Biographer Tellechea Idígoras lays out a colorful, detailed list. "There were married men and women, young unmarried women, students, and monks."[23] Even some names of particular supplicants were recorded: "[T]here was Juan the saddler; the wife of Davila the baker, who had been a woman of loose morals before her marriage"; one of the young daughters of Isidro, the tax collector; Isabel the prioress; a hospital orderly; widows; university professors and students.[24] There were "a number of servants, some weavers, and a woman who, at one time, had wanted to hang herself."[25] (Suicidal ideation, of course, was something about which Íñigo was familiar, dating to his Manresa Episode.)

Certain inquirers were discouraged. In a foundational text from the Ignatian tradition, Jerónimo Nadal (1507–80), a close companion of Íñigo, noted: "It sometimes happens that a man is frequently in our company and yet never gets to the point where he is willing to talk of the things of God bearing on the salvation of his soul. With such a person the best course is not to waste time on trivia even though that is what he wants to discuss."[26] The package of exercises was for the spiritually injured or distressed who invoked God, or desired instruction on how to do so. Such people are distinguished by their felt readiness—perhaps after years of conscious or unconscious resistance—to cry out both *to* God and, conversationally, about their need *for* God. The distressed population drawn to the Íñiguistas in Alcalá, like bees to honey, very *much* wished to talk of

23. Tellechea Idígoras, *Ignatius of Loyola*, 250–51.

24. Tellechea Idígoras, 250–51.

25. Tellechea Idígoras, 250–51.

26. Jerónimo Nadal, "Sixth Exhortation," *The Conversational Word of God*, trans. Thomas H. Clancy (St. Louis: Institute of Jesuit Sources, 1978), 52–56.

God. They were an eclectic, broad audience, many lacking in educational or religious literacy. They were "*the afflicted*, the marginal, not those who were content with themselves and their lot."[27]

The Verdict

The Inquisition, under the jurisdiction of the archbishop of Toledo, delegated the investigations to local authorities in Alcalá and Salamanca. Vicar General Figueroa, of the former, found Íñigo innocent after each Process brought against him, but fired an ecclesial shot across his bow. A sanction was imposed: the *Íñiguistas* must dress in ordinary clothes and wear shoes. Subsequently, Dominican authorities in Salamanca ruled that they must not teach the distinction between venial and mortal sin, and must cease all public speaking and preaching about matters of faith, unless and until they were to complete a master of arts degree in theology.

Íñigo was surely relieved. But he remained impatient with the Processes, as beneficial as they proved. The seemingly endless scrutiny deprived him of valuable time and energy to preach the Gospel, to beg and study, and to assist restless, afflicted souls in spiritual conversation. One anecdote recalls how, seemingly exasperated, Íñigo displayed the ferocious combativeness by which he had earned his battlefield reputation. After being formally exonerated on one charge by Figueroa, Íñigo said to him: "I do not know what use there is in these investigations."[28] And then, he risked a pointed question: " 'We would like to know if they found any heresy in us,' [Íñigo] said. 'No,' replied Figueroa, 'if they had, they would have burned you.' 'They would likewise have burned you,' retorted [Íñigo], 'if they found heresy in you.' "[29]

Despite his annoyance, Íñigo recognized the hand of God at work. His package of spiritual exercises had won initial church approbation, of paramount importance in sixteenth-century Europe. The intense heat of the various inquisitorial processes had helped the sinner/saint refine the Exercises into gold for the ages. Indeed, they were an important first step toward eventual papal approval, enabling Íñigo and his first companions to continue spiritual outreach to the afflicted with church approval.

27. Tellechea Idígoras, *Ignatius of Loyola*, 251, emphasis added.

28. Dudon, *St. Ignatius of Loyola*, 112.

29. Tellechea Idígoras, *Ignatius of Loyola*, 244.

The ecclesial sanctions were surely reasonable at a time of religious witch hunts, arguably even a blessing. Obedient to the verdict, Íñigo faced a long journey to ordained priesthood, which now required enrollment at the University of Paris, and, finally, a more sustained commitment to academics. The pilgrim had no doubt that he had received the gift of the Exercises from God, but on one condition—he must share them. If that meant four or more years of study in Paris, so be it. Dedication was not an issue, only direction. Of course, there was another advantage to leaving Spain forthwith, given the scurrilous gossip about his relations with women. "The verdict of the Inquisition was not the only reason for Ignatius' move to Paris," as he faced continuing hostility from many who thought he was an *Alumbrado* "or who mistrusted his close relationships with women."[30] In order to pursue more freely the conversational help of souls, it was again time for the pilgrim to move along. Going forward, Basque Íñigo was moving toward a global platform, and he would adopt the Latinized version of his name, "Ignatius."

A Spirituality of Affliction

Pursuant to several manageable stipulations, Íñigo and his devotees had been cleared to offer a spiritually healing conversational package, which over time became the officially approved *Spiritual Exercises*. The Íñiguistas consoled the afflicted through an innovative package born of their master's excruciating Manresa Episode, and which addressed key symptoms of spiritual injury and distress. Today's survivors of violence can recognize in Íñigo's documented soul wounds a kindred spirit, and in his exercises tailored guidance that can mediate renewed divine encounter. Spiritual exercises, as Ignatius conceived them, are structured practices designed to bring the anguished God-seeker into the comfort and joy of personal relationship with God.

Beneficiaries were those such as the shamed and distressed María de la Flor. Her term "poenas" is rooted in the Latin *poena*, or "pain" in English. Presumably, not all those who asked for spiritual assistance were enduring some type of *poenas*. But Flor's testimony offers an intriguing historical snapshot of Íñigo's early practice, which loosely grounds a contemporary spirituality of affliction for a very troubled zeitgeist. The

30. *Auto.*, 146n8.

light Exercises package was quite flexible, suitable for future adaptation according to changing contexts and needs.

Spiritual guides in any of the Abrahamic religions will find many citations about affliction in their sacred texts, since it is a common theme highlighting trials and tribulations as opportunities for personal growth, purification of ego, and trust in God. "When the righteous cry for help, the LORD hears, and rescues them from all their troubles. The LORD is near to the brokenhearted and saves the crushed in spirit. Many are the afflictions of the righteous, but the LORD rescues them from them all. He keeps all their bones; not one of them will be broken" (Psalm 34:17-20).

What might be the significance today for those afflicted by moral injury trauma? In her groundbreaking 1992 book *Trauma and Recovery*, Harvard Medical School professor emerita of psychiatry Judith Herman characterizes psychological trauma as "an affliction of the powerless."[31] It is hardly a clinical diagnosis but a broad appeal to a skeptical public disinclined to notice the overwhelming pervasiveness of a horrific modern phenomenon.

Herman's landmark research and clinical practice led her to conclude that violence was ubiquitous in society. She wrote well before popular movements such as #MeToo made it possible for victim-survivors to publicize more broadly their experience of sexual harassment, abuse, and rape culture. Her practice also included Vietnam veterans. "It is now apparent also that the traumas of one are the traumas of the other. The hysteria of women and the combat neurosis of men are one. . . . There is a 'commonality of affliction.' "[32] Evidently, there is also a commonality of discourse between Íñigo and Herman. It seems likely, in this regard, that many of today's afflicted present with some degree of trauma. If so, more intentional trauma-informed spiritual and pastoral care is recommended. Following is some preliminary guidance to that end.

Follow the Symptoms

"La poena" in medieval Castilian, sometimes spelled "la pena" or "la penna," corresponds to "pain," "hardship," "sorrow," or "grief" in English. It is an expansive term whose meaning often depends upon the context. It

31. Judith Herman, *Trauma and Recovery: The Aftermath of Violence—from Domestic Abuse to Political Terror* (New York: Basic Books, 1992), 33.

32. Herman, *Trauma and Recovery*, 32.

can denote emotional or psychological suffering, including fear or anxiety, as well as bodily distress, torment, or physical harm.[33] In this sense, *penas* impact all human capacities of soul. The affliction can be *active* (a cause of pain or distress) or *passive* (being afflicted by something or someone who causes suffering or anguish).

Would it be a stretch to consider many of Íñigo's afflicted supplicants, such as Flor, presenting with symptoms that today overlap with the estimated 70 percent of people worldwide exposed to a traumatic event?[34] Physical and sexual violence are nothing new; indeed, late medieval Castile was characterized by a culture of chivalric violence, including sexual conquest of women. There were limits to the population suitable for the light Exercises, certainly, but those limits pertained primarily to the relative self-awareness and intentionality of supplicants' hunger for divine intervention.

Afflicted casualties of violence in the twenty-first century, distressed in conscience, may well be enduring some form of moral injury trauma. They include those who personally experience cruelty, perpetrate it, or witness it (in person or on social media). This large population can find empathetic resources in the Ignatian paradigm. Spiritual and pastoral caregivers should recall that evidence-based research indicates that 30–70 percent of individuals who experience a traumatic event subsequently report positive change and growth grounded in that very tribulation.[35] In this regard, it is a psychospiritual opportunity. Afflictions are akin to soul wounds, whose symptoms display interconnection among the faculties of body, mind, psyche, and brain, all fused to Divinity through the human spirit. The soul also keeps the score because, according to Hebrew and Christian scriptural tradition, these powers holistically comprise the one person.

Sorrow, shame, and confusion, among other symptoms, all plagued Íñigo's conscience because of his willing participation in the excesses and contradictions of medieval chivalric culture. Leaning in to—and humbly acknowledging—those painful symptoms is the first step toward

33. "Pena," *Diccionario Medieval Español: Tomo II, CH-Z* (Salamanca: Universidad Pontificia de Salamanca, 1986), 1485.

34. Chapter 2 noted this estimate of trauma counselor Lisa López Levers and her associated list of the multiple events at stake.

35. Lisa López Levers, *Trauma Counseling: Theories and Interventions for Managing Trauma, Stress, Crisis, and Disaster*, 2nd ed. (New York: Springer Publishing, 2023), 19.

being healed from their enslaving tyranny. This blessed step, when one is ready, is pivotal to a person's reconciliation and reconnection—with God, others, and one's very self—and among the divine gifts sought in the Exercises. The distressing symptoms described by Íñigo at Manresa are readily on view within both contemporary trauma theory and the Exercises. Moreover, one can follow them to God, as Hansel and Gretel trusted their shiny white pebbles to lead them home safely through the forest darkness.

Of course, recalling the interdisciplinary guidance of psychiatrist and theologian Warren Kinghorn, the reduction and healing of psychological symptoms—so that someone should "feel better"—is not the ultimate goal of spiritual care. At root, the purpose is so that sins (of commission or omission) may be forgiven and that the supplicant finds reconciliation in the intimacy of divine embrace. Relationship, relationship, relationship.

Psychological and body-oriented therapies are immeasurably valuable, but some people of faith and seekers also seek methods to reconnect their humanity with the bliss of Divinity. Íñigo was not the only Christian mystic to see divine opportunity in the distress of affliction. In the following century, the great English metaphysical poet and clergyman John Donne articulated his own spirituality of affliction: "For affliction is a treasure, and scarce any man has enough of it; no man hath affliction enough that is not matured and ripened by and made fit for God by that affliction."[36]

Expert Companionship

Given the pervasiveness of various forms of trauma, spiritual and pastoral caregivers of this special needs population are well advised to lean into professional development of insights and practices. Trauma counseling specialist Levers suggests trauma be viewed as a "scaffold"[37]—the learning process builds upon basic knowledge and skills as preparation for increasingly more complex issues in the field, like ascending the rungs of a ladder. The construct of trauma has evolved since 1980 from psychological understanding of the individual client to a more systemic, intergenerational, and psychosocial perspective, to the current neurobiological

36. John Donne, *The Works of John Donne*, vol. 3, ed. Henry Alford (London: John W. Parker, 1839), 574–75.

37. López Levers, *Trauma Counseling*, 2.

realizations about the effects of trauma.[38] The next generation promises to include the realm of the spirit and soul. With certain types of trauma, licensing is not necessarily required to begin the process of accompaniment. Readiness to consult with mental health practitioners, of course, is always presumed.

Psychologists Lawrence G. Calhoun and Richard G. Tedeschi promote the role of "expert companions" trained to accompany those journeying through posttraumatic growth. This could be considered a lower rung of the trauma scaffold. "We call the stance we take as professionals in helping people who are coming to us for assistance in coping with trauma and its aftermath *expert companionship*. The term emphasizes the view that both professional expertise and human companionship are crucial for the people seeking our help. . . . We see ourselves as *facilitators* rather than creators of growth."[39]

Many experienced spiritual and pastoral caregivers will find that, at this lower rung, they are more qualified than they imagine to accompany the population of survivors of one or more traumatic events. "Companionship first" is the basic principle in the psychological literature of posttraumatic growth. Calhoun and Tedeschi continue: "We use the term *companion* to emphasize that simply *being with* a survivor of trauma who is experiencing misery and confusion can bring significant comfort to this person. . . . Especially in the early phases of helping trauma survivors, the expertise that trauma clinicians offer should be expertise in relating and listening."[40]

Ignatian guides are trained to listen with a third, discerning ear; to establish trust with those they accompany; and to be surprised by—much less judgmental of—nothing. With a modicum of mentoring, some will discover how suitable their skills are to accompany survivors, perpetrators, and witnesses of traumatic events who are enduring some form of moral injury trauma. Scholars today, for example, have begun to recall that Íñigo's First Spiritual Exercises "are a special form of spiritual conversation."[41] Guided conversations may well prove to be the most ef-

38. López Levers, 23.

39. Lawrence G. Calhoun and Richard G. Tedeschi, *Posttraumatic Growth in Clinical Practice* (New York: Routledge, 2013), 23, emphases in original.

40. Calhoun and Tedeschi, *Posttraumatic Growth*, 24, emphases in original.

41. Nicholas Austin, "The Ignatian Art of Spiritual Conversation," *The Way* 62, no. 3 (July 2023): 13.

fective modality for midwifing care to faith-based, traumatically injured survivors.

Trauma-Informed Intake

Intake procedures, adaptable to spiritual retreat, direction, and pastoral counseling settings, might piggyback on current practice for routine inquiry about any particular needs the supplicant desires. For example, intake forms typically ask about special dietary needs, or whether the supplicant prefers a male or female guide on a private directed retreat. The list of options has begun to (or likely should) include preference for a director familiar with twelve-step-program dynamics. For seekers unsettled by one or more traumatic events, and who feel ready to engage those symptoms, intake options could stipulate: "If possible, I prefer a director comfortable with trauma dynamics." Such a procedure indicates staff and program preparedness, through an effort to provide an ambience of safe spatial settings.

Another informed approach for consideration would be to train qualified spiritual guides and pastoral counselors in how to introduce themselves at orientation meetings with careseekers. This is becoming a standard procedure for trauma-informed care in a variety of other service settings. For example, one might describe her or his openness to accompany careseekers impacted by traumatic injury, stipulate that she or he is not a licensed medical professional qualified to address a formal diagnosis of posttraumatic stress disorder, and invite careseekers to name a concrete traumatic event, symptom, or area of uncertainty, at whatever point in the relationship sufficient trust might develop. The more this becomes gently routinized and demystified during orientation, over introductions, and throughout the course of care, the more likely this special needs population will feel safe enough to speak up. The initiative, of course, remains with the careseeker. But some claim they have been waiting years for the right cue from the caregiver.

The Powers of Soul as Method of Prayer

"They told him their afflictions, and he consoled them." One concrete way that Íñigo did so, according to Benavente's testimony, was by teaching supplicants how to pray with Augustine's three powers of soul: memory, understanding, and will. Her declaration has left an important clue to posterity, a historic snapshot suitable for adaptation of an Ignatian meditation practice tailored for trauma-informed spiritual and pastoral care. A brief introduction to those Augustinian capacities, and Íñigo's appropriation of them, illustrates the significance for those journeying through posttraumatic growth.

In the very first exercise of the First Week, the retreatant is asked to pray about the "sin of the angels."[42] "The First Point will be to use my memory, by going over the first sin, that of the angels; next, to use my understanding, by reasoning about it; and then my will."[43] These three powers of the soul "operate in all prayer . . . where their application constitutes a method."[44]

Memory is a faculty of soul responsible for recalling past experiences, cognitions, impressions, and knowledge. It encompasses personal memories, most obviously, but also the intellect's storage of more general truths, apprehensions, and beliefs. This makes it possible to apply one's "memory" to things beyond personal experience, such as Íñigo's exercise on the "first sin of the angels." Memory is not independent of understanding or any other capacity, and no power connects with God apart from the human spirit. Rather, memory permits individuals to draw upon past experiences (including traumatic events), perceptions, mystical encounters with Divinity, and discernments to inform present construction of meaning and related decision-making. All three powers are at work simultaneously. It is evident that both Augustine and Ignatius considered these powers in a holistic fashion, since the human person is one. The challenge for spiritual and pastoral care is that trauma can obstruct, shroud, or wholly erase the memory bank.

Understanding (sometimes conceived or expressed as *intellect* or *thought*) is the power of soul responsible for cognition and comprehension. It includes the ability to grasp truths, engage in rational reflection, decipher existential meaning and purpose, and form coherent judgments. For Augustine, it involves the capacity for self-awareness. Understanding, just as

42. Revelation 12:7-9 references the war in heaven between Michael with his army of angels and the disobedient Satan with his. The result was the latter's banishment from heaven.

43. *SpEx* no. 50.

44. Michael Ivens, *Understanding the Spiritual Exercises: Text and Commentary* (Leominster, England: Gracewing, 1998), 46.

memory and will, is never an isolated capacity but operates in conjunction and interplay. The challenge for spiritual and pastoral care is that traumatic events can result in confusion manifesting as impaired memory, ability to think or focus, or diminished self-awareness. From a medical perspective, confusion can be regarded as a possible symptom of brain activity disruptions or neurological breakdown of cognitive functions.

Will is a power of soul responsible for choosing and desiring. It is the seat of intentionality and decision-making, governing human agency and moral choices. Augustine believed that the human will was free and, therefore, that people are responsible for their choices. The will can choose for good or evil. But the question arises, post-trauma, about whether or not freedom of human agency any longer exists. Trauma is an affliction of the powerless, and may manifest in the individual's sense of powerlessness. The first step in trauma recovery, according to psychiatrist Herman's paradigm, is to establish personal safety and security through recovery of human agency.

Moreover, recent scientific examination of neural circuits, as highlighted in research such as van der Kolk's, demonstrates that trauma renders countless victims impaired by overwhelming force—for example, by *freezing* their emotions and faculty of volition.[45] In this regard, trauma is not a failure of agency or unwillingness to "fight back," as is so often erroneously alleged of victim-survivors of rape or sexual assault. Rather, it is now scientifically demonstrable that freezing can be *involuntary* from a medical perspective because the brain paralyzes the will. The acute stress response of fight-or-flight here expands to fight, flight, or freeze.

The genius of Íñigo was to articulate a disciplined method of meditation utilizing all three powers of soul in repeated practice. It could be deployed to pray other exercises from the full package in service of spiritual growth, healing, and reconciliation. The soul seeks truth through meaning and understanding, exerts agency toward healthy and holy decisions, and retains the experience of Divinity in memory. Today, therapeutic practices—some of them somatic—can assist seekers and clients to safely reclaim their memories, restore existential understanding and meaning, and unlock and empower their interior agency. Here, Íñigo's

45. Jennifer Percy, "What People Misunderstand about Rape," *New York Times Magazine*, August 22, 2023.

traditional Christian anthropology and method of consoling the afflicted find interdisciplinary resonance in a troubled world.

Of course, the pilgrim's offering of the Exercises at Alcalá included instruction in the gospels and Pauline letters. For people of faith of any Abrahamic tradition, sacred texts are a central healing resource. The following chapter introduces a contemporary reading of the most famous gospel story of affliction in the Western canon and religious imagination, placing casualties of violence at the center. Is it possible that injury and vulnerability can broker God's compassionate embrace? Certainly the Sufi mystic Rumi believed so: "the wound is the place where the Light enters." Let the bloodied crime victim discarded at roadside in the famous parable of the Good Samaritan make the case.

7

The Invisible Mugged Traveler

Encountering God as Hero or Casualty

25 An expert in the law stood up to test Jesus. "Teacher," he said, "what must I do to inherit eternal life?" 26 He said to him, "What is written in the law? What do you read there?" 27 He answered, "You shall love the Lord your God with all your heart and with all your soul and with all your strength and with all your mind and your neighbor as yourself." 28 And he said to him, "You have given the right answer; do this, and you will live."

29 But wanting to vindicate himself, he asked Jesus, "And who is my neighbor?" 30 Jesus replied, "A man was going down from Jerusalem to Jericho and fell into the hands of robbers, who stripped him, beat him, and took off, leaving him half dead. 31 Now by chance a priest was going down that road, and when he saw him he passed by on the other side. 32 So likewise a Levite, when he came to the place and saw him, passed by on the other side. 33 But a Samaritan while traveling came upon him, and when he saw him he was moved with compassion. 34 He went to him and bandaged his wounds, treating them with oil and wine. Then he put him on his own animal, brought him to an inn, and took care of him. 35 The next day he took out two denarii, gave them to the innkeeper, and said, 'Take care of him, and when I come back I will repay you whatever more you spend.' 36 Which of these three, do you think, was a neighbor to the man who fell into the hands of the robbers?" 37 He said, "The one who showed him mercy." Jesus said to him, "Go and do likewise."

Luke 10:25-37 (New Revised Standard Version Updated Edition)

Some called it the "Way of Blood," others the "Bloody Path." The steep downhill road from Jerusalem to Jericho in first-century Palestine was notoriously dangerous for lone travelers. Loosely organized bands of ruthless highwaymen preyed upon the vulnerable with little fear of sanction. It provided an ideal foundation upon which Jesus could build a violent story of a mugged Jewish traveler. "A man was going down from Jerusalem to Jericho," Jesus began, "and fell into the hands of robbers, who stripped him, beat him, and took off, leaving him half dead" (Luke 10:30). "Lestes," the Greek word for robber, connotes "violent criminal."[1]

Listeners would have nervously recalled their own anxiety when journeying the precipitous switchbacks, descending more than three thousand feet over seventeen miles of isolated Judean desert resembling a hilly moonscape. Each successive bend afforded an opportunity for ambush. Jesus's parable about a victim of violent crime drew upon such frightful village lore to highlight the precariousness of life and, in so doing, offer a scathing period critique of religious elites. "Now by chance a priest was going down that road, and when he saw him he passed by on the other side. So likewise a Levite, when he came to the place and saw him, passed by on the other side" (Luke 10:31-32).

"The Good Samaritan" Parable, Reconsidered

This chapter presents a close reading of Jesus's parable of "The Good Samaritan," drawing upon modern scriptural and theological scholarship to foreground the victimized traveler. Because the story is so familiar, it is difficult to hear afresh. The interpretive key is that, using a period stylistic technique common to all four evangelists, Luke joined an actual tale from Jesus's lips (verses 30-35) to a framing narrative of his own composition (verses 25-29 and 36-37). That is, he took an authentic Jesus-story about a victim of violent crime, which had circulated orally, and incorporated it into his own written narrative centered on a lawyer's two questions. First, "Teacher, what must I do to inherit eternal life?" Second, "And who is my neighbor?" Both were issues of pressing pastoral concern to Luke's community and help explain his editorial perspective and final

1. Amy-Jill Levine and Marc Zvi Brettler, eds., *The Jewish Annotated New Testament: New Revised Standard Version* (New York: Oxford University Press, 2011), 123.

composition. Together, Jesus's prior tale—and Luke's bookending of it—form the inspired, canonical text known to posterity as the parable of the Good Samaritan. But it is crucial, according to Scripture scholar Bernard Brandon Scott, to understand that the Jesus-story "originally circulated separately from the question about neighborliness."[2]

For all its sublimity, Luke's creative artistry has come at considerable cost. An unanticipated outcome has been the submersion of the point of view of the battered traveler, bereft in the roadside ditch. The existential pathos, understood in the biblical sense as the cry of the poor and in the Greek philosophical sense as "complaints of the soul," has grown fainter. The evangelist's tale obscures the precious assertion that human and spiritual vulnerability can invite and mediate divine encounter and redemption. Australian Scripture scholar Brendan Byrne echoes Scott on the pivotal point of compositional history. "As originally told by Jesus (abstracted, that is, from the setting Luke has provided), the original parable draws the hearer into the perspective of the wounded, half-dead traveler."[3] The point of the Jesus-story, according to Scripture scholar Luke Timothy Johnson, is therefore not a contrast between Jews and Samaritans but rather "a contrast between those who were established . . . and those who were not."[4] At stake, spiritually, is the clarity of a person's existential awareness of their vulnerability or even impotence, and how that very powerlessness can midwife divine encounter. It is akin to completing the first step toward recovery in any twelve-step addiction program: "We admitted that we were powerless."

Prophet Jesus's tale of the bloody traveler in the ditch strikingly exemplifies the important Lukan theme of *reversal of fortune* in favor of outsiders and the poor; the Good Samaritan parable should be considered through that lens. "Human security and complacency are challenged" by a "Great Reversal" of religious expectations and social values.[5] The outcast are those rejected by conventional society and religion—literally in the case of the

2. Bernard Brandon Scott, *Hear Then the Parable: A Commentary on the Parables of Jesus* (Minneapolis: Augsburg Fortress Press, 1989), 191.

3. Brendan Byrne, *The Hospitality of God: A Reading of Luke's Gospel*, rev. ed. (Collegeville, MN: Liturgical Press, 2015), 100.

4. Luke Timothy Johnson, *The Gospel of Luke*, Sacra Pagina, ed. Daniel J. Harrington (Collegeville, MN: Liturgical Press, 1991), 173.

5. Johnson, *Gospel of Luke*, 22.

mugged traveler—but all the more cherished by God. "Among them are the crippled, the lame, the blind and deaf, the sexually mutilated, lepers, and all those ritually excluded from full participation in the life of the people."[6] The representative figures of priest and Levite "see" the bloodied traveler at roadside, but with such mistaken, self-serving understanding of the Torah that they are blind to the authentic mercy and compassion required by God.[7] They look but do not perceive (Mark 4:12).

Jesus thereby issues a prophetic challenge to established religious interests, personified in the priest and Levite. They "see" but do not " notice," perhaps for reasons of narcissistic and exaggerated ritual purity (see Matt 13:1). Jesus aims to challenge their misreading of the Torah through his presentation of a tragic scene of humanity, wounded by senseless violence and often invisible to conventional church and society, yet noticed and cherished by God. To encounter one's neighbor in a full Lukan sense, one must cultivate a spiritual capacity to notice from the perspective of the mugged traveler, bloodied and spurned like roadkill, attentive to the voice of excluded others on the underside of history, society, and current events.

Mary's Magnificat vividly expresses the fundamental Lukan theme of the Great Reversal: "He has brought down the powerful from their thrones and lifted up the lowly" (Luke 1:52). The point, not necessarily obvious, readily resonates for many marginalized casualties of violence today, some of them estranged from institutions such as family or church, perhaps even a past supportive relationship with their Higher Power.[8] The good news is that "Jesus' parables . . . reimagine a world that subverts the status quo."[9] Outsiders, or those who self-identify as such, are

6. Johnson, 22.

7. "Your neighbor as yourself" (Luke 10:27) is a precise citation from Leviticus 19:18: "You shall not take vengeance or bear a grudge against any of your people, but you shall love your neighbor as yourself: I am the LORD."

8. A decorated and devout Marine first lieutenant, just returned from the battle of Fallujah in Iraq, once recounted to me his search for a welcoming Christian church in southeastern Pennsylvania. On one Sunday in 2021 he and his middle-aged wife were stopped by greeters at the entrance to a nondenominational church. They summoned the pastor, who sized up the couple and told the veteran he was not welcome because of his tattooed forearms and neck. "We don't want any gang members here," he said icily.

9. Bernard Brandon Scott, *Reimagine the World: An Introduction to the Parables of Jesus* (Santa Clara, CA: Polebridge Press, 2001), 15.

invited to trust that they are dear to Divinity. "Those ordinarily deemed unworthy, lowly, marginal, or even outcast, are accepted by God."[10]

The plot thickens at the recognition that Luke's rendering of the parable has resulted in a one-sided emphasis on the person of the Samaritan champion to the rescue. This is evident in contemporary catechetics and homiletics, as Sunday churchgoers can attest. Luke's compelling figure of the Good Samaritan has even entered the lexicon and iconography of Western culture. His composition draws the reader into the perspective of the neighborly Samaritan who passes by, sees but also *notices* with heartfelt mercy the festering wounds of the traveler in the ditch, and stops to assist him. The concluding injunction to "go and do likewise" is memorable, ethically compelling, and arguably a foundation of Western values. The hearer is challenged to identify with the Samaritan. (Everyone loves hero-to-the-rescue stories.)

Later Christian interpreters, of course, would go even further, viewing him as Savior in the person of Christ. "To do likewise" develops into a Christology and spirituality of identification and encounter with God *in the Samaritan*. Early interpreters such as Irenaeus, Origen, Ambrose, and Augustine set the pattern with allegorical interpretation of the Samaritan *as Christ*, healing the wounds caused by sin.[11] This reading has largely prevailed down the centuries.

However, a different perspective is front and center in the Jesus-story versus the wider Lukan composition. According to Scott, "[t]he all-important question in this parable is that of point of view: from where do I hear the parable?"[12] It is Jesus's intention to draw the listener into identification with the character and point of view of the bloodied traveler. This is also the perspective of theologian Gustavo Gutierrez and his liberation school, for whom the fundamental hermeneutical question is: Who is the most important person in Luke's parable?[13] Few, certainly in the United States, will answer this question like Scott or Gutierrez. To do

10. Johnson, *Gospel of Luke*, 22.

11. *Ancient Christian Commentary on Scripture: New Testament III, Luke*, ed. Arthur A. Just Jr. (Downers Grove, IL: InterVarsity Press, 2003), 177–81.

12. Scott, *Hear Then the Parable*, 190.

13. Gustavo Gutierrez, "Church Must Be Samaritan, Reaching Out to Others," *National Catholic Reporter*, February 28, 2014, https://www.ncronline.org/blogs/ncr-today/gutierrez-vatican-church-must-be-samaritan-reaching-out-others. Gutierrez points out that the

so may require "perspective-taking." Psychologists associate this trait with empathy, requiring the ability to consider a situation from a viewpoint other than one's customary frame of reference.[14]

Many first-century travelers would have identified readily with the crime victim assaulted along the Bloody Path—if not directly, surely vicariously through violated family, friends, and fellow villagers. The tale cut awfully close to the bone, drawing them into solidarity with the half-dead traveler, whose "restoration is the narrative's goal."[15] A penny for the real-time reactions of the beaten and stripped traveler in the ditch as he watched religious leaders and scholars pass him by. Did he experience the metallic taste of paralyzing fear for his life, the breathlessness or racing heart of a panic attack, the degradation of shame, or the determination never to frequent the Temple again? Might listeners and readers today pray the parable of "The Battered Traveler" to seek psychospiritual access to the anxious affect, bodily tension and headaches, and painful memories that accompany (perceived) threats to their personal or familial safety?

Seekers and persons of faith, therefore, are invited to imagine themselves at roadside, bloodied or bewildered of conscience, there to encounter the kingdom of God. For most, it does not come naturally. For survivors of past traumatic injury, it can even be risky; in so doing they may well trigger unwanted memories and associated symptoms. Hence, they must be *ready* to choose this perspective. It may be prudent for this special needs population, therefore, to consult with a spiritual guide or sponsor before praying in such fashion. They can take heart from the original Jesus-story, which clearly promises that recognition of one's existential vulnerability can elicit a heartfelt experience of the goodness and mercy of God.

---

church in Latin America and the Caribbean understands itself as "a Samaritan church" by virtue of its identification with Christ's suffering and being forgotten at roadside.

14. The capacity to modify perspective is considered by developmental psychology a key to cognitive development. Social psychological research has demonstrated the benefits of viewing a situation or concept from a different frame of reference—including increased altruism, decreased stereotyping, and an ability to establish stronger social bonds with others.

15. Scott, *Hear Then the Parable*, 193.

Though the wounded victim arguably owes the Samaritan his life, nevertheless, the compelling force of Luke's masterful version has overshadowed Jesus's account. Treasure though it is, Luke's memorable telling shrouds the invitation to notice the point of view of the nearly dead man in the ditch. In the primal Jesus-story the hearer plays *casualty*; in Luke's composition the hearer plays *champion and hero*. The evangelist's edit has backgrounded the presenting incidence of criminal violence, virtually canceling it in the Christian spiritual, pastoral, interpretive, catechetical, and homiletic traditions. A variety of interpretive issues are at stake but beyond this chapter's scope. The central spiritual question, though, is clear enough: Which perspective do the parable's hearers adopt in order to encounter God most profoundly—champion or casualty?

Contemporary exegetes have pondered the conundrum at some length. Some argue that, like many parables, the Good Samaritan is a marvelous riddle best approached as a Zen koan. There is wisdom and spiritual profit in this. Nevertheless, greater theological clarity is available. When the point of view of the Jesus-story is recaptured, thereby restoring casualties of violence to the narrative foreground, Luke's clarion theme of reversal of fortune shimmers more brightly. Here, "the wall between *us* and *them* no longer exists."[16] Here, would-be Samaritans-to-the-rescue discover yet more profound entrée to Divinity in meaningful interpersonal *encounter* with survivor-neighbors.

It is the difference between charity and solidarity, the latter overcoming the dehumanizing risk of viewing people on the societal or ecclesial margins as *objects* of religious duty. These might include, for example, the economically poor; racial minorities; those who are elderly, infirm, or mentally incapacitated; survivors of ecclesial sexual abuse; or those who identify as LGBTQ. "Solidarity differs from charity because it replaces unilateral doing for with the mutuality of being with."[17] Samaritan neighborliness is reframed as the human solidarity of sisters and brothers, an egalitarian recognition of voluntary reciprocity and encounter between and among children of God, each equal in dignity.

16. Scott, *Reimagine the World*, 64.

17. Marcus Mescher, *The Ethics of Encounter: Christian Neighbor Love as a Practice of Solidarity* (Maryknoll, NY: Orbis, 2020), 59.

The parable's riddle suggests that "my *place* in the world changes. To 'go and do likewise' is to be a neighbor who courageously and compassionately goes into the ditch in order to draw near to neighbors in need."[18] To reclaim that gentleman's dignity after all these centuries, perhaps the parable should more aptly be called "The Battered Traveler." Pope Francis has exhorted the people of God to seek more profound encounter with Christ in those who suffer, to look directly into their eyes, and "to put them at the center of the Church's pilgrim way."[19] Christians can thereby "recognize Christ himself in each of our abandoned or excluded brothers and sisters."[20] In this fashion, "The Battered Traveler" becomes an ideal scriptural resource for Ignatian contemplation of Jesus's passion narrative, as presented in the "Third Week" of the Spiritual Exercises. The stripped, beaten, invisible, mugged victim personifies and reveals the crucified Christ on Calvary.

EverySurvivor

Anyone startled by this reversal of perspective would do well to recall that both the original Jesus-story and Luke's wider Good Samaritan parable are meant to achieve just such incredulous reaction, beginning with the account of brutal crime perpetrated along the forlorn Bloody Path. The road was a source of nightmares for frequent travelers, especially those required to journey alone. Parents who wished to promote children's good behavior could recite stories about a boogeyman along the wilderness path. "The violence done to the traveling Judean is overt: he is stripped, beaten, left half dead. This is not a sentimental tale."[21] Nevertheless, over the centuries the parable has in fact been domesticated. Few homilists, religious educators, spiritual guides, or pastoral counselors display much interest in the raw story of violent crime at the heart of Jesus's tale. In so doing they appear aloof from the twenty-first-century context of their congregations, thereby impoverishing an authentic reading of the Good News and obscuring healing entrée to the suffering Christ.

18. Mescher, *Ethics of Encounter*, 61.
19. Pope Francis, *Evangelii Gaudium* 198, Vatican, November 24, 2013.
20. Pope Francis, *Fratelli Tutti* ("All Brothers") 85, Vatican, October 3, 2020.
21. Johnson, *Gospel of Luke*, 175.

Trauma psychiatrist van der Kolk points out that the majority of Americans, or their loved ones, will experience a violent crime at some point during their lifetimes, and that three million children are reported annually as victims of child abuse or neglect.[22] In 2023, according to the Kaiser Family Foundation, firearms were reported as "the number one cause of death for children and teens in the United States, surpassing motor vehicle deaths and those caused by other injuries."[23] According to the National Domestic Violence Hotline, "an average of 24 people per minute are victims of rape, physical violence or stalking by an intimate partner in the United States—more than 12 million women and men over the course of a single year."[24] Each of these numbers represents one human being, perhaps someone who has been too ashamed to report the crime or tell their story.

Such close, contemporary reading of a cherished sacred text offers a striking example from New Testament studies of the challenge faced by casualties of violence today. As the mother of a murdered transgender man observes, "When you're misgendered, it becomes a daily trauma of not being seen."[25] Those who draw close enough to the bloodied ditch might hear a lament echoing that of the central character in Ralph Ellison's novel *Invisible Man:* "I am an invisible man. No, I am not a spook like those who haunted Edgar Allen Poe: Nor am I one of your Hollywood movie ectoplasms. I am a man of substance, of flesh and bone, fiber and liquids, and I might even be said to possess a mind. I am invisible, simply because people refuse to see me."[26]

22. Bessel van der Kolk, *The Body Keeps the Score: Brain, Mind, and Body in the Healing of Trauma* (New York: Viking, 2014), 20.

23. Matt McGough et al., "Child and Teen Firearm Mortality in the U.S. and Peer Countries," KFF, July 18, 2023, https://www.kff.org/global-health-policy/issue-brief/child-and-teen-firearm-mortality-in-the-u-s-and-peer-countries/.

24. "Domestic Violence Statistics," *The Hotline*, https://www.thehotline.org/stakeholders/domestic-violence-statistics/.

25. Kathy Lynch, referring to her transgender son, Aaron. At age twenty-six, he was shot and killed by police during a psychotic episode, "the culmination of his years of mental health struggles" according to his mother. Tom Jackman, "After Years of Turmoil, A Fatal Night: Fairfax Officers Were Called to Help a Transgender Man in Crisis. One Killed Him," *Washington Post*, June 14, 2024, 1.

26. Ralph Ellison, *Invisible Man* (New York: Random House, 1995 [1952]), 3. The novel won the 1953 National Book Award for fiction.

One scriptural commentator recently noted that the stricken traveler "is simply a generic human being of the male sex. . . . The description of the victim is significant: naked and mute, the person is stripped of identity."[27] Absent distinctive clothing, passersby lacked any clues to identify the battered traveler with a particular village, clan, or even social class. Had he died, it might have been difficult to restore the anonymous corpse to the family for dignified, ritual burial. Ignominy upon invisibility upon injury.

Venerable Bede, an eighth-century Doctor of the Church, viewed the parable's victim as *Adam*, a term used throughout the Hebrew Scriptures as an allegorical representation of mankind to designate an individual human person or humanity in general.[28] In other words, the focal point of the Jesus-story is an *Everyman* figure, a battered crime victim who more properly can be designated *EverySurvivor.* The very absence of distinctive features, voice, clothing, or personality leaves *EverySurvivor* to find his or her identity precisely *qua* battered and invisible. Luke's parable here displays a further facet of artistic and mystical genius. His shocking theme of reversal of fortune underlines Jesus's unpalatable challenge to his followers to see themselves not first as heroes to the rescue but as those very casualties of violence themselves. "It will not be so among you, but whoever wishes to be great among you must be your servant" (Matt 20:26).

The Christian heritage suggests that those with eyes to see can encounter a hidden God in *EverySurvivor*, one who is front and center in the passion narrative. The disciples once asked Jesus: " 'Lord, when was it that we saw you hungry or thirsty or a stranger or naked or sick or in prison, and did not take care of you?' Then he will answer them, 'Truly I tell you, just as you did not do it to one of the least of these, you did not do it to me' " (Matt 25:44-45). Today, the roadsides remain strewn with those frantically awaiting first-responder solidarity and assistance.[29] The

27. M. Dennis Hamm, "Luke," *Paulist Biblical Commentary* (Mahwah, NJ: Paulist Press: 2018), 1066.

28. Cited in James F. Keenan, *The Works of Mercy: The Heart of Catholicism* (Lanham, MD: Rowman and Littlefield, 2017), 4.

29. More than three women are killed every day in the United States by husbands or boyfriends as victims of intimate partner violence, according to the Grady Nia Domestic Violence and Suicide Prevention Project of the Emory University School of Medicine in Atlanta. Domestic Violence/Intimate Partner Violence Facts, https://med.emory.edu/departments/psychiatry/nia/resources/domestic_violence.html.

first step is recognition of epochal violence as one of the "signs of the times." After all, recognition is "the threshold of ethics . . . the beginning of the moral life."[30]

Spiritual and pastoral caregivers who wish to upgrade their tool kits in service of survivors of violence, as well as ecclesial leaders and influencers, may have homework to do regarding the sometimes subtle symptoms and triggers of spiritual injury trauma. A measure of familiarity with the damaged voices from the ditch may be a contextual skill required in an epoch of trauma. Here is an aspirational best-practices standard for an upgraded ethics and spirituality of encounter.

Íñigo's "Cannonball Moment," Reconsidered

EverySurvivors know the numbing grief of invisibility, stigma, or isolation within their families and communities, their marriages, among their (former) friends, or even in the most well-intentioned of popular and religious discourse. For example, those who have experienced suicidal ideation, perhaps even attempted death by suicide, lament that they have never heard a homily or any public catechetical guidance about what is, in fact, a very common affliction.[31] If they feel left out of the church's proclamation of the Gospel, that is because they are. The following illustration puts a familiar name and face on the phenomenon of invisibility and demonstrates the distressing risks of exclusion of the casualty's point of view as well as the healing benefits of inclusion at the table.

To celebrate the five hundredth anniversary of Íñigo de Loyola's battlefield wound at Pamplona in May 1521, the worldwide Society of Jesus in 2021 effectively marshaled an intensive spiritual renewal campaign as part of a broader "Ignatian Year" celebration whose motto was "To See All Things New in Christ." Jesuit leadership promoted an impressive array of social media, artistic, publishing, and spiritual initiatives to commemorate the "conversion" of young Íñigo occasioned by the French cannonball wound to his leg. The chosen meme was "Cannonball Moments." The

30. James F. Keenan, "The Great Religious Failure: Not Recognizing a Person in Need," *America*, June 17, 2024.

31. According to the American Foundation for Suicide Prevention, on a typical day approximately 132 people will die from suicide. "Suicide Statistics," American Foundation for Suicide Prevention, afsp.org/suicide-statistics/.

Ignatian network around the world was invited to celebrate their own "Cannonball Day" in solidarity with the Jesuit founder: "Today, we invite you to contemplate 'cannonball moments' in your own lives"[32] by spending time contemplating your place of conversion.

The motif is appealing and continues to meet popular global success in capturing the imaginations of the extensive Ignatian network. It has enabled individuals to renew or deepen their faith, spirituality, and mission-driven identity, a commendable outcome. A quick sampler provides a random potpourri of initiatives based on the "cannonball moment" meme:

- Scores of short YouTube videos, in various languages, featuring individuals from around the world who narrate a personal "cannonball moment" that changed their life. These conclude by asking some variation of the question: "And what about you? What's the moment that changed your life? Or shifted your perspective? What's YOUR cannonball moment?"[33]
- A book entitled *Cannonball Moments* from Loyola Press, highlighting stories of "those big moments of conversion that are reflective of Ignatius's own life story"[34] as an invitation to others to consider their own faith journeys.
- Jesuit high school reenactments of the Pamplona battle highlighting the cannonball moment.
- Jocular memes popping up on the internet, featuring cartoonish images of Ignatius with slogans like "Cannonized Before He Was Canonized" or "I used to be a sinner like you, then I took a cannonball to the knee."

Unfortunately, the "cannonball moment" campaign strongly alienated certain military veterans, including otherwise sympathetic retired U.S. Marine colonel Robert Seamus Macpherson. The psychiatric help and medications he received through the Veterans Administration, Macpherson

32. "Celebrating Cannonball Day," jesuits.org/stories/celebrating-cannonball-day.

33. "Cannonball Moment," *Jesuits Global*, www.youtube.com/watch?v=GSpLXpOwkaI&list.

34. Eric A. Clayton, *Cannonball Moments: Telling Your Story, Deepening Your Faith* (Chicago: Loyola Press, 2022), 3.

noted, were an important step in recovery from PTSD. But, in the end, "the Spiritual Exercises saved my sanity." (His heartfelt gratitude for the transformative power of the Exercises was highlighted in a personal testimony after chapter 1.)[35]

Colonel Macpherson, despite his profound identification with Íñigo as a military man exposed to live fire, found himself bewildered and angered by the "cannonball moment" meme—bewildered because it rendered the bitter experience of so many courageous, patriotic vets invisible, and angered because the motif is potentially triggering for survivors of battlefield violence. It was tone-deaf, in the extreme. Had he been consulted, he would have explained that such triggers can be subtle and difficult to predict. For some of those traumatically injured by violence, the meme can spark past horrific memories, leading to belligerent, unfocused rage, panic attacks, and other destructive personal and social symptoms. Notable triggers, according to trauma counselor Levers, include "feeling left out."[36]

> The phrase "cannonball moment" trivializes the pieces of metal shredding your body and all you hear over the sounds of bombs, artillery, and bullets are men screaming in pain. The Jesuits are using the horrors of war to promote their own agenda. Unfortunately for anyone who has been victimized by war and battle, the naïveté of their promotion sets them apart from the people they are trying to reach. Their promotion of this theme demonstrates how far out of touch they are with the veterans. Because if you survive the holocaust of war, there are many people you respected and loved who did not. The meme is trivial and an assault on their memory and sacrifice(s).
>
> Let me give you my take on the cannonball moments motif I keep seeing on Ignatian websites and social media. It makes me ask if people who are this far from reality have lost the core of the meaning of the Spiritual Exercises. I mean, after Jesus' crucifixion, would any of the Apostles have referred to their own "crucifixion moment"?

35. All citations are from private correspondence and conversations with the author and quoted with permission.

36. Lisa López Levers, *Trauma Counseling: Theories and Interventions for Managing Trauma, Stress, Crisis, and Disaster*, 2nd ed. (New York: Springer Publishing, 2023), 410.

Colonel Macpherson is not alone in his painful military experience. "The U.S. Department of Veterans Affairs estimates that 13.8 percent of the veterans returning from the wars in Iraq and Afghanistan currently have PTSD. For comparison, a male veteran of those wars is four times more likely to develop PTSD than a man in the civilian population. PTSD is probably at least partially at the root of an even more alarming statistic: upwards of 22 veterans commit suicide every day."[37]

Happily, according to Levers, "attitudes about trauma and violence have begun to change; the current public climate has shifted, and there is greater support for *hearing* the voices of survivors rather than *silencing* them."[38] Though Colonel Macpherson makes no claim to speak for all veterans of live fire across history, listening to his viewpoint illustrates the importance of perspective-taking from point of view of battlefield casualties. He is able to notice potential psychospiritually destructive aspects of war, such as leadership betrayal, collateral damage, sadistic atrocities, and emotionally damaged family and loved ones back home.

In a word, some battlefield veterans experienced the chosen meme as exclusionary and trauma-*uninformed*. Consider the thousands of Iraq War veterans who lost a leg—or two—to an improvised explosive device. Would anyone dare speak about "IED Moments" to veterans of that war who lost friends to an IED or to family members of paraplegics or amputees injured by one? Would anyone seriously run a social media campaign called "IED Moments"?

Ecclesial leaders and social media influencers of the future should be more attentive to the science-based conclusions of diagnostic research by including the casualties' voice and profile from the periphery, where applicable. How better to say to a veteran: "Thank you for your service"? The same principle applies to casualties of other forms of violence, for example crime victims like "The Battered Traveler." As the following chapter points out, evidence-based diagnostic insights about distinctive traits associated with crime victimization—or different traits associated with molestation, wartime violence, and so on—are available to thoughtful caregivers who search for them.

37. MaryCatherine McDonald, Marisa Brandt, and Robyn Bluhm, "From Shell-Shock to PTSD, a Century of Invisible War Trauma," *PBS News Hour*, November 11, 2018.

38. López Levers, *Trauma Counseling*, xix.

Witnessing—much less participating in—the bloodletting and pervasive horror of battlefield combat, the killing of innocent civilians, or the loss of a comrade's life can result in *spiritual*, even *religious*, injury, as Colonel Macpherson can attest. The symptoms are well documented in the research-based, military moral injury trauma literature, including "having anger at God; stopping attendance at religious services; experiencing emptiness or meaninglessness; feeling God has failed . . . and being angry or cynical towards clergy. Counseling professionals who are trauma-informed understand that these are 'normal' responses to 'abnormal' events."[39]

Colonel Macpherson's testimony greatly enriches the Christian perspective precisely by including the voice and perspective of *EverySurvivor* of violence, as envisioned by the original Jesus-story and Jesus's passion itself. If Macpherson is angry and denounces, he does so like novelist Ellison's central character: "I denounce because though implicated and partially responsible, I have been hurt to the point of abysmal pain, hurt to the point of invisibility."[40]

Pamplona, Reconsidered

History can never determine how many husbands, brothers, and fathers were among the deceased and wounded at Pamplona's 1521 artillery duel. The online edition of the Encyclopedia Britannica describes the losses as "unknown."[41] Given the new generation of deadly, rapid-firing cannons employed by the French, "cannonball moment" casualties could be gruesome. They used solid iron balls rather than the shot that had been used previously in Europe. The balls "crushed battlements, careened wildly and sprayed shards of stone in all directions."[42]

Íñigo, of course, was no ordinary casualty of war. It was his brave leadership that had galvanized the Spanish to fight, and *to keep* fighting

39. López Levers, 410.

40. Ellison, *Invisible Man*, 579–80.

41. Jacob F. Field, "Battle of Pamplona," *Encyclopedia Britannica*, https://www.britannica.com/event/Battle-of-Pamplona.

42. Phil Klay, "Can the Trauma of War Lead to Growth, Despite the Scars?," *New York Times*, July 6, 2020.

until he went down, when they capitulated to the French. His heroism in defeat was undeniable. Even the French combatants were impressed by his relentless valor, which glorified the Pamplona battlefield upon which *both* sides had fought. As offensive as it may be to modern sensibilities, Íñigo's embrace of arms and derring-do—the votes of his comrades be damned—marked his emergence into manhood in an age of chivalry. He had boldly demonstrated to his older, conquistador brothers—indeed to the larger clan with its bellicose heritage—his bona fides as one of the Loyola boys.

In a gallant display of their own, the French did Íñigo the rare honor of carrying their heroic enemy on a well-appointed conveyance back to the family's small Loyola Castle in Azpeitia. It would have been "a large wooden box with a door and windows, and with a bed or seat inside."[43] Surely Íñigo suffered greatly, but one can imagine the fanfare en route, not to mention family acclaim back home upon his arrival in a state-of-the-art military litter carried by uniformed French soldiers. This was surely an honor no one in Guipúzcoa had previously witnessed, and more than compensated the wounded Íñigo for his painful journey.

Hagiographic lore surrounding Íñigo's so-called "cannonball moment" has become part of the popular Ignatian landscape. Yet the hero's questionable judgment proved fatal for other combatants, and surely occasioned severe distress and receptive MIT for the families of casualties back home. Today, most soldiers would rush to assist a fallen buddy, but Íñigo is silent about fellow casualties, many of whom would have survived without his intervention. Did subsequent Jesuit redactors of his memoirs purge compromising information about the swashbuckler? In any case, the Ignatian heritage makes no mention of this detail.

Might Íñigo's status as Pamplona's champion require a certain tempering through perspective-taking? In the wake of atomic weaponry, the Vietnam War, and ongoing Forever Wars in the Middle East, cloaking combat service in heroic narrative sometimes rings morally off-key. Perhaps a timely opportunity is at hand. Reconsideration of "cannonball moments" can yet lead to more profound reckoning. Upgraded trauma-

43. Ignatius of Loyola, *A Pilgrim's Testament: The Memoirs of Saint Ignatius of Loyola*, ed. Barton T. Geger (Chestnut Hill, MA: Institute of Jesuit Sources of Boston College, 2020), 111n5.

informed care, for example, would challenge the global Ignatian network to accompany more closely, and listen more attentively to, the unique voices of casualties of violence as a potential source of revelation, in keeping with the Jesus-story.

Moral myopia, tragically, permits the traumatic aftereffects of violence to perdure—endlessly and intergenerationally. The concept describes what happens when persons, organizations, or churches fail, often innocently enough, to recognize the full implications of a matter, or even a meme. The divine lens of Jesus's story about "The Battered Traveler" serves as baseline corrective that points to a trauma-informed shift in point of view for noticing and supporting soul-wounded survivors of violence. "As with the Samaritan, it is a movement out of one's way and into the ditch." Conversion, in this view, "demands an intentional change of place."[44] Greg Boyle, founding director of Homeboy Industries in Los Angeles, puts it simply: "All Jesus asks is, 'where are you standing?' "[45]

Don Íñigo's undoubted heroism at Pamplona can now be respectfully reframed through a wider twenty-first-century lens of military moral injury trauma research and fresh theological and scriptural insights. "The study of trauma and the rise of trauma studies have had a necessary impact on Christian theology."[46] Recall those severely wounded Spanish casualties on the Pamplona battlefield or inside the fortress. Is it too late to honor their memory by listening to the voices of contemporary survivors of violence? The Ignatian heritage and Christian spirituality, more broadly, have long displayed a remarkable capacity for reinvention and reformulation. Now, amid an epoch of surpassing violence, these unvarnished voices may attract devotees whom heroes cannot.

44. Mescher, *Ethics of Encounter*, 60.

45. Greg Boyle, *Tattoos on the Heart* (New York: Free Press/Simon and Schuster, 2011).

46. Shelly Rambo, "How Christian Theology and Practice Are Being Shaped by Trauma Studies," *Christian Century*, November 1, 2019.

8

Noticing Hibakusha

A Trauma-Informed Reading of the Incarnation Contemplation

On the morning of August 6, 1945, a thirty-seven-year-old Spaniard was gazing serenely out the window of his Jesuit residence in the Nagatsuka neighborhood on the outskirts of Hiroshima. He was composed, having spent almost two hours in prayer seated on his heels in traditional Japanese meditation posture, silent and immobile on a tatami bamboo mat. But life as he knew it was about to erupt like a volcano. Almost ten thousand feet overhead, a United States B-29 bomber had just changed history by releasing *Little Boy*, the code name for the first atomic bomb deployed in wartime. For Basque Jesuit Father Pedro Arrupe, henceforth, there would be *before* Hiroshima and *after* Hiroshima.

On the far side of a nearby hilltop an incandescent flash lit the sky, followed immediately by an earthquake-like roar. Despite severe damage to the compound's buildings, Arrupe and his Japanese and German Jesuit companions were unhurt. Ascending the rise, they were aghast at the sight of the city below. "A desolate panorama opened before their eyes. A huge, dark, smoking cloud hovered menacingly over a desert of ashes, the devastating remains of what had been Hiroshima. . . . Smoke, fire, ruins, screams—this was truly hell."[1]

1. Pedro Miguel Lamet, *Pedro Arrupe: Witness of the Twentieth Century, Prophet of the Twenty-First* (Chestnut Hill, MA: Institute of Jesuit Sources at Boston College, 2021), 22–23.

There was no time to waste. The resourceful Arrupe had trained as a medical doctor before his spiritual call, and immediately began to organize daily forays into the city to visit local hospitals and sweep the streets for survivors. He recalls seeing a child with glass in one eye here, a man caught between two pillars with legs calcified to his knees there.[2] His small Christian community immediately converted their chapel into a field hospital, where Arrupe treated hundreds of the wounded, many of whom survived. *Proximity to Ground Zero was crucial*—a lesson he would never forget. Some 150,000 persons died before the end of the year—about 90 percent in the first two weeks after the explosion.[3]

Pedro Arrupe, famously, would go on to serve as the twenty-eighth superior general of the Society of Jesus from 1965 to 1983. According to Peter Hans-Kolvenbach, the Dutch Jesuit who succeeded him, his predecessor was "a spiritual master in the line of St. Ignatius Loyola."[4] His temperament evinced a visceral attraction to God encountered in the "plight of the suffering, especially refugees and the victims of war and violence."[5] Arrupe could never be accused of moral myopia, and he felt instinctive, actionable solidarity with bloodied casualties. Hiroshima had left an indelible mark on his soul, transforming him into a *hibakusha*—an "explosion-affected person"—as the Japanese called survivors of an atomic bomb.

After Arrupe passed away in 1991, his dramatic reform program for the Society of Jesus, overlapping with the broader ecclesial reforms of the Second Vatican Council, left him both reviled and revered. Only in the past generation has Arrupe's momentous legacy been fully appreciated, and his continuity with Íñigo himself celebrated and admired.[6] However, the significance played by *proximity to physical violence* in the personal narratives of both Basque Jesuits has gone unremarked.

Chapter 8 suggests that these bloody formative experiences ground fresh Christian spiritual insights and tools suitable for an age of trauma. Ety-

2. Pedro Arrupe, *Recollections and Reflections of Pedro Arrupe*, trans. Yolanda T. DeMola (Wilmington, DE: Michael Glazier, 1986), 30.

3. Lamet, *Pedro Arrupe*, 183n16.

4. Peter-Hans Kolvenbach, "Foreword," in Kevin Burke, *Pedro Arrupe: Essential Writings*, selected with intro. by Kevin Burke (Maryknoll, NY: Orbis Book, 2004), 12.

5. Kolvenbach, "Foreword," 12.

6. February 5, 2025, marked the sixth anniversary since the process for Arrupe's beatification and canonization was introduced.

mologically, "[t]he ancient Greek word for trauma means a 'wound' or 'an injury inflicted upon the body by an act of violence.' "[7] In service of anyone damaged or distressed, Ignatian spirituality has an opportunity—indeed a duty—to be of service. According to Michael Kirwan at Trinity College in Dublin, "[t]here are in 2018 so many indicators of cultural sickness and danger that to ignore them would be irresponsible."[8] Surely trauma is among them. The most important Ignatian spiritual exercise in this regard is the *Incarnation Contemplation*, grounded in violent imagery and language, positioned at the beginning of the Second Week of the Exercises.[9] This imaginative prayer finds fresh, striking currency in an epoch of trauma.

Spirituality for an Age of Trauma

It is time for Ignatian spirituality and pastoral care to notice that "we're living through an age of trauma, and it's taking its toll."[10] Theology and, more slowly, spirituality are beginning to respond to this special needs population. For example, Christian practice today features any number of spiritual retreats that begin in the "bad news" of traumatic violence personally suffered—which can leave the faculties of human *volition* paralyzed, *affect* numb, *memory* blank, *understanding* meaningless, and *imagination* stunted. Specialized retreats are expressly designed for adults who have been abused, perhaps as minors, by clergy or other authority figures in the church.[11] Others are offered for female survivors of intimate partner violence; male staff may or may not be welcome. Retreats open to men and women of any denomination who have served in the United States Armed Forces are available, with consideration of any traumatic events that may accompany military experience.

7. Serene Jones, *Trauma + Grace: Theology in a Ruptured World*, 2nd ed. (Louisville, KY: Westminster John Knox Press, 2019), 12. Jones is president of Union Theological Seminary in New York City.

8. Michael Kirwan, "Swearing, Blaspheming, Wounding, Killing, Going to Hell . . . The World, as Seen and Heard by Ignatius," *The Way* 57, no. 4 (October 2018): 81.

9. Note the continuity with the closing exercise of the First Week, the *Meditation on Hell.*

10. S. I. Rosenbaum, "The Age of Trauma," *Harvard Public Health Magazine*, September 30, 2021.

11. In 2023 the Jesuit Conference of the United States and Canada commissioned such a weekend Ignatian retreat for men.

Such practice respects those who, for whatever reason, struggle to experience God's creation as good—"*In the beginning was the subhuman howl.*"[12] Though this can be accommodated within "standard" Ignatian retreats and caregiving, the distinctive symptoms and dynamics of traumatic injury nevertheless present contextual challenges to personal relationship with Divinity. "Now the earth was corrupt in God's sight, and the earth was filled with violence" (Gen 6:11). In this regard the *Incarnation Contemplation* stands out as a tailored spiritual prayer method.

The *Incarnation Contemplation*

A diagnosis of trauma, obviously, postdates Íñigo and Arrupe. The connection to the *Incarnation Contemplation*, though, is more foundational. The centrality of violence in this prayer exercise can be associated with Pamplona, Manresa, and now Hiroshima, and is a stark reminder that the Exercises were born in bloodshed endured and inflicted. Íñigo was both product and snapshot of the violence of medieval chivalric culture. Regarding the context of this *Contemplation*, one wonders: "Is Ignatius remembering here his own swaggering past life?"[13]

Ignatius invites the retreatant to notice the Three Divine Persons of the Trinity, who are depicted gazing down intently from the heavens at the world. What the Divinity observes is horrific—a world swearing, blaspheming, wounding, and killing. (In the age of social media, one might add trolling, doxing, ghosting, and swatting.) Michael Ivens's guidance directs retreatants to personalize in prayer, unsparingly and only if ready, that appalling vision. "The exercitant contemplates the world in its totality, with particular emphasis on diversity of race and culture and on the tragic, fragile and violent aspects of human life. It is essential that the world thus contemplated be, or at any rate include, the exercitant's own world."[14]

Today's *hibakusha* thereby find assurance from the classical spiritual tradition that their Higher Power notices them and acts on their behalf.

12. Kirwan, "Swearing, Blaspheming," 84, emphasis in original, alluding to the work of British philosopher Gillian Rose (1947–95).

13. Kirwan, 79.

14. Michael Ivens, *Understanding the Spiritual Exercises: Text and Commentary* (Leominster, England: Gracewing, 1998), 92.

"[T]he emphasis is on the way Creation has turned out disastrously and on the need for someone (the Second Person) to come down and fix things."[15]

The *Incarnation Contemplation* exercise is available to guide persons of faith and seekers how to open their eyes—safely—and stand courageously in their dark place. Five times it makes use of the phrase "and so on," a technical Ignatian usage variously translated as "etc.," "and so forth," and "et cetera."[16] For example: "Here I will consider what the persons on the face of the earth are doing: How they wound, kill, go to hell, and so on."[17] Regarding the Ignatian et cetera, Ivens comments: "In Ignatius' usage this is an invitation to the exercitant to develop a general idea in one's own way."[18] For *hibakusha* and those who accompany them, the invitation is a shorthand cue to stamp the exercise with personal, perhaps anxious, narrative authenticity. One is invited to pray from the existential experience of traumatic or spiritually injurious events personally endured, perhaps utilizing the method Íñigo taught at Alcalá based on the powers of memory, understanding, and will.

In this fashion, the exercise can promote "trauma-informed care," a quasi-technical term in mental health and trauma counseling literature. Levers notes, "Trauma-informed care represents a means to address trauma throughout a system of care. . . . As we learn more about traumatic events across the lifespan, along with the lifelong effects of some trauma, it is increasingly evident that all care systems share the need and responsibility for identifying and responding to trauma."[19]

Consideration of a "trauma-informed" *Incarnation Contemplation* can thereby serve as a spiritual step to personalized encounter with God tailored for a world of hurt. It reflects toxic aspects of the present zeitgeist, for example, the alarming increases in rape and sexual violence among teen girls,[20] not to mention nightmare scenarios such as sex trafficking.

15. Kirwan, "Swearing, Blaspheming," 78.

16. George E. Ganss, *The Spiritual Exercises of Saint Ignatius: A Translation and Commentary* (St. Louis: Institute of Jesuit Sources, 1992), no. 106; no. 107 twice; no. 108 twice. Hereafter, *SpEx*.

17. *SpEx*., 108.

18. Ivens, *Understanding the Spiritual Exercises*, 93.

19. Lisa López Levers, *Trauma Counseling: Theories and Interventions for Managing Trauma, Stress, Crisis, and Disaster*, 2nd ed. (New York: Springer Publishing, 2023), 432.

20. Donna St. George, "Teen Girls 'Engulfed' in Violence and Trauma, CDC Finds," *Washington Post*, February 14, 2023. The report and accompanying data can be accessed

Having observed one's Higher Power looking down upon and even come, lovingly and mercifully, to save a damaged, fallen creation, one can notice—through *God's* merciful eyes—events in her or his own troubled personal or family history. Or, one can choose to notice current troubling events, viewed on the news or social media, that offend or distress one's moral conscience. Use of the faculties of memory and imagination are required. Evident to anyone ready and willing to pay attention—which should never be assumed, out of concern for triggering—are people abusing and *being* abused; shooting up primary and secondary schools and *being* shot; bombing and *being* bombed; trafficking children . . . "and so on." Many experienced Ignatian caregivers are capable, by God's grace, of learning to be more attentive to a world in which violence, and the trauma it engenders in many, is unfathomably pervasive.[21] Such prayer opens their eyes to notice the many battered travelers by the wayside who await Good News and desire spiritual companionship.

Trauma-Informed Spiritual Noticing

It was early in Íñigo's third-person account of his spiritual awakening, while still convalescing at the Loyola family castle, that "his eyes were opened a little."[22] What he had begun to notice interiorly he subsequently described, unsurprisingly, in language familiar to him. God must always be in conflict, since an evil power whom Íñigo designates "the enemy of our human nature" has invaded the world and must be overcome. The inevitable result is warfare within the human soul between the Kingdom

---

at https://www.cdc.gov/healthyyouth/data/yrbs/pdf/YRBS_Data-Summary-Trends_Report2023_508.pdf. This population also displays record levels of feeling sad or hopeless, based on data collected in autumn 2021. Suicidal ideation, planning, and attempts all display increasing trendlines.

21. In a September 2020 report, *Creating Refugees*, the Costs of War Project at Brown University concluded that refugee flows have never been higher. "The U.S. post-9/11 wars have forcibly displaced at least 37 million people." The authors consider that number a "very conservative estimate," and one that *excludes* those killed or injured. https://watson.brown.edu/costsofwar/files/cow/imce/papers/2020/Displacement_Vine%20et%20al_Costs%20of%20War%202020%2009%2008.pdf.

22. Ignatius of Loyola, *A Pilgrim's Testament: The Memoirs of Saint Ignatius of Loyola*, ed. Barton T. Geger (Chestnut Hill, MA: Institute of Jesuit Sources, 2020), no. 8. Hereafter, *Auto*.

of Christ and the kingdom of Satan, archetypal representatives of good versus evil spiritual forces.[23]

Such inner spiritual battle, parenthetically, is of increasing interest to psychologists open to the numinous from various Abrahamic traditions, for example, in the exploration of mental health, posttraumatic growth, and Islam. "We frame spiritual jihad as a mindset that Muslims may adopt when coping with religious/spiritual struggles, particularly those of a moral nature."[24] Jihad may have significant ramifications for "drawing closer to God."[25] Perhaps unaware of Ignatian spirituality, the authors view this dynamic of spiritual struggle as "unique to the Islamic traditions."[26] Conversely, some Christians might be shocked by any positive reference to jihad. However, interior conflict between good and evil spirits, arguably, is fundamental to *both* Ignatian and Islamic theology.

"So began a practice that underpinned Ignatius' conversion and his journey with God: noticing."[27] Obstacles to noticing the dynamics and symptoms of traumatic injury—including loss of faith in a God who is good—are legion for *hibakusha* and those who accompany them. Most obvious, perhaps, is that traumatic events can be shameful, triggering, frightening, disgusting, nightmarish, or paralyzing to name, much less recall to memory. In the wake of trauma, "shame becomes the dominant emotion and hiding the truth the central preoccupation."[28]

In his thirteenth rule for discernment, Ignatius cautions that "the enemy acts like a false lover, insofar as he tries to remain secret and undetected."[29] In spiritual warfare over the human soul, trauma enables

23. The imagery and theology are most famously captured in two exercises—the *Contemplation of the Kingdom of Christ* (*SpEx*, nos. 91–99) and the *Meditation on Two Standards* (*SpEx*, nos. 136–47).

24. S. N. Saritoprak, J. J. Exline, and H. Abu-Raiya, "Spiritual Jihad as an Emerging Psychological Concept: Connections with Religious/Spiritual Struggles, Virtues, and Perceived Growth," *Journal of Muslim Mental Health* 14, no. 2 (2020): 109.

25. Saritoprak, Exline, and Abu-Raiya, "Spiritual Jihad," 109.

26. Saritoprak, Exline, and Abu-Raiya, 110.

27. Gail Paxman, "When His Eyes Were Opened a Little: The Role of Noticing in the Spiritual Exercises," *The Way* 61, no. 2 (April 2022): 1. This chapter is indebted to Paxman's insightful presentation.

28. Bessel van der Kolk, *The Body Keeps the Score: Brain, Mind, and Body in the Healing of Trauma* (New York: Viking, 2014), 67.

29. *SpEx*, no. 326.

the enemy to open a clandestine new front. It will likely be very well defended, whether consciously or unconsciously.

For seventy-one years, this seems to have been the evil spirit's strategy for Hiroshima survivor Tomiko Shoji. She was a nineteen-year-old tobacco factory secretary at the time of the blast. Until she was almost ninety, she had never talked about her experience of the atomic bomb. A paralyzing terror had left her no option but to isolate herself in the shadows for the entirety of her adult life. " 'I'm scared to meet people,' she finally acknowledged publicly, speaking in the present tense Japanese of her teen-age self . . . 'Something could just blow up.' "[30]

Casualties of violence like Shoji must be interiorly ready and able to notice their symptoms. For some it takes a lifetime; others, tragically, never develop the requisite freedom to seek access to healing resources, especially following painful childhood traumatic event(s). It is conceivable that a trauma-informed spiritual conversation with a trained companion, at the right moment, may assist some *hibakusha* to begin their recovery, by naming the event(s) at stake. Might it even assist them to discover God's compassionate presence and mercy at work, as unlikely as it sounds, in and through those events?

The stakes could not be much higher. Prominent addictions and trauma physician Gabor Maté believes that the attempt to escape from pain creates more pain. But how does one escape the prison of the siren song popularized by Simon and Garfunkel? "I am a rock, I am an island. And a rock feels no pain, and an island never cries."[31]

The twenty-first century requires a more trauma-sensitive approach to the Exercises, one that thoughtfully accounts for "unconscious resistance to conflicts and pain."[32] Rarely is that a facile or speedy process. The tendency to "fight, flight, or freeze" is well documented in the psychological literature. But, with informed guidance, there is a healthier option. Noted Jesuit spiritual directors William A. Barry and William J. Connolly sug-

30. Sarah Stillman, "Hiroshima and the Inheritance of Trauma," *New Yorker*, August 12, 2014.

31. Paul Simon, "I Am a Rock," *The Paul Simon Songbook*, https://www.paulsimon.com/track/i-am-a-rock-2/.

32. Paxman, "When His Eyes," 34.

gest that the "willingness to notice" can over time become "a process of progressively greater openness to reality."[33]

The importance of noticing as a key spiritual tool is creatively cultivated for Jesuit novices in training. As part of their formation, some are given five dollars in cash, stripped of their cell phone, and asked to spend a month on pilgrimage from one destination to another, hundreds of miles distant. No hitchhiking is permitted. One recently spent an overnight on cardboard just outside New York City's Port Authority Midtown Bus Terminal, the country's largest. The next day at Times Square, he begged bus fare to his next destination. After completing his probationary test and safely returned to the novitiate, the young man recounted that the most difficult aspect of begging was that passersby turned their eyes away, choosing not to notice, much less greet or acknowledge him in any way. Ignatius, himself a legendary beggar, surely knew the painful dehumanization of relational and societal invisibility.

Horrendous events cannot be undone or permanently deleted, and it would be cruel to propose otherwise. God does not come to take away *EverySurvivor's* human pain and toxic bitterness so much as to accompany and sustain them through the heavy lifting of posttraumatic growth and reconnection to one's Higher Power. "I can see no way out but through—Leastways for me."[34] Though the road is long and winding, with proper support one can gradually learn to trust that resources for the journey are sufficient. "It is not the amount of darkness in the world that matters. It is not even the amount of darkness in ourselves that matters. In the end, it is how we stand in that darkness that is of essence."[35]

Using Case Studies with the Incarnation Contemplation

A vivid case study can demonstrate the existential traction of noticing—or not noticing—*hibakusha*. Tina Cordova is a seventh-generation New Mexican and co-founder of the Tularosa Basin Downwinders Con-

33. William A. Barry and William J. Connolly, *The Practice of Spiritual Direction*, 2nd ed., rev. (New York: HarperOne, 1982), 83.

34. Robert Frost, *The Poetry of Robert Frost: The Collected Poems, Complete and Unabridged*, ed. Edward Connery Lathem (New York: Henry Holt, 1969), 62–67.

35. Robert Wicks, *Bounce: Living the Resilient Life* (New York: Oxford University Press, 2010), 164.

sortium. She describes watching the Oscar-decorated film *Oppenheimer* at a packed screening in Santa Fe, New Mexico, when it first opened in July 2023.[36] The audience of local people was tense, wondering if, finally, their story as "the first human test subjects of the world's most powerful weapon," ironically code-named "Trinity," would be told.

For eighty years there has been a popular perception that the area in southern New Mexico, where the Manhattan Project's atomic bomb was tested on July 16, 1945, was uninhabited. In fact, "[t]here were more than 13,000 New Mexicans living within a 50-mile radius." But most were Hispanic. Racism was surely a factor in the community's invisibility and powerlessness. Regrettably, the blockbuster film failed to note this shameful piece of the history, though the atomic test was conducted, as Cordova observes, "in a place where my family and many others had lived for generations." Those marginalized by race, over generations, understand that skin color and ethnicity play a role in just solutions. The Holy Trinity, as well, looking down from heaven at the Tularosa Basin on that historic day, presumably noticed the pervasive discrimination among people "so diverse in dress and behavior, some white and others black . . . "[37]

"My community and I are being left out of the narrative again," laments Cordova. Her dad was four years old on the day of the atomic test, living a happy family life in the historic Hispanic town of Tularosa. The test left radioactive ash covering his home, but the family unwittingly carried on as before, eating fresh fruit and vegetables grown in the contaminated soil. "By age 64, he had developed three cancers that he didn't have risk factors for, two of which were primary oral cancers. He died at the age of 71." Cordova herself is the fourth generation in her family to have had cancer since the atomic test. Her 23-year-old niece, a college student studying art, was recently diagnosed with thyroid cancer.

To this day, the U.S. government has refused to acknowledge the injustice, leaving the Downwinders without the financial compensation available to other survivors of nuclear test radiation. They have been excluded from eligibility for financial redress under the Radiation Ex-

36. Tina Cordova, all citations are from "What 'Oppenheimer' Doesn't Tell You about the Trinity Test," *New York Times*, Tuesday, August 1, 2023, A22. The website of the Downwinders Consortium is https://www.trinitydownwinders.com/.

37. *SpEx*, no. 106.

posure Compensation Act (RECA), passed in 1990 to support Cold War survivors exposed during subsequent tests on U.S. soil or during uranium mining. The blockbuster film maintains the fiction that no one was harmed as a result of the *Trinity* test. "This, too, is the legacy of J. Robert Oppenheimer and the government he worked for." Moral injury trauma is not only personal and institutional but sometimes sociopolitical as well.

Using Poetry with the Incarnation Contemplation

English Jesuit martyr and noted poet Robert Southwell (1561–95) surely recognized a sixteenth-century hellscape when he prayed the pivotal *Incarnation Contemplation* spiritual exercise. Ignatius had only died in Rome five years before Southwell's birth. A contemporary and likely cousin of Shakespeare, Southwell in his famous 1595 Christmas poem "The Burning Babe" highlighted the limited corpus of a priest executed for treason in defense of his faith at age thirty-four.

The cruelty inflicted on the gifted Southwell only amplified his public celebrity, such that the poem was immediately and prolifically published, with outsized influence upon English poetry. At the time, religious sorrow was viewed as a form of spiritual conversation between the soul and God, such that the poem was a signature example of the cultural legacy "performed by the poetry of tears . . . popularized by Southwell."[38] Holy mourning in post-Reformation England presents not only a theology but also a literary window into the psychospiritual soul of the traumatically injured, afflicted, and grieving. One specialist on early modern lyric and narrative poetry makes the remarkable claim that Southwell not only influenced Shakespeare but that his life and writings "instructed William Alabaster, provoked Edmund Spenser, prompted George Herbert, haunted John Donne, inspired Richard Crashaw and consoled Gerard Hopkins."[39] The poetry and spirituality of religious sorrow is an untapped

38. Gary Kuchar, *The Poetry of Religious Sorrow in Early Modern England* (New York: Cambridge University Press, 2008), 31.

39. Gary M. Bouchard, *Southwell's Sphere: The Influence of England's Secret Poet* (South Bend, IN: St. Augustine Press, 2018), 8.

resource of the literary and Christian traditions well suited for trauma-informed care.[40]

"The Burning Babe" is a lyric lament that pictures a disturbing image of the newly born Christ Child. Baby Jesus is "scorched with excessive heat" and sheds "floods of tears."[41] To modern eyes the child is either an infant avatar of an anthropomorphized, traumatized Deity or God in the person of a crucified Jesus Christ, according to one's beliefs. In either case, the infant is a suffering Supreme Being come for the spiritual rescue and redemption of *hibakusha*.

As I in hoary winter's night
Stood shivering in the snow,
Surprised I was with sudden heat
Which made my heart to glow;
And lifting up a fearful eye
To view what fire was near,
A pretty babe all burning bright
Did in the air appear;
Who, scorchèd with excessive heat,
Such floods of tears did shed,
As though His floods should quench His flames,
Which with His tears were bred:
"Alas!" quoth He, "but newly born
In fiery heats I fry,
Yet none approach to warm their hearts
Or feel my fire but I!
My faultless breast the furnace is;
The fuel, wounding thorns;
Love is the fire, and sighs the smoke;
The ashes, shames and scorns;
The fuel Justice layeth on,
And Mercy blows the coals,

40. Those familiar with the Exercises will recognize the foundational influence on the poem of the Second Meditation of the First Week (no. 55), in which the supplicant prays for the grace of "sorrow and tears."

41. Robert Southwell, *The Complete Works of R. Southwell: With Life and Death* (New York: Andesite Press, 2017), reproduced from the original 1876 edition, 98.

The metal in this furnace wrought
Are men's defilèd souls:
For which, as now on fire I am
To work them to their good,
So will I melt into a bath,
To wash them in my blood."
With this He vanish'd out of sight
And swiftly shrunk away,
And straight I callèd unto mind
That it was Christmas Day.

At stake in the poet's mystical vision is a newborn God-Child who, though without guilt, already suffers redemptively on behalf of Adam's sin and fallen humanity. God's innocent heart identifies and burns—literally and painfully in the poet's vision—for love of injured and vulnerable humans, purifying them like gold in the refiner's fire. Southwell's personal narrative allowed no saccharine, Hallmark-card entrée to the Nativity. The motif of the "suffering of innocents" can hardly be missed in the twenty-first century, and is an important component of a trauma-informed reading of the *Incarnation Contemplation*.[42]

"The Burning Babe" provides an essential gloss nearly contemporaneous with Íñigo himself. It spotlights the perils of childhood, and exemplifies how literature and art can be incorporated, for those ready and willing, into a prayerful, retrospective dive into any adverse childhood experiences. Here, for example, medieval religious iconography featuring the child Jesus holding a cross takes on fresh import. Wounded adults can benefit spiritually by praying an imaginative prayer of personal reminiscence (to be described in the following chapter) with such paintings and sculptures.[43]

42. According to the Substance Abuse and Mental Health Administration (SAMSA), a U.S. government public health agency, more than two-thirds of children report at least one traumatic event by age sixteen. These include abuse or assault of any sort, community or school violence, witnessing or experiencing domestic violence, refugee or war experiences, and neglect. https://www.samhsa.gov/child-trauma/understanding-child-trauma.

43. Ivens, *Understanding the Spiritual Exercises*, 88, insists that attention must be centered on the human reality of Jesus's childhood as "an implication of the Incarnation." This, in turn, suggests that retreatants consider their own personal experience of childhood in light of the Christ Child. Most persons of faith and seekers would be prudent

The poet composed from bitter, violent life experience in which he mystically experienced a suffering God who accompanied him. Southwell was a victim but not a survivor of the persecution of Catholics in Queen Elizabeth's reign. Brutally tortured and remanded to solitary confinement, he was finally hanged, drawn, and quartered in 1595, just months before publication of his celebrated poem. The searing tone and content of "The Burning Babe" were doubtless influenced by the martyrdom of scores of innocent Catholics in Elizabethan England.

Earlier in the century, of course, Catholic Queen Mary I (Mary Tudor)—"Bloody Mary"—had massacred many Protestants in her zeal to reverse the English Reformation. In the world of the subhuman howl, life is cheap. What goes around, comes around. So it goes. Who could fairly blame anyone who distrusts a Deity whose warring devotees vie to exceed the other in barbarity, all in "honor" of that same God's glory?

It is unsurprising that so many *hibakusha* stumble through life with eyes tightly shut, fearful of triggers or the next panic attack. Moral or spiritual injury trauma can rob them of healthy lives, as it did Hiroshima survivor Shoji. Perhaps she could relate to these words of writer Anne Lamott: "And I felt like my heart had been so thoroughly and irreparably broken that there could be no real joy again, that at best there might eventually be a little contentment. Everyone wanted me to get help and rejoin life, pick up the pieces and move on, and I tried to, I wanted to, but I just had to lie in the mud with my arms wrapped around myself, eyes closed, grieving, until I didn't have to anymore."[44]

Interdisciplinary Dialogue and Collaboration

The modern field of trauma studies complements the practice of Ignatian noticing—indeed Christian spirituality and pastoral care more broadly—in significant ways. "Trauma has become a key interpretative category of our time."[45] To promote superior trauma-informed care, the

only to pray this exercise on the recommendation of, and accompanied by, a qualified spiritual or pastoral guide.

44. Anne Lamott, *Operating Instructions: A Journal of My Son's First Year* (New York: Pantheon, 1993), 161.

45. Nicole A. Sutterlin, "History of Trauma Theory," *The Routledge Companion to Literature and Trauma*, ed. Colin Davis and Hanna Meretoja (New York: Routledge, 2020), 11.

following are suggestions for further interdisciplinary exploration, in no particular order, subject to review and correction by additional research, collaboration, and field experience.

Bodily Sensations

Since noticing is "an indispensable ingredient of the Spiritual Exercises,"[46] it is worthwhile to correlate insights from social and neurobiological science. Van der Kolk claims that one of the two most important phrases in trauma therapy is: "Notice that."[47] He thereby complements Ignatian spiritual care with psychological and neuroscientific tools of a similar nature. He starts with *physicality* and *sensuality*. One must befriend bodily sensations. "In my practice," he says, "I begin the process by helping my patients to first notice and then describe the feelings in their bodies—not emotions such as anger or anxiety or fear but the physical sensations beneath the emotions: pressure, heat, muscular tension, tingling, caving in, feeling hollow, and so on."[48]

Here, van der Kolk echoes the incarnational methodology of spiritual writer Ronald Rolheiser: "Thus, God deals with us through our senses. The Jesus who walked the roads of Palestine could be seen, touched, and heard. In the incarnation, God became physical because we are creatures of the senses who, at one point, need a God with some skin."[49] Pioneering Indian Jesuit Anthony de Mello (1931–87) promoted a related, sensual method of prayer: "There is a very close connection between the body and the psyche and any harm done to one seems to affect the other. . . . [R]est in the awareness of your body. . . . This will bring you the spiritual benefits of opening your Heart to the divine, plus the benefits to psyche and body that go with this exercise."[50]

Modern neuroscience was not the first to grasp the healing powers of bodily sensations. For half a millennium, the Exercises have tapped into that transformative capacity. "As a wise and challenging coach, Ignatius explains to the exercitant exactly what can be gained through

46. Paxman, "When His Eyes," 27.

47. Van der Kolk, *Body Keeps the Score*, 208.

48. Van der Kolk, 101.

49. Ronald Rolheiser, *The Holy Longing: The Search for a Christian Spirituality* (New York: Doubleday, 1999), 77.

50. Anthony de Mello, *Sadhana, a Way to God: Christian Exercises in Eastern Form* (St. Louis: Institute of Jesuit Sources, 1978), 56.

an intentional and careful contemplation of each sensation."[51] Ivens comments: "The *subject matter* is now myself as sensate. The ways I lead my life as sensate are examined in the light of a developing appreciation of this dimension of human existence, a perfect understanding of the fact that precisely as sensate, we are made for God's glory and praise."[52] Understood accordingly, the *Incarnation Contemplation* is a reminder that the soul, holistically, keeps the score.

Diagnostic Insights

Because of impressive mental health and clinical advances, certain social psychological characteristics of casualties, such as Luke's battered traveler, can be sketched based on the nature of the presenting wound and related symptomology. For example, according to the clinical and forensic psychologist Laurence Miller, particular traits are distinctive to victims of crime.

> Society often regards victimization as contagious. . . . In modern American culture . . . victims are often equated with losers. Most of us want to believe that crime victimization is something that happens to somebody else. The victim must have done something to bring it on him or herself; otherwise, I'm just as vulnerable too, and who wants to believe that. We may thus be reluctant to associate with the victims for fear that their bad luck will "rub off." All of these beliefs and reactions further contribute to the feelings of blame and shame that many crime victims experience.[53]

Such evidence-based indicators provide invaluable social psychological data cues to spiritual and pastoral guides—and not only regarding crime victimization. Diagnostic insight about distinctive traits is available for other populations as well—for example, war refugees, or survivors of incest, molestation, or intimate partner violence. Caregivers working with such individuals can upgrade their professional skills by familiarizing themselves with such data.

51. Chris Krall, "Trauma, Imagination, and Sensation," *Thinking Faith,* posted May 11, 2018. https://www.thinkingfaith.org/articles/trauma-imagination-and-sensation.

52. Ivens, *Understanding the Spiritual Exercises*, 185.

53. Laurence Miller, *Practical Police Psychology: Stress Management and Crisis Intervention for Law Enforcement* (Springfield, IL: Charles C. Thomas, 2006), 38

Perspective Taking

The American Psychological Association's online Dictionary of Psychology defines "perspective taking" as "looking at a situation from a viewpoint that is different from one's usual viewpoint."[54] It is a trait associated in the psychological literature with *empathy*. Psychologists suggest it may be required to notice potentially traumatic events, perhaps many years later. For example, Ignatian devotees are understandably attracted to the heroic figure of Íñigo and his so-called "cannonball moment" during the bloody Pamplona siege. But what of other battlefield casualties? Perspective taking suggests that authentic gospel neighborliness requires a capacity to notice *all* those wounded and killed that day, as well as to consider their loved ones back home. Surely the God of the *Incarnation Contemplation* exercise did. It is a virtue well worth cultivating today through this spiritual exercise.

Imagination

Imagination is an important psychospiritual noticing skill, one that can be cultivated. The Ignatian heritage is well aware that an ability to deploy one's imagination effectively is required in order to pray the Exercises as Íñigo intended. Its formal use in contemplative practice in the Western tradition dates at least to a popular fourteenth-century bestseller by Ludolph of Saxony called *Vita Christi*. It was subsequently reinterpreted and popularized for wide usage by the Exercises. "Ignatian imaginative contemplation" today is widely practiced globally, with popular applications and teaching workshops regularly featured on social media and in the literature of spirituality. The ability to benefit spiritually from the *Incarnation Contemplation*, for example, requires some access to the faculty of imagination.

Trauma is so insidious, van der Kolk notes, precisely because it "affects the imagination."[55] It deprives the individual of the mental flexibility for perspective taking, "the hallmark of imagination." Those suffering from the memory of past horrific events "simply keep replaying an old reel." Stunted imagination can result in "no hope, no chance to envision a better future, no place to go, no goal to reach." Indeed, imagination

54. "Perspective Taking," APA Dictionary of Psychology, https://dictionary.apa.org/perspective-taking.

55. Van der Kolk, *Body Keeps the Score*, all citations in this paragraph, 17.

is of such critical significance in the healing and reconciliation process that interdisciplinary collaboration between mental health and clinical professionals, on the one hand, and spiritual and pastoral guides, on the other, may be decisive for certain individuals. For careseekers of faith, interdisciplinary practice in this regard is an obvious place to begin to scale the traumatic injury ladder.

Proximity to Ground Zero

Hibakusha and those who companion them in seeking divine encounter can take heart, and learn, from the compassionate perspective of yet a *third* Jesuit. Like Pedro Arrupe and Ignatius Loyola before him, Jorge Mario Bergoglio—Pope Francis—proclaims good news for battlefield casualties, forsaken crime victims, and other survivors of violence in a world of hurt.[56] This is a man profoundly gifted with skills of expert companionship, noticing, imagination, and perspective taking. For Francis, as was the case for Arrupe at Hiroshima, *proximity to Ground Zero* is crucial. "I see clearly that the thing the church needs most today is the ability to heal wounds and to warm the hearts of the faithful; it needs nearness, proximity. I see the church as a field hospital after battle. It is useless to ask a seriously injured person if he has high cholesterol and about the level of his blood sugars! You have to heal his wounds. Then we can talk about everything else. Heal the wounds, heal the wounds . . . And you have to start from the ground up."[57]

56. Cf. Michael Hansen, *God's Field Hospital: Ignatian Spiritual Exercises Healing Wounds of Life* (New York/Mahwah, NJ: Paulist Press, 2024). Jesuit Father Hansen provides sixty original Ignatian spiritual exercises around themes such as "Emergency Care," "First-Aid," "Mental Health Care," "Pain Management," and "Recovery Ward."

57. Antonio Spadaro, "A Big Heart Open to God: An Interview with Pope Francis," *America*, September 13, 2013.

9

Memory, Understanding, and Will

A Trauma-Informed Reading of the Ignatian Suscipe

All of me—why not take all of me
Can't you see—I'm no good without you
Take my lips, I wanna lose them
Take my arms, I'll never use them.[1]

Frank Sinatra's torch song rendition of the 1930s ballad "All of Me" helped establish his reputation as one of the premier singers of his era. The song explores the theme of unconditional love and the vulnerability associated with a total gift of self to the beloved. The lyrics indicate an ardent desire to give everything as a measure of one's devotion. "You took the part that once was my heart, so why not take all of me?"[2] Curiously, "All of Me" also captures something of the wholehearted expanse of the famous *Suscipe* prayer of Ignatius of Loyola, which climaxes the Exercises in unreserved self-offering to God. Both the song and classic Christian prayer express total, loving surrender of one soul into intimate embrace with another.

1. "All of Me," lyrics by Gerald Marks and Seymour Simons (1931).
2. Marks and Simons, "All of Me."

Various saints over the ages have composed different versions of a *Suscipe* (rendered "Take and Receive" in English), reflective of their own distinctive relationships with Divinity. For Ignatius, it points to the full human person, understood holistically as the soul in all its many faculties. His *Suscipe* may well be the most famous prayer in the Exercises, commonly associated with the saint and his spirituality. Jesuits in training learn to pray it regularly, frequently as part of their morning offering to God or prayer before retiring: *"Take, Lord, and receive all my liberty, my memory, my understanding, and all my will—all that I have and possess. You, Lord, have given all that to me. I now give it back to you, O Lord. All of it is yours. Dispose of it according to your will. Give me love of yourself along with your grace, for that is enough for me."*[3]

The *Suscipe* appears at the end of the Exercises as part of a larger prayer called the "Contemplation to Stir Up Spiritual Love of God in Ourselves," itself considered "the conclusion and apt climax of the retreat experience."[4] The *Suscipe*, as well as the broader exercise that encloses it, are at the core of the Ignatian vision and spiritual practice.

Chapter 9 offers a selective, trauma-informed reading of the *Suscipe*, specifically the three Augustinian powers of soul that Íñigo taught at Alcalá—memory, understanding, and will. Introduced at the beginning of the *Exercises*, they find consequential, sustainable significance in their self-surrender to God at the climax. "The prayer consists, then, in an 'examination' of the Powers, a reflection on the nature and purpose of each, leading to appreciation and gratitude."[5] At this point the supplicant is looking toward integrating God more organically into her or his daily life—finding God in all things. The goal is a life entrusted to God's good pleasure, enjoying the associated personal relationship with a Divinity increasingly experienced as benevolent.

3. George E. Ganss, *The Spiritual Exercises of Saint Ignatius: A Translation and Commentary* (St. Louis: Institute of Jesuit Sources, 1992), no. 234. This rendering of the *Suscipe* is based on the official 1548 Latin version of the *Spiritual Exercises* called the "Vulgate," the one used by Ignatius in his later years. It is the English translation preferred by Ganss. Hereafter, *SpEx*.

4. *SpEx*, FN 183n117.

5. Michael Ivens, *Understanding the Spiritual Exercises: Text and Commentary* (Leominster, England: Gracewing, 1998), 184.

But how can spiritual seekers possibly offer themselves wholeheartedly to God if their memory bank is sealed shut, their understanding confused or distorted, their will aimless or compromised? Spiritual seekers carrying symptoms of trauma—including haunted consciences from exposure to any sort of disturbing visual or auditory content—can benefit from interdisciplinary insights into the *Suscipe*, invoking God's mercy for the gradual healing of symptoms such as shame, confusion, and sorrow. As always, suffering souls are best served when both psychology and spirituality have a seat at the table.

Ignatius of Loyola Meets Judith Lewis Herman

The discourse begins with Harvard emerita psychiatrist Judith Lewis Herman's three-stage model of trauma recovery, regarded as the gold standard. She introduced the paradigm in her 1992 magnum opus *Trauma and Recovery*,[6] described at the time as "one of the most important psychiatric works to be published since Freud."[7] It has weathered the test of time, and still today stands as "a therapeutic template in the field of psychiatry."[8] Probing for interdisciplinary wisdom, a constructive examination of the Ignatian powers of soul in succinct counterpoint with Herman's stages of recovery can prompt assorted insights and spiritual practices conducive to healing efficacy.

Here is an encounter between two titans of their respective fields, Ignatius from Christian spirituality and Herman from trauma studies. Can a beginning conversation, across centuries and disciplines, prove worthwhile to caregivers today? Establishing a credible affirmative is the ambitious goal of this chapter. The simplest procedure is to specify briefly Herman's first stage of trauma recovery, then toggle immediately to a loose religious corollary. The same procedure will be followed for Herman's second and third stages of trauma recovery, each immediately

6. Judith Herman, *Trauma and Recovery: The Aftermath of Violence—from Domestic Abuse to Political Terror* (New York: Basic Books, 1992).

7. Phyllis Chesler, "The Shellshocked Woman," *New York Times*, August 23, 1992.

8. Eren Orbey, "A Trailblazer of Trauma Studies Asks What Victims Really Want," *New Yorker*, May 2, 2023.

followed by a proposed Ignatian consideration responsive to the genius of her system.

Herman's Stage One: Overcoming Powerlessness of Will through Personal Safety and Security

Herman's first stage of recovery is the establishment of personal safety and security by survivors rendered impotent by one or more traumatic events. Trauma is an affliction of the powerless, requiring the reconstitution of shattered human agency; it renders the victim helpless by overwhelming force. "Ordinary" care systems typically prove minimally effective. Survivors of traumatic events may *internalize* their helplessness, making life—for example, getting out of bed—an existential risk. Choice becomes unpredictable, perhaps even dangerous, because it is out of a survivor's control. For this reason, it can feel safer to cede any pretense of volitional capacity. Agoraphobia is common at this stage. The temptation to turn over and put the pillow over one's head, some days, is viscerally real. In the logic of the traumatically wounded, to decide is not to decide.

The central *psychological* task of the first stage of recovery is to establish personal safety and stability by restoring self-esteem through reclaimed confidence in one's decision-making capabilities. For survivors of a single traumatic event in adulthood, Herman believes that safety can, in principle, be reestablished reasonably soon. (Childhood traumatic events and more complex traumas are different.) This can include learning self-care and emotion-regulation skills. The way forward often begins in one's body through "routine" choices such as good hygiene, as well as the capacity to plan and execute tasks such as grocery shopping and running simple errands successfully.

This in turn builds growing self-confidence and the desire to consider further recovery steps. The capacity of willpower must be rebuilt—one decision at a time. Neuroscience has now demonstrated that particularly frightful events, or a series of traumatic events in childhood, can *paralyze* a person's will—the phenomenon of "freezing" in situations of extreme danger such as sexual assault. Thus, specialized professional care may be required during stage one, indeed at any point in recovery.

Spiritual Considerations

Powerlessness—or the surrender of power—is also at the heart of a trauma-informed consideration of the *Suscipe* and suggests important spiritual and moral corollaries. Astute careseekers and caregivers should be aware of all three dynamics—psychological, spiritual, and moral—and monitor any interplay. The input of skilled spiritual and pastoral care professionals may be required at this point, or anywhere during trauma recovery.

Herman's emphasis on trauma as an affliction of the powerless will remind experienced caregivers of the significant comorbidity between trauma and substance use disorder, particularly in cases of early traumatic experiences dating to adolescence or childhood. "It is important that individuals entering treatment for substance use disorder or PTSD be assessed for this comorbidity."[9] Substances offer temporary relief and a (false) sense of control, but the slope toward dependency is slippery. Neuroscientists today describe certain changes in brain chemistry and function, which may explain a biological cycle in which symptoms of one condition exacerbate the other.

The tendency toward comorbidity suggests possible corollary benefits of making connections among twelve-step addiction programs such as Alcoholics Anonymous (AA), trauma recovery, and the Exercises. Each is about compromised freedom of choice, but only the first and third explicitly incorporate key spiritual and pastoral perspectives. For Ignatius, of course, the goal of the Exercises is human flourishing and divine encounter grounded in God's mercy. Evil aims to restrain and corrupt free will by means of what Ignatius calls "inordinate attachments." This is a period term for moral flaws such as sin, but also habit-forming or compulsive obsessions with money, comfort, appearance, youth, pleasure, honor, and so on. The corollary in AA, Step Four, requires "making a searching and fearless moral self-inventory."

9. Katherine L. Mills et al., "Trauma, PTSD, and Substance Use Disorders: Findings from the Australian National Survey of Mental Health and Well-Being," *American Journal of Psychiatry* 163, no. 4 (April 2006).

Psychiatrist Gerald May, fluent in the Christian spiritual tradition, uses the term "addiction" interchangeably with Ignatian "attachment."[10] The malice of evil, manifesting through both trauma and substance abuse dynamics, undermines free will at every opportunity. Addiction, too, is an affliction of the powerless. "People take up the 12 Steps largely because they have been throwing will-power at things and people over which in fact they have no control—alcohol and alcoholics—to name two."[11]

What is distinctive about spiritual models like twelve-step programs is that the way forward—the only way forward—is precisely by acknowledging one's *powerlessness* and need for God. "We admitted we were powerless over alcohol," in the words of Step One. "We made a decision to turn our will and our lives over to the care of God as we understood Him," according to Step Three. The spiritual corollaries, in effect, flip Herman's script. Here is the *Take and Receive* surrender of one's will, writ boldly.

The first step of Herman's paradigm—to establish personal safety and security through recovery of human agency—is of crucial importance from a psychological perspective, but many careseekers aspire to interdisciplinary inclusion of *spiritual* insights and tools. They must learn to accept, even embrace with trust, the self-surrender of agency to God as a necessary healing tool. This is a road-more-traveled to personal encounter with one's Higher Power. AA offers an outstanding, proven model, which those recovering from trauma should note. It does not come naturally and may initially seem counterintuitive, but with repetition and (the desire for) faith, the seeker is on a rewarding—liberating—path toward personal encounter with a merciful God.

The twelve-step "Serenity Prayer" has become a world-famous beacon of a "spirituality of powerlessness"—a beautiful formulation that simultaneously respects human agency—and is frequently prayed at the beginning of AA meetings: "God grant me the serenity to accept the things I cannot change, courage to change the things I can, and wisdom to know the difference." The Serenity Prayer and the *Suscipe* both require a personal spiritual surrender to God, frequently baffling for those beginning

10. Gerald G. May, *Addiction and Grace: Love and Spirituality in the Healing of Addictions*, reissue ed. (San Francisco: HarperOne, 2007).

11. Jim Harbaugh, *A 12-Step Approach to the Spiritual Exercises of St. Ignatius* (Franklin, WI: Sheed and Ward, 1997), 3.

their recovery from addiction or traumatic injury. Dynamics, timing, and choices will play out differently for mental health and trauma counselors versus spiritual and pastoral caregivers, and a measure of expertise or interdisciplinary collaboration may be required. The role of powerlessness is a key pivot point in recovery and healing whose interplay should be monitored carefully. Certain careseekers may need encouragement to step up and take *more* ownership of their lives, whereas others may need guidance toward *surrender* of control and agency to God.

A final spiritual consideration is that both the Ignatian and twelve-step traditions strongly emphasize that a seeker's journey to recovery should prioritize human fellowship. For the former, that person is the spiritual director, the guide, the expert companion. For AA, it is the sponsor. AA founder Bill Wilson relied on both. For twenty years, his spiritual guide was a Jesuit priest, Ed Dowling.[12] In a letter of October 6, 1964, Wilson described to a mutual friend his enormous debt to Father Ed: "He became just about the closest friend I shall ever have—and my spiritual advisor, too. He took me through some of my rough going, which, without his counsel and love, I might never have survived."[13]

Moral Considerations

In addition to the psychological and spiritual aspects of powerlessness, there are important *moral* considerations for people in recovery from trauma (and/or addictions.) Herman herself astutely recognizes the critical significance of severely limited human agency. Even in situations of limited free will, "[t]he moral emotions of shame and guilt . . . are not obliterated."[14] One assumes that to be the case, as well, for other difficult emotions. The client of impaired willpower, for example, must find a way forward to a set of beliefs that overcomes confusion, anger, or bitterness because of any undeserved past suffering.

For Herman, however, these are philosophical questions. But many careseekers present for assistance with a more explicit religious heritage and belief system, perhaps inclusive of sin. They need to know that the

12. Dawn Eden Goldstein, *Father Ed: The Story of Bill W.'s Spiritual Sponsor* (Maryknoll, NY: Orbis Books, 2022).

13. Goldstein, *Father Ed*, 135.

14. Herman, *Trauma and Recovery*, 66.

absence of free will precludes the possibility of religious responsibility for one's choices. This can be enormously liberating, perhaps the very interdisciplinary cue that is lacking for recovery on the part of those burdened by toxic guilt or shame. Trauma-informed caregivers should recognize that seekers' volition, if (severely) compromised, precludes the requisite freedom to sin. For healing to progress, that illusory religious burden must be relinquished.

The Catholic *Catechism*[15] is quite clear in this area, and an authoritative source with which caregivers should be familiar. Regarding moral culpability, it notes: "Freedom is the power, rooted in reason and will, to act or not to act, to do this or that, and so to perform deliberate actions on one's own responsibility" (1731). "Freedom makes man *responsible* for his acts to the extent that they are voluntary" (1734). "*Imputability* and responsibility for an action can be diminished or even nullified by ignorance, inadvertence, duress, fear, habit, inordinate attachments, and other psychological or social factors" (1735). The official ecclesial teaching, notably, includes the traditional terminology associated with Ignatius—"inordinate attachments," as well as specifying psychological factors associated with certain types of trauma, such as fear.

The *Catechism* wisely notes that not only fear or duress but "other psychological or social factors" can undermine moral culpability because of a lack of freedom and human agency. Experienced caregivers—whether from mental health, trauma counseling, spiritual, pastoral, or sacramental care backgrounds—should be familiar with relevant religious traditions, or refer to someone who is. Failure to understand the spiritual and theological nuances of sin explained the serious limitations on successful therapy encountered by the psychological caregivers in the case studies in chapters 3 and 4.

Herman's Stage Two: Remembrance and Mourning

By the time a survivor of some sort of trauma establishes safety and stability in the successful management of daily life, she or he has typically established a secure bond with a therapist, sponsor, pastor, or trusted

15. *Catechism of the Catholic Church*, 2nd ed. (United States Catholic Conference—Libreria Editrice Vaticana, 1997).

spiritual companion. (If not, it is well advised to do so.) Herman's second stage of recovery can begin. "The survivor is now ready to tell the story of the trauma, in depth and detail."[16] The principle of empowerment remains operative at all stages, such that the choice to face and describe an existentially disruptive past resides with the survivor. Herman calls this stage of recovery "remembrance and mourning." One grieves past abusive events and lost innocence, as well as positive experiences on which one missed out. "I feel like I never had a childhood."

To move safely and successfully through stage two, there are three identifiable psychological components. The first, and perhaps most difficult, is to remember, and narrate, the traumatic loss; the second is to mourn or grieve it; and the third is to transform traumatic memories from "what's wrong with me?" to a more emotionally neutral "what happened to me?" Here, some who understand themselves as "victims" begin to experience and name themselves as "survivors"; others prefer the term "victim-survivor." Regardless of nomenclature, they must tell their stories. For some, once will be sufficient; for others, repeated recounting is required, slowly becoming free of and surrendering any toxic overlay. "Survivors . . . come to a point in their testimony where all questions are reduced to one, spoken more in bewilderment than in outrage: Why? The answer is beyond human understanding."[17]

The survivor seeks an authentic way to grieve her profound feelings of shame, sorrow, guilt, and confusion. "The major work of the second stage is accomplished . . . when the patient reclaims her own history and feels renewed hope and energy for engagement with life . . . When the second stage has come to its conclusion, the traumatic experience belongs to the past."[18] At some indeterminate point, the intensity of the feelings begins to diminish. "It occurs to the survivor that perhaps the trauma is only one part, and perhaps not even the most important part, of her life story."[19] (Note that Herman relies on feminine pronouns for victim/survivors.

16. Judith Herman, "Recovery from Psychological Trauma," *Psychiatry and Clinical Neurosciences* 52, no. S1 (January 2002).

17. Herman, *Trauma and Recovery*, 178.

18. Herman, "Recovery from Psychological Trauma."

19. Herman.

While recognizing that trauma is an equal-opportunity affliction, in this section that choice will be followed for purposes of symmetry.)

Any tool, technique, or process takes as long as it takes. Each person is different; recovery may be quick, or it may take months or even years, depending on the type of trauma, the age when the event was experienced, the quality and availability of suitable resources, and so on. Pacing and timing, of course, should be regularly reviewed by the individual with associated caregivers. It may be that, occasionally, the survivor needs to retrace her steps back to stage one to reestablish a sense of safety and security.

Van der Kolk notes that "people cannot put traumatic events behind until they are able to acknowledge what has happened and start to recognize the inevitable demons they're struggling with . . . and without memory you cannot imagine how things can be different."[20] The ordinary response to horrific past events or vicarious exposure is to banish them from memory, of course, because it is so often a shameful, haunted place. Remembering the past, for some, is a journey begun with great fear, anxiety, or other obstructive emotions. The decision to open oneself to the past should not be taken lightly, but there *are* safe ways forward when a person is ready. And the fact remains that the failure to mourn past painful events leaves the survivor trapped. Grieving enables her to reclaim her voice and identity, and further a sense of self-ownership.

Spiritual Considerations

Herman is not shy about the use of arguably religious language. "The traumatic events challenge an ordinary person to become a theologian, a philosopher, and a jurist. The survivor is called upon to articulate the values and beliefs that she once held and that the trauma destroyed. She stands mute before the emptiness of evil."[21] Various reputable models and prayer practices for the spiritual (and ritual) healing of memories are available. In trusting dialogue, caregivers and careseekers in the Abrahamic religious traditions can explore options to identify one or more that is congenial. The best models typically resemble the light form of the Exercises in their reliance on God's power and mercy to overcome shame,

20. Bessel van der Kolk, *The Body Keeps the Score: Brain, Mind, and Body in the Healing of Trauma* (New York: Viking, 2014), 219.

21. Herman, *Trauma and Recovery*, 178.

sorrow, confusion, and other potentially debilitating symptoms of evil and sin. Ignatius's focus on personal sin early in the Exercises is an invitation to the supplicant to discover that the very name of God is mercy. Mercy is God's identity. This is similar to Islam's understanding of the two most important names of God as "the Compassionate" and "the Merciful." It is time to surrender any remaining shame and guilt to this Divinity.

Some supplicants will likely be challenged to embrace fresh images of God at this stage of spiritual recovery, poignantly captured by the following example from Jewish history. The celebrated rebbe of the Warsaw Ghetto, Kalonymos Kalmish Shapiro (1889–1943), taught the beleaguered Jewish community how it is possible to maintain a radiant faith amid the evil and despair of Nazi genocide:

> God, blessed be He, is to be found in His inner chamber weeping, so that one who pushes in and comes close to Him by means of studying Torah, weeps together with God, and studies Torah with Him. Just this makes the difference: the weeping, the pain which a person undergoes by himself, *alone*, may have the effect of breaking him, of bringing him down, so that he is incapable of doing anything. But the weeping which the person does *together with God*—that strengthens him. He weeps—and is strengthened.[22]

From the "Jewish Residential District" (so called by the Nazis) Rabbi Shapiro describes a mystical vision of a weeping God who empowers the violently and cruelly oppressed to meet Him in shared tears. In so doing, he challenges subsequent generations of beleaguered, wounded believers and seekers to ask themselves: *Are these tears my own, or God's as well?*

Examples abound in the folk religious heritage:

Master to disciple: "I feel so sorry for God."
Disciple: "Why?"
Master: "Because no one notices Him weeping."

22. Kimberley Christine Patton and John Stratton Hawley, eds., *Holy Tears: Weeping in the Religious Imagination* (Princeton, NJ: Princeton University Press, 2005), 89–90, emphasis added. The rebbe buried the manuscript in 1943 as the Warsaw Ghetto was annihilated. Estimates of fatalities range up to 400,000. After the war the manuscript was discovered and later published in Israel under the title *Esh Kodesh* (Fire of holiness).

Rendered powerless by meager human resources and at wits' end, some seekers are thereby freed for healing encounter with a suffering Divinity in the weeping mode.

Capturing this perspective, the Catholic Ignatian tradition offers concrete models of remembrance and mourning for the healing of trauma. Recently, Dawn Eden, a courageous and perceptive survivor of childhood sexual abuse, described growing up in the years following her parents' separation. "I had been living in an environment I would now consider sexually porous. I don't recall any clear boundaries; I was not well shielded from adults' nudity, substance abuse, dirty jokes, sex talk, and swearing."[23]

The first abuse she can recall occurred at a temple, where her Jewish mother took her and her sister on Friday nights for Shabbat. Dawn was five years old. Growing up, she retained only the most confusing of memories, none of them pleasant, about what happened to her in the temple's library.

Years later, having embraced Catholicism, she continued trying to make some sense of those memories, wondering if healing was ever possible. Finally, thirty years after the traumatic events, she found it with the help of the *Suscipe* prayer. In her book, *Remembering God's Mercy: Redeem the Past and Free Yourself from Painful Memories*,[24] Eden juxtaposes the painful experience of childhood sexual abuse with her love for Jewish and Christian sacred texts, Catholic sacraments, and Marian devotion. Chapter by chapter and phrase by phrase, she offers specific spiritual exercises and religious insights based on the precise language of the *Suscipe*, which taught her how past traumas can be healed and transformed into an offering back to God. "PTSD is a miserable disease to live with," concludes Eden. "But it is truly a great disease to recover from" because it teaches us how to live.[25]

What Eden discovered was that the *Suscipe* was an earthy prayer for the traumatically wounded and beleaguered of conscience because it can heal not only the spirit, but also other human faculties such as memory

23. Dawn Eden, *My Peace I Give You: Healing Sexual Wounds with the Help of the Saints* (Notre Dame, IN: Ave Maria Press, 2012), xviii.

24. Dawn Eden, *Remembering God's Mercy: Redeem the Past and Free Yourself from Painful Memories* (Notre Dame, IN: Ave Maria Press, 2016).

25. Eden, *Remembering God's Mercy*, 116.

and human agency. How so? "The saint acknowledges there are things he cannot change—the events of his past—and at the same time displays the bold hope that his Maker will accept him as he is now, with everything he did and everything that was done to him."[26] Like Ignatius, Eden surrendered her powerlessness, jaundiced memories, and any lingering shame to a merciful God—*Take and Receive*. The result, over time, was reclaimed self-possession and transcendence of confusing, painful childhood memories of sexual abuse. It is a fine example of how to pray the *Suscipe* from a trauma-informed perspective.

One other spiritual method from the Catholic tradition, Christ- and Ignatian-based, deserves attention. The late Jesuit David J. Hassel called it the "prayer of personal reminiscence."[27] As a longtime professor of philosophy at Loyola University in Chicago, Hassel was aware of the prayer's roots in St. Augustine; he presents the latter's fourth-century autobiographical *Confessions* as the saint's own prayer of personal reminiscence.[28] "[M]emory is not a set of dusty photographs at the back of a person's head but an evaluative act of recall pulsing at the front of his consciousness, filled with colorful detail from the past, and interpreted in terms of the timely confronting situations."[29]

Prayer of personal reminiscence invites the survivor/supplicant, when ready and under the proper conditions, to relive certain difficult memories with Christ alongside and organically part of the imaginative prayer exercise. The qualifying conditions include consultation with and, likely, personal accompaniment by one's spiritual guide or trained companion, since the person praying in reminiscence may be inviting God into a stored memory or generic situation in which evil or sin was at work. A second condition would require a safe environment. "The praying person slowly begins to see the self and the past as Christ sees them,"[30] which is to say with affection, tears, loving mercy, and divine acceptance. This is not a psychological technique (though there are analogous imaginal

26. Eden, *My Peace*, 3.

27. David J. Hassel, *Radical Prayer: Creating a Welcome for God, Ourselves, Other People and the World* (Ramsey, NJ: Paulist Press, 1983). Cf. chap. 2.

28. Augustine, *The Confessions of Saint Augustine* (New York: Penguin Random House, 1960).

29. Hassel, *Radical Prayer*, 21.

30. Hassel, 23.

therapies) but a traditional spiritual exercise available to persons of faith and seekers.

The following first-person narrative, "Maggie's Story," recounts one person's experience of what might more properly be called a prayer of *imaginative* personal reminiscence in the wake of a traumatic event that occurred when she was a young woman. The autobiographical account is a true case study used with permission, though the name "Maggie" is a pseudonym. She moves through all three psychological components of Herman's second stage of recovery from trauma. Though Maggie's experience is remarkable, it is hardly exceptional in the spiritual literature.

Maggie's Story

The most important hour in my spiritual life is one I never talk about.

It was winter break of my senior year as an undergraduate theology major at a Jesuit university. Thanks to Campus Ministry activities, my faith had evolved from simply "knowing the right answers" to finding joy in community and becoming passionate about social justice. Something was missing, though. I just didn't know it yet.

Then I made my first silent Ignatian retreat—five days of prayer and contemplation in a large retreat house, punctuated by daily meetings with a trained spiritual director. I already had a trusting relationship with my assigned guide, an experienced Jesuit priest who was one of our campus ministers. He'd celebrated with me at my best and hung in with me through my worst. He knew me. Even so, it took me until the last night of retreat to tell him why I was such a well-controlled mess.

I had worked at the Jersey Shore during the summer between my sophomore and junior years. It was a childhood dream come true—except that the dream had never included being raped in the middle of a Friday afternoon, in my own bed, by a guy I'd just met. I carried that traumatic memory through the second half of my college years—battling anorexia, damaging my relationships, struggling at every turn to be an academic and co-curricular success while my insides felt like broken glass.

On that last night of retreat, I told my director the story. He responded with gentle words of empathy, cautionary wisdom, and spiritual insight. He suggested a prayer assignment—if I felt ready. "Revisit the day in your imagination," he said, "but let God take your hand for comfort and strength. If you believe that God is always with you—and I know you do—it means God was there, somehow. So, walk back through the day, trying to see yourself through God's eyes. But don't be foolish. STOP the prayer exercise if you feel frightened or emotionally overwhelmed, and come knock on my door." I told him I got it—don't try this spiritual exercise at home, alone—and felt quite safe in the retreat house environment, with support nearby. This sounded like a rare healing opportunity, and I wanted to go for it.

Years later, a therapist raged against my spiritual director's guidance. "Clergy should leave the therapy to the therapists," she said. "It was totally irresponsible to send you off alone like that to revisit a traumatic memory."

But I wasn't alone, I said. I was with God. And this wasn't therapy, it was prayer.

She scoffed.

I found a new therapist.

Here's what happened. Following my director's guidance, I settled into the big, comfortable chair in my private retreat center room. Then, in my imagination, I walked to the cavernous chapel and knelt in front of the cross, praying for the courage to do this. I asked Jesus for help, and he reached out and took my hand, then walked with me to the doorway of a room I had been afraid to enter. I opened the door, and together we walked through the events of that painful day, from the first moments I could remember.

I tried to pay attention to what Jesus was feeling and how he was regarding me. I experienced his joy in the morning, as I baked cookies on my day off then headed to the beach with a book to top off my tan. I felt his apprehension as I allowed a stranger to strike up a flirtatious conversation. I felt his anxiety rise as I ignored what I now know were red flags. I felt his helplessness as I agreed to let the guy walk me back to my sweet little apartment.

And I felt him rage and weep—as I had not been able to—at what ensued. God's tears enabled me—finally—to weep. I never knew God could cry!

We went through the day more than once. We went through it until my feelings gentled and a sense of calm washed over me. The guilt, shame, and confusion gradually lifted. Now I was ready to finish my prayer and go out the door on the other side.

Never having let go of my hand, Jesus escorted me at last into a beautiful garden.

Although it would take many years and more than one good therapist to put back together everything that was undone in that awful afternoon, I can hardly describe just how important to me was the spiritual healing that came from my imaginative prayer experience on that retreat. Although I usually stay away from gendered pronouns for God, at the time all I knew was that the God who revealed himself to me that night was the one I wanted to follow. God beheld me, knew me, and cherished me. He did not judge or shame me for the naïve choices and reckless decisions without which the rapist could not have wound up in my room. He did not condemn, criticize, or lecture me. Jesus wanted my good, my healing, even more than I wanted it for myself. He was so far from the God of right answers that it was a wonder they answered to the same name.

This is the God who has kept me working in ministry for thirty years. Because this merciful God who took my hand in prayer and showed a desire to be intimately involved in each aspect of my life—including the most shameful—is just as interested in every *other* person's life. Out of gratitude, I try to be as well.

Herman's Stage Three: Reconciling with Oneself, Reconnecting with the Wider Community, and Exploring a Survivor Mission

By this time in the trauma recovery process, if not earlier, it is no longer possible to do justice to Herman's three-stage model without noting that she peppers her writings with references rich in religious and spiritual significance. "Morality," "ethics," "survivor's mission," "faith," "moral injury," "belief," "justice," and so on. She should be read in light of her respect for such frameworks. The boundary between psychological and spiritual grows increasingly thin and porous. Nevertheless, it is the responsibility of spiritual and pastoral caregivers to tailor Herman's insights. Following the lead of Duke University psychiatrist and theologian Warren Kinghorn, they will understand that the reduction and healing of symptoms is not the ultimate goal of spiritual and pastoral care, but rather so that a survivor may discover divine mercy and that this person "is reconciled to God and to the human community."[31]

As the third stage unfolds, the survivor is beginning to develop an exciting opportunity to make new friends, rediscover a meaningful life corresponding to the existential moment, and freely create a new way of being in the world. Trauma has in a real sense destroyed the old self, perhaps including important relationships. "Having come to terms with the traumatic past, the survivor faces the task of creating a future."[32] This requires substantial progress in reconciliation with oneself and reconnection with others, as well as beginning to construct a safe and positive future personally meaningful to her. For many people of faith and seekers, reconciliation and reconnection with Divinity top the list of aspirations.

Meaning and purpose play a central interdisciplinary role in the final stage, serving to clarify a survivor's past *confusion*, a debilitating symptom in both the Exercises and moral injury trauma. She is no longer captive to a force outside herself but displays self-possession and ownership of the healing process. Stage three is an act of resistance and agency, during which the survivor can immerse herself in a freely chosen care circle and consider next life steps. "Who do I want to be?" the survivor asks, beginning to rediscover and reclaim her imagination, personal dreams, and goals.

The third stage is a meaning-making process that invites the survivor, with trusted companions and allies alongside, to uncover a survivor's mission in life. "The old beliefs that gave meaning to her life have been challenged; now she must find a new sustaining faith."[33] Herman believes that survivors who recover most fully are those who discover some

31. Warren Kinghorn, "Combat Trauma and Moral Fragmentation: A Theological Account of Moral Injury," *Journal of the Society of Christian Ethics* 32, no. 2 (Fall/Winter 2012): 70.

32. Herman, *Trauma and Recovery*, 196.

33. Herman, 196.

wider social meaning in past traumatic events. It is an effective way to befriend, and transcend, the past. At this stage, many survivors "recognize a political or religious dimension to their misfortune."[34] The "survivor's mission" is a construct in psychiatry that dates back to research on the *hibakusha* survivors of Hiroshima.[35]

Hunger for interdisciplinary meaning and purpose is evident at the conclusion of Maggie's testimony. The role of religious beliefs and prayer is obvious, but she also acknowledges that "*it would take many years and more than one good therapist to put back together everything that was undone in that awful afternoon.*" Survivors are symbols and wisdom figures of pain, possibility, and hope; the wider human community will be enriched by receptivity to casualties in its midst. The recovery process for Colonel Macpherson, Helen, and Maggie all flowered into a grateful survivor's mission of outreach to the wider human community and desire to share their testimonies. Maggie: "*This is the God who has kept me working in ministry for thirty years—this merciful God who took my hand in prayer and showed a desire to be intimately involved in each aspect of my life . . . out of gratitude, I try to care for others in the same way.*

Spiritual Considerations

Russian novelist Leo Tolstoy believed that the two most powerful warriors were patience and time. He was not speaking as a military strategist but as an astute chronicler of history and the human soul. Nevertheless, when Napoleon began his campaign east across the steppes, senior Russian generals in the Patriotic War of 1812 surely anticipated Tolstoy's perspective, correctly viewing the weather as their most potent ally against the ill-supplied French invaders. Foolishly, the latter had prepared for a quick, decisive victory. But Moscow—choosing delay by strategic retreat—weaponized the intense summer heat, then the onslaught of a brutal Russian winter. The result was disaster for France, with fatalities estimated at one million. Patience and time, time and patience.

34. Herman, 207.

35. Robert Jay Lifton, "The Concept of the Survivor," in J. E. Dimsdale, ed., *Survivors, Victims, and Perpetrators: Essays on the Nazi Holocaust* (New York: Hemisphere Publishing, 1980), 123.

Spiritual care in the Ignatian heritage takes the long view, wary of the quick fix in favor of the more measured nurture often required for sustainable enlightenment and intimacy in relationships. After all, the context for religion and spirituality is eternity; fast-food devotees will be stretched. The expectation is neither sudden miracles nor inexplicable magic, though neophytes may be tempted down those rabbit holes. The paradigm of relationship—with oneself, others, and Divinity—is fully open-ended to the boundless possibilities of a benevolent future.

Spirituality's greatest contribution to interdisciplinary, trauma-informed care for people of faith and seekers is twofold: first, the recognition that it may take time and require patience; and second, that they are not alone on the journey. *Are these tears my own, or God's as well?* Reasonable people understand that the road may be long and winding, though progress along the way is always sufficient to sustain hope and resilience. In the Ignatian perspective, what happens *after* any formal retreat is just as important as the retreat itself. This is the so-called "Fifth Week"—the rest of a person's life. It would be professionally irresponsible for caregivers to suggest quick fixes as normative. Patience and time.

One spiritual practice, briefly noted, stands out in this regard. The Ignatian model explicitly recommends *repeating* particular exercises as long as the seeker finds them rewarding and appealing. This is prayer of "repetition." The Exercises suggest that where the supplicant has experienced healthy, holy, and healing dynamics, she repeat that particular prayer, or some variation thereof. The first two exercises of the First Week, for example, are practices by which the supplicant asks God's curative mercy through remembrance, mourning, and repentance of past shameful memories of sinful events or evil situations—for which one may or may not bear any responsibility. Exercises Three and Four immediately invite the supplicant to slow down and repeat the first two. "I have used the word repetition because the intellect, aided by the memory, will without digressing reflect on the matters contemplated in the previous exercises."[36] (Of course, repetition is not exclusive to the Exercises; a Chinese Shaolin master may advise his students that they cannot call a specific maneuver their own until they have practiced it at least one thousand times.)

36. *SpEx*, no. 64.

To begin a prayer of repetition, as an entry point one might recall particular affective feelings, bodily sensations or postures, meaningful insights, or visual imaginative images from a previous prayer exercise. Perhaps the seeker has recorded these in her journal. This is a step "back" to a previous exercise in order to allow God's goodness to ripen more profoundly in one's soul. Maggie's imaginative prayer of personal remembrance, for example, could be repeated endlessly, following her free decision as to what she thinks best for her. Endless variations are possible—perhaps recalling *different* memories, including those which are happy—according to what appeals to her and the wisdom of her care companion(s). One step back with the prayer of repetition may be two spiritual steps forward. She is moving forward purposively in developing personalized prayers which she can call upon from her memory, with growing facility and trust in God's benevolent presence in and through the exercises chosen. The contribution to stage one–related human agency and self-possession is obvious.

Devotional litanies, mantras, bead prayers such as the rosary, and other repetitive prayer practices can offer precious resources in the healing of moral or spiritual distress. Repetition with sacred texts and hymnody can be fruitfully employed when praying the *Incarnation Contemplation*, for example. Looking down from above, Divinity considers the role of race in a violence-scarred world. "There is a balm in Gilead to make the wounded whole. There is a balm in Gilead to heal the sin-sick soul."[37] This popular African American hymn hauntingly highlights the direct relation between sin and soul-sickness in the Jewish and Christian traditions. Historians have noted the contribution of "gospel hymns," or "American Negro Spirituals," to the resilience of the African American community in the face of the sin—and intergenerational trauma—of chattel slavery. A rousing version of "There Is a Balm," available on YouTube and repeated as frequently as efficacious, can serve as cost-free holistic soul medicine, fortification against the despair and related self-destructive behaviors triggered by ongoing atrocities such as those perpetrated against George Floyd on May 25, 2020.

Building on Herman's work, certain trauma specialists in psychology have now begun to normalize religion and spirituality into their thera-

37. "There is a Balm in Gilead" is a nineteenth-century African American spiritual drawing on language from Jeremiah 8:22. "Is there no balm in Gilead? Is there no physician there? Why then has the health of the daughter of my people not been restored?"

peutic modalities. "Religion is clearly a path for finding meaning in life and especially for restoring meaning following traumatic events (accidents, illnesses, twists of fortune, and the loss of loved ones)."[38] In his *Memoirs*, Íñigo describes intense, torturous confusion during his Manresa Episode about whether to pray more or less; to sleep more or less; to fast or not; to visit a priest again for confession or not; and so on. He was frighteningly addled, disoriented to the point of despair.

Ignatian scholars view the prayer of repetition as readily oriented toward greater understanding and coherence. Ivens notes that it is through repetition that "prayer moves into synthesis: a coming together of details and the emergence of meaning from the interplay between them."[39] In this sense, the underappreciated prayer of repetition joins the imaginative prayer of personal reminiscence as two prominent Ignatian practices from the Christian tradition that are adaptable for an epoch of trauma. Ongoing bouts of confusion can be surrendered in the *Suscipe* to the hopeful desire for forthcoming enlightenment and meaning regarding past, present, or future events, situations, or decisions. Clarity of understanding, a virtue widely associated with Buddhism, emerges as a preeminent Ignatian recovery practice.

The Exercises are a school of prayer and repetitions play a significant role in the curriculum. This is far from a cloistered spirituality; in fact, it is quite worldly. It understands that busy supplicants rarely have the leisure to generate fresh prayer options each Monday morning, say, or while on the road. Though Ignatian prayer apps are readily available, they are not required for a repetition. In an age of dehumanization from excessive gadgetry, human agency can be fostered by spiritual exercises free of earbuds or other electronic bells and whistles. Some claim that silence is God's first language.

Finally, exciting evidence-based neurological research has now demonstrated measurable benefits to the practice of regular and repetitive prayer and meditation. This emerging field is called "neurotheology," in which scientists study the brains of people who are diligent in their spiritual practice. The discipline is not without its detractors, and critical

38. C. L. Park and D. Edmondson, "Religion as a Source of Meaning," in *Meaning, Mortality, and Choice: The Social Psychology of Existential Concerns*, ed. Phillip R. Shaver and Mario Mikulincer (Washington, DC: American Psychological Association, 2012), 145–62.

39. Ivens, *Understanding the Spiritual Exercises*, 61.

consideration of the topic is well beyond the scope of this primer. Nevertheless, astute spiritual caregivers should be aware that neurological evidence suggests that diligence in prayer can actively contribute to healing from trauma—for example, through the release of feel-good chemicals such as dopamine and endorphins.[40] Scientists have described the brain as a muscle that can be sculpted and toned by repetition, not unlike bodily muscles at the local fitness center. Some scientists go further and provocatively suggest God is a "muscle" that can be developed.

The latter goes too far, obviously. But the brain does exhibit plasticity, as the nerve cells (neurons) that serve as building blocks can change, adjust, reorganize, and grow new pathways. There is scientific evidence that a concerted, regular effort to progress in the spiritual life demonstrably modulates brain wave activity and rewrites neural connections. What to make of that fact is a matter of ongoing debate, confronting the limits of the scientific method.

In one intriguing study, neuroscientist Andrew Newberg scanned the brains of Buddhists in meditation, Sikhs in communal chant, and Catholic nuns at prayer.[41] He then compared the neurological results with a control group of test subjects whose brains were at rest. After eight weeks, scans confirmed dramatic changes in the brains of the former group. "[O]ur model of brain activity during meditation indicates that there may be very demonstrable reasons why people who frequently practice meditation experience lower blood pressure, lower heart rates, decreased anxiety, and decreased depression."[42]

Research psychiatrist Jeffery M. Schwartz (at University of California, Los Angeles) takes the neurotheological data further. "[T]here is significant experimental evidence that directing your attention towards spiritual growth changes your brain in ways that are conducive to spiritual growth."[43] In this sense, it may be that regular prayer practices (presum-

40. Cf. the work of neuroscientist Allan N. Schore, *Affect Regulation and the Origin of the Self: The Neurobiology of Emotional Development* (New York: Routledge, 2015).

41. Andrew Newberg and Mark Robert Waldman, *How God Changes Your Brain: Breakthrough Findings from a Leading Neuroscientist* (New York: Ballantine Books, 2009).

42. Andrew Newberg, "Neurotheology: This Is Your Brain on Religion," National Public Radio author interview, December 15, 2010, https://www.npr.org/2010/12/15/132078267/neurotheology-where-religion-and-science-collide.

43. Schwartz writes: "Another way of saying this is that as our brain changes in ways that are conducive to spiritual growth, as we come closer to the imitation of Christ through

ably including Ignatian repetition) can shape neural pathways of the brain in ways that positively impact moods, cognitions, memories, and perceptions of meaning. Can this be correlated with Divinity? That will always be a matter of faith and discernment. But neuroscience, it seems, may one day become a valued partner of traditional spiritualities, as it continues to plumb the significance of repeated prayer and meditation exercises.

Back to the Future

Memory, understanding, and will are faculties explicitly drawn from the early Christian tradition. Today they can be adapted into interdisciplinary insights and effective prayer practices suitable for survivors of MIT or anyone journeying through posttraumatic growth. Traditional faculties of soul taught by Íñigo to Alcalá's afflicted in 1526–27 find fresh, twenty-first-century healing applications.

What does it mean to surrender one's faculties to God, much less one's whole self? "Give up my memory, my freedom, my mind? Yikes! Why, for goodness' sake, would I ever want to do that?" Point taken—this will never be an easy sell. If the *Suscipe* prayer feels like too much of a blank check, one can always limit the spiritual self-offering to something more existentially meaningful in the moment.

Seekers legitimately wary of entrusting too much to God, too soon, can scale the offering prayer back, maintaining a felt sense of safety and security. A particular God-seeker might know herself as blessed with gifts of leadership, or music, for example, and choose to offer those to God's purposes. Or the gift of friendship, creativity, one's marriage and family, time, treasure, or talents. Perhaps a person has settled on a particular survivor's mission and wants to offer that to God, invoking divine blessing and guidance upon it. Perhaps a supplicant finds the prayer of imaginative personal reminiscence particularly timely. Then she should

---

the reception of grace by the work of the Holy Spirit, the dynamic and powerful lower animal drives—which it may be reasonable, from a Christian perspective, to describe as close to identical with what we call sin nature—lose their control over how our mind works. Thus, our mind is less distracted and directed away from the goals of spiritual growth." Jeffrey M. Schwartz, "Neuroplasticity and Spiritual Formation," Biola University Center for Christian Thought, April 18, 2019, https://cct.biola.edu/neuroplasticity-and-spiritual-formation/.

start there. The *Suscipe*, in this sense, should come from the heart, and reflect the uniqueness of each person at their particular stage in life.

Nevertheless, there are some people who *are* ready for a fuller surrender of self; one meets them all the time at twelve-step meetings, for example. Colonel Macpherson, Helen, and Maggie see no reason to hold back, not after years of excruciating alienation from self, others, the world, and God. Their instinct was that something *more*—something spiritual—was required to complement their therapeutic healing, and they would not give up until they found it. "If it's broken, fix it." Each person must be true to herself as she recovers, and caregivers should respect and prepare for that.

Through trauma-informed insights and methods adapted from the Ignatian heritage, the Exercises can offer spiritual value-added for certain special needs persons of faith and seekers. Fresh interdisciplinary healing modalities, oriented toward divine encounter, are available for exploration. Through the "trauma-informed *Suscipe*," as it might be designated, Íñigo's traditional Christian understanding of the human person finds foundational application in a world characterized by a commonality of affliction. Spiritual and pastoral caregivers can find here a worthwhile source of professional development and may wish to explore further any implications for their own practice.

Epilogue

Body and Soul Keep the Score

When King David and his men moved the sacred ark of the covenant to the newly established capital of Jerusalem, they could not restrain their celebratory bodily worship to vigorous musical accompaniment upon arrival: "David and all the house of Israel were dancing before the Lord with all their might, with songs and lyres and harps and tambourines and castanets and cymbals" (2 Sam 6:5). In the New Testament, the tax collector who goes up to the temple to pray stands at a respectful distance, lowers his eyes, and beats his breast—details that give locational significance and somatic expression to his spoken prayer: "God, be merciful to me, a sinner!" (Luke 18:13). The Hebrew and Christian Scriptures are replete with references to the physicality of prayer.

Chapter 8 highlighted the role of the body in Ignatian prayer, and the human person as sensate. Yet, over the centuries, the living tradition has increasingly come untethered from flesh and blood. "Although Ignatian spirituality definitely involves all the senses—sight, hearing, taste, smell, and touch—as well as the emotions, and indeed the whole body, there has been a noticeable intellectualizing tendency in the Ignatian literature of our time. The dominant view is to play down the physical and to be most interested in reason or 'soul.' "[1] This epilogue briefly addresses that valid concern, bringing the discourse full circle, pointing to a balanced way forward grounded in neglected *bodily* guidance from the Exercises.

1. Fredrik Heiding, "Body Language before the Face of God," *The Way* 63, no. 3 (July 2024): 15–24.

Ignatius explicitly emphasized somatic guidelines for prayer through what he called "Additions" (*Adiciones* in Latin).[2] A vague term, Ganss translates it as "Additional Directives."[3] The fourth is the most applicable: "I will enter upon the contemplation, now kneeling, now prostrate on the floor, or lying face upward, or seated, or standing—but always intent on seeking what I desire."[4] Such guidance, Ignatius was convinced, helped the person on retreat to "make the Exercises better."[5] One might compare him to a Zen master in this regard; for both, posture is crucial.

The Additional Directives are designed to involve the whole person, including "emotions, thoughts, imagination, senses, posture,"[6] choice of prayer environment (light or dark), location of prayer (indoors or out), time of prayer (before retiring or immediately upon waking), and so on. Kneeling, for example, can communicate—without words—reverent self-offering to God. Depending upon the individual, praying on one's knees may also bespeak heartfelt spiritual supplication, repentance, humility, or submission. Experienced spiritual guides today attend to breathing, gesture, facial expression, body language, and prayer location. Words are not always required and may be a distraction as the relational intimacy with one's Higher Power deepens. Need two longtime lovers speak words to convey their affection, or grief? Van der Kolk's emphasis on somatic healing modalities, including yoga,[7] can be read as an invitation to reclaim the physical aspect of spirituality as one more interdisciplinary modality for trauma-informed recovery. This is critical for survivors of sexual trauma, for whom "the threat of dissociation between the mind and the body is both debilitating and ever-present."[8]

2. George E. Ganss, *The Spiritual Exercises of Saint Ignatius: A Translation and Commentary* (St. Louis: Institute of Jesuit Sources, 1992), nos. 73–86. Henceforth, *SpEx*.

3. *SpEx*, 158n48.

4. *SpEx* no. 76.

5. *SpEx* no. 73.

6. Michael Ivens, *Understanding the Spiritual Exercises: Text and Commentary* (Leominster, England: Gracewing, 1998), 65.

7. Joanne Spence, *Trauma-Informed Yoga: A Toolbox for Therapists* (Eau Claire, WI: PESI Publishing, 2021), can be highly recommended in this regard.

8. Julie Feder, *Incarnating Grace: A Theology of Healing from Sexual Trauma* (New York: Fordham University Press, 2024), 27.

The Additional Directives present open-ended guidance that brokers more intimate encounter with God. Perhaps they are all the more valuable in an age of virtualization, when human and physical connection is being lost. It is a point to which spiritual caregivers should attend. In an essay called "To Make the Exercises Better," Jesuit Father Brian Grogan explains that "the purpose of the additions is to mobilize the whole person in his search for the divine will. Ignatius had a comprehensive view of man: body, imagination, mind, senses, feeling, and will were all to be brought into play to reach the goal of the Exercises."[9] Today, those human faculties must include consideration of the brain.

A more holistic bio-psycho-neural-spiritual healthcare model is on the horizon. Groundbreaking neurobiological advances and somatic-oriented therapies can be complemented by examining trauma's fingerprints on the soul and spirit. Body *and* soul, mental health *and* spirituality: two languages, one voice in trauma recovery. The implications for healing are thrilling. Wounded careseekers who hunger for God's touch need not settle for less.

9. Brian Grogan, "To Make the Exercises Better: The Additional Directions," *The Way Supplement* 27 (1976): 15–26.

Acknowledgments

The journey from research to manuscript completion spanned two continents and almost four years. Countless individuals contributed to the project—reading various chapters, making valuable suggestions, and holding my hand. May they recognize their contributions reflected in the finished product, and forgive the impossibility of naming them all. Errors and omissions, of course, are mine.

The book would never have been possible without the blessing of my Jesuit Provincial, Very Reverend Joseph M. O'Keefe, SJ, who afforded me the opportunity for research and writing.

Jesuit Brother Chris Derby was a steadfast believer from the beginning and had my back until the end.

Jesuit Father Stephen V. Sundborg read every page, restraining my literary excess and improving the writing on many of them.

Jesuit Father Ben Hawley graciously offered the spiritual guidance and personal companionship required to soothe the occasional meltdown.

The Georgetown Jesuit Community, in particular my guys at Andrew White House, were endlessly patient and respectful of a writer's peculiarities.

Siblings Mike, Dave, Kath, and Weed—time has a way of showing us what matters most.

Ditto Marcey, Jenny, Kristen, Mary Ellen, and all my amazing cousins.

Jesuit Father Philip Harrison, editor of *The Way*, whose early support for this venture was consequential for its successful outcome.

Liturgical Press editorial director Hans Christoffersen's embrace of an unproven author was unwavering. His production team of Stephanie Lancour, Michelle Verkuilen, Tara Durheim, and Angela Steffens offered personalized, timely, and professional guidance.

Bo Karen Lee, associate professor of spiritual theology and Christian formation at Princeton Theological Seminary and prayer warrior.

Mary Gautier—you opened the door, and so much more.

Lisa López Levers—how I enjoyed our monthly Zooms! Your professional expertise in the field of trauma was indispensable. Who would have imagined interdisciplinary collaboration could be as enjoyable as it is productive? Two languages, one voice.

Christine Marie Eberle—your enthusiasm regularly buoyed my own. You changed my approach to the writing life when you taught me about the genre of "essay." Thank you for slogging with me through the muddy field of details. We did it, my friend!

And—first and last—dear Mom and Dad.

Bibliography

Aist, Clark S. "The Recovery of Religious and Spiritual Significance in American Psychiatry." *Journal of Religion and Health* 51, no. 3 (September 2012).

Alonso, Martín. *Diccionario Medieval Español: Tomo II, CH-Z.* Salamanca: Universidad Pontificia de Salamanca, 1986.

"Alumbrado." *Encyclopedia Britannica.* April 23, 2020. https://www.britannica.com/event/Alumbrado. Accessed May 15, 2024.

Ancient Christian Commentary on Scripture: New Testament III, Luke. Edited by Arthur A. Just Jr. Downers Grove, IL: InterVarsity Press, 2003.

Arrupe, Pedro. *Recollections and Reflections of Pedro Arrupe.* Translated by Yolanda T. DeMola. Wilmington, DE: Michael Glazier, 1986.

"Art, Trauma, and PTSI: An Interview with Dr. Frank Ochberg." *Journal of Military and Veteran's Health* 28, no. 3 (July 2020).

Augustine. *The Confessions of Saint Augustine.* New York: Penguin Random House, 1960.

Augustine. *On the Immortality of the Soul.* Translated by George G. Leckie. New York: D. Appleton-Century, 1938.

Austin, Nicholas. "The Ignatian Art of Spiritual Conversation." *The Way* 62, no. 3 (July 2023).

Bangert, William V. *A History of the Society of Jesus.* St. Louis: Institute of Jesuit Sources, 1972.

Barnes, Charles. "To Stand before the Cross and Not Run Away: A Practical Guide to Directing the Spiritual Exercises for Retreatants with Post-traumatic Stress Disorder and Moral Injury." *STUDIES in the Spirituality of Jesuits* (Summer 2021).

Barry, William A., and William J. Connolly. *The Practice of Spiritual Direction.* 2nd ed., rev. New York: HarperOne, 1982.

Bible. *New Revised Standard Version Updated Edition.* Grand Rapids, MI: Zondervan, 2022.

Bouchard, Gary M. *Southwell's Sphere: The Influence of England's Secret Poet.* South Bend, IN: St. Augustine Press, 2018.

Boyle, Greg. *Tattoos on the Heart.* New York: Free Press/Simon and Schuster, 2011.

Brodrick, James. *Saint Ignatius Loyola: The Pilgrim Years 1491–1538.* New York: Farrar, Straus and Cudahy, 1956.

Burge, Ryan. *The Nones: Where They Came From, Who They Are, and Where They Are Going.* 2nd ed. Minneapolis: Fortress Press, 2023.

Burke, Kevin. *Pedro Arrupe: Essential Writings.* Selected with an introduction by Kevin Burke. Foreword by Peter-Hans Kolvenbach. Maryknoll, NY: Orbis Book, 2004.

Byrne, Brendan. *The Hospitality of God: A Reading of Luke's Gospel.* Rev. ed. Collegeville, MN: Liturgical Press, 2015.

Calhoun, Lawrence G., and Richard G. Tedeschi. *Posttraumatic Growth in Clinical Practice.* New York: Routledge, 2013.

"Cannonball Moment." Jesuits Global. https://www.youtube.com/watch?v=GSpLXpOwkaI&list. Accessed June 23, 2024.

Caruth, Cathy, ed. *Trauma: Explorations in Memory.* Baltimore: Johns Hopkins University Press, 1995.

Catechism of the Catholic Church. 2nd ed. United States Catholic Conference—Libreria Editrice Vaticana, 1997.

"Celebrating Cannonball Day." https://www.jesuits.org/stories/celebrating-cannonball-day/. Accessed June 12, 2024.

Chesler, Phyllis. "The Shellshocked Woman." *New York Times.* August 23, 1992.

Claussen, Samuel A. *Chivalry and Violence in Late Medieval Castile.* Suffolk, England: Boydell & Brewer, 2020.

Clayton, Eric A. *Cannonball Moments: Telling Your Story, Deepening Your Faith.* Chicago: Loyola Press, 2022.

Coady, Alanna, Jessica R. Carney, Sheila Frankfurt, and Brett T. Litz. "The Emergence and Development of the Concept of Moral Injury." In *Moral Injury: A Guidebook for Understanding and Engagement*, edited by Brad E. Kelle. Lanham, MD: Rowman and Littlefield, 2020.

Coady, Alanna, Lataya Hawkins, Ruth Chartoff, Brett Litz, and Sheila Frankfurt. "Trauma, Spirituality, and Moral Injury: Assessing and Addressing Moral Injury in the Context of PTSD Treatment." *Current Treatment Options in Psychiatry* 8, no. 8 (December 2021).

Cordova, Tina. "What 'Oppenheimer' Doesn't Tell You about the Trinity Test." *New York Times.* Tuesday, August 1, 2023, A22.

Crete, Gerry Ken. *Litanies of the Heart: Relieving Post-traumatic Stress and Calming Anxiety through Healing Our Parts.* Manchester, NH: Sophia Institute Press, 2023.

Currier, Joseph M., Kent D. Drescher, Jason Nieuwsma, eds. *Addressing Moral Injury in Clinical Practice*. Washington, DC: American Psychological Association, 2021.

Currier, Joseph M., Timothy D. Carroll, and Jennifer H. Wortmann, "Religious and Spiritual Issues in Moral Injury." *Addressing Moral Injury in Clinical Practice,* edited by Joseph M. Currier, Kent D. Drescher, and Jason Nieuwsma. Washington, DC: American Psychological Association, 2021.

Davies, Murray. "Assessing Spiritual Wounds and Injuries." *Journal of Military and Veterans' Health*. Forthcoming.

Davies, Murray. "Spiritual Injuries—An Australian Defense Force Experience." *Journal of Veterans Studies* 6, no. 1 (May 18, 2020).

de Cervantes, Miguel. *Don Quixote*. Translated with an introduction and notes by John Rutherford. London: Penguin Classics, 2000.

de Dalmases, Candido. *Ignatius of Loyola, Founder of the Jesuits: His Life and Work*. Translated by Jerome Aixala. St. Louis: Institute of Jesuit Sources, 1985.

DeMarco, Patricia. Review of *Chivalry and Violence in Medieval Europe*, by Richard W. Kaeuper. *Studies in the Age of Chaucer* 23 (2001).

de Mello, Anthony. *Sadhana, A Way to God: Christian Exercises in Eastern Form*. St. Louis: Institute of Jesuit Sources, 1978.

Diagnostic and Statistical Manual of Mental Disorders. 5th ed., Text Revision (DSM-5-TR). New York: American Psychiatric Association Publishing, 2022.

Dictionary of American Family Names. Edited by Patrick Hanks. New York: Oxford University Press, 2003.

"Domestic Violence/Intimate Partner Violence Facts." Nia Project. https://med.emory.edu/departments/psychiatry/nia/resources/domestic_violence.html. Accessed June 11, 2024.

"Domestic Violence Statistics." The Hotline. https://www.thehotline.org/stakeholders/domestic-violence-statistics/. Accessed June 14, 2024.

Dominguez-Morano, Carlos. *Sigmund Freud and Oskar Pfister on Religion: The Beginning of an Endless Dialogue*. Translated by Francisco Javier Montero. New York: Routledge, 2024.

Donne, John. *The Works of John Donne*. Vol. 3. Edited by Henry Alford. London: John W. Parker, 1839.

Dudon, Paul. *Saint Ignatius of Loyola*. Translated by William J. Young. Milwaukee: Bruce Publishing, 1949.

Eden, Dawn. *My Peace I Give You: Healing Sexual Wounds with the Help of the Saints*. Notre Dame, IN: Ave Maria Press, 2012.

Eden, Dawn. *Remembering God's Mercy: Redeem the Past and Free Yourself from Painful Memories*. Notre Dame, IN: Ave Maria Press, 2016.

Ellison, Ralph. *Invisible Man*. New York: Random House, 1995 [1952].

Endean, Philip. "Who Do You Say Ignatius Is? Jesuit Fundamentalism and Beyond." *Studies in the Spirituality of Jesuits* 19, no. 5 (November 1987).

Feder, Julie. *Incarnating Grace: A Theology of Healing from Sexual Trauma.* New York: Fordham University Press, 2024.

Field, Jacob F. "Battle of Pamplona." *Encyclopedia Britannica.* https://www.britannica.com/event/Battle-of-Pamplona. Accessed June 12, 2024.

Fleming, David L. *Draw Me into Your Friendship: A Literal Translation and a Contemporary Reading of the Spiritual Exercises.* 2nd ed. Chestnut Hill, MA: Institute of Jesuit Sources, 1978.

Frame, Tom. "Moral Injury and the Influence of Christian Religious Conviction." In *War and Moral Injury: A Reader*, ed. Robert Emmet Meagher and Douglas A. Pryer. Eugene, OR: Cascade Books, 2018.

Freud, Sigmund. *Psychoanalysis and Faith: The Letters of Sigmund Freud and Oskar Pfister.* London: Forgotten Books, Classic Reprint Series, 2018.

Frost, Robert. *The Poetry of Robert Frost: The Collected Poems, Complete and Unabridged.* Edited by Edward Connery Lathem. New York: Henry Holt, 1969.

Ganss, George. *The Spiritual Exercises of Saint Ignatius: A Translation and Commentary.* Chicago: Loyola Press, 1992.

Geger, Barton T. "Six Little-Known Facts—Really—About the Society of Jesus." *Chronicles on Jesuit Higher Education*, March 1, 2022.

Goetz, Stewart, and Charles Taliaferro. *A Brief History of the Soul.* Hoboken, NJ: Wiley-Blackwell, 2011.

Goldstein, Dawn Eden. *Father Ed: The Story of Bill W.'s Spiritual Sponsor.* Maryknoll, NY: Orbis Books, 2022.

Graham, Larry Kent. *Moral Injury: Restoring Wounded Souls.* Nashville: Abingdon Press, 2017.

Griffin, Brandon J., et al. "Moral Injury: An Integrative Review." *Journal of Traumatic Stress*, no. 3, *Special Issue on Moral Injury* (June 2019).

Grogan, Brian. "To Make the Exercises Better: The Additional Directions." *The Way Supplement* 27 (1976): 15–26.

Gutierrez, Gustavo. "Church Must Be Samaritan, Reaching Out to Others." *National Catholic Reporter*, February 28, 2014. https://www.ncronline.org/blogs/ncr-today/gutierrez-vatican-church-must-be-samaritan-reaching-out-others.

Habito, Ruben L. F. *Zen and the Spiritual Exercises.* Maryknoll, NY: Orbis Books, 2013.

Hagerty, Barbara B. *Fingerprints of God: The Search for the Science of Spirituality.* New York: Riverhead Books, 2009.

Hamm, M. Dennis. "Luke." *Paulist Biblical Commentary.* Mahwah, NJ: Paulist Press, 2018.

Hansen, Michael. *The First Spiritual Exercises: Four Guided Retreats.* Notre Dame, IN: Ave Maria Press, 2013.

Hansen, Michael. *God's Field Hospital: Ignatian Spiritual Exercises Healing Wounds of Life.* New York/Mahwah, NJ: Paulist Press, 2024.

Harbaugh, Jim. *A 12-Step Approach to the Spiritual Exercises of St. Ignatius.* Franklin, WI: Sheed and Ward, 1997.

Harris, J. Irene, and Timothy Usset et al. "Spiritually Integrated Care for PTSD: A Randomized Controlled Trial of 'Building Spiritual Strength.'" *Psychiatry Research* 267 (September 2018).

Hassel, David J. *Radical Prayer: Creating a Welcome for God, Ourselves, Other People and the World.* Ramsey, NJ: Paulist Press, 1983.

Healey, Mary. *The Gospel of Mark.* Ada, MI: Baker Academic, 2008.

Heiding, Fredrik. "Body Language before the Face of God." *The Way* 63, no. 3 (July 2024).

Herman, Judith. "Recovery from Psychological Trauma." *Psychiatry and Clinical Neurosciences* 52, no. S1 (January 2002).

Herman, Judith. *Trauma and Recovery: The Aftermath of Violence—from Domestic Abuse to Political Terror.* New York: Basic Books, 1992.

Ignatius of Loyola. *A Pilgrim's Testament: The Memoirs of Saint Ignatius of Loyola.* Edited with revised translation by Barton T. Geger. Chestnut Hill, MA: Institute of Jesuit Sources, 2020.

Ivens, Michael. *Understanding the Spiritual Exercises: Text and Commentary.* Leominster, England: Gracewing, 1998.

Jackman, Tom. "After Years of Turmoil, A Fatal Night: Fairfax Officers Were Called to Help a Transgender Man in Crisis. One Killed Him." *Washington Post*, June 14, 2024.

James, William. *The Varieties of Religious Experience.* Oxford: Oxford University Press, 2012 [1902].

Jamieson N., M. Maple, D. Ratnarajah, and K. Usher. "Military Moral Injury: A Concept Analysis." *International Journal of Mental Health Nursing* 29, no. 6 (December 2020).

Johnson, Luke Timothy. *The Gospel of Luke.* Sacra Pagina, edited by Daniel J. Harrington. Collegeville, MN: Liturgical Press, 1991.

Jones, Serene. *Trauma + Grace: Theology in a Ruptured World.* 2nd ed. Louisville, KY: Westminster John Knox Press, 2019.

Joseph, Stephen. *What Doesn't Kill Us: The New Psychology of Posttraumatic Growth.* New York: Basic Books, 2013.

Judicial Processes of Íñigo Loyola. Third Process, Declaration of María de la Flor, X.3, *Archivum historicum Societatis Iesu.* Rome: Institutum Scriptorum de Historia S.I., 1932.

Kaeuper, Richard W. *Chivalry and Violence in Medieval Europe*. Oxford: Oxford University Press, 1999.

Kaeuper, Richard W., and Elspeth Kennedy. *The Book of Chivalry of Geoffroi de Charny: Text, Context, and Translation.* Philadelphia: University of Pennsylvania Press, 1996.

Keenan, James F. "The Great Religious Failure: Not Recognizing a Person in Need." *America*. June 17, 2024.

Keenan, James F. *The Works of Mercy: The Heart of Catholicism.* Lanham, MD: Rowman and Littlefield, 2017.

Kelle, Brad E., ed. *Moral Injury: A Guidebook for Understanding and Engagement.* Lanham, MD: Rowman and Littlefield, 2020.

Kinghorn, Warren. "Combat Trauma and Moral Fragmentation: A Theological Account of Moral Injury." *Journal of the Society of Christian Ethics* 32, no. 2 (Fall/Winter 2012).

Kirwan, Michael. "Swearing, Blaspheming, Wounding, Killing, Going to Hell . . . The World, as Seen and Heard by Ignatius." *The Way* 57, no. 4 (October 2018).

Klay, Phil. "Can the Trauma of War Lead to Growth, Despite the Scars?" *New York Times*. July 6, 2020.

Koenig, Harold G., Donna Ames, and Michelle Pearce. *Religion and Recovery from PTSD.* Philadelphia: Jessica Kingsley Publishers, 2020.

Krall, Chris. "Trauma, Imagination, and Sensation." *Thinking Faith*. May 11, 2018. https://www.thinkingfaith.org/articles/trauma-imagination-and-sensation. Accessed June 24, 2024.

Kuchar, Gary. *The Poetry of Religious Sorrow in Early Modern England.* New York: Cambridge University Press, 2008.

Kurtz, Ernest, and Katherine Ketcham. *The Spirituality of Imperfection.* Bantam Reissue. New York: Bantam Books, 2002.

Lamet, Pedro Miguel. *Pedro Arrupe: Witness of the Twentieth Century, Prophet of the Twenty-First.* Chestnut Hill, MA: Institute of Jesuit Sources at Boston College, 2021.

Lamott, Anne. *Hallelujah Anyway: Rediscovering Mercy.* New York: Riverhead Books, 2017.

Lamott, Anne. *Operating Instructions: A Journal of My Son's First Year.* New York: Pantheon, 1993.

Lee, Joseph. "The Brain and the Soul." *The Way* 53, no. 1 (January 2014).

Lettini, Gabriella. "Moral Injury and Its Causes, Symptoms, and Responses." In *Moral Injury: A Guidebook for Understanding and Engagement,* edited by Brad E. Kelle. Lanham, MD: Rowman and Littlefield, 2020.

Levers, Lisa López. *Trauma Counseling: Theories and Interventions for Managing Trauma, Stress, Crisis, and Disaster.* 2nd ed. New York: Springer Publishing, 2023.

Levine, Amy-Jill, and Marc Zvi Brettler, eds. *The Jewish Annotated New Testament: New Revised Standard Version.* New York: Oxford University Press, 2011.

Liebert, Elizabeth, and Annemarie Paulin-Campbell. *The Spiritual Exercises Reclaimed: Uncovering Liberating Possibilities for Women.* 2nd ed. New York/ Mahwah, NJ: Paulist Press, 2022.

Liebscher, Martin, ed. *Jung on Ignatius of Loyola's Spiritual Exercises.* Princeton, NJ: Princeton University Press, 2023.

Lifton, Robert Jay. "The Concept of the Survivor." In *Survivors, Victims, and Perpetrators: Essays on the Nazi Holocaust.* Edited by J. E. Dimsdale. New York: Hemisphere Publishing, 1980.

Litz, Brett T., Nathan Stein, Eileen Delaney, Leslie Lebowitz, William P. Nash, Caroline Silva, and Shira Maguen. "Moral Injury and Moral Repair in War Veterans: A Preliminary Model and Intervention Strategy." *Clinical Psychology Review* 29 (2009).

Macpherson, Robert Seamus. *Stewards of Humanity: Lighting the Darkness in Humanitarian Crisis.* Durham, NC: Torchflame Books, 2021.

Mallard, Timothy S. "The (Twin) Wounds of War." *Providence Magazine.* February 17, 2017.

Maté, Gabor. *In the Realm of Hungry Ghosts: Close Encounters with Addiction.* Berkeley, CA: North Atlantic Books, 2010.

May, Gerald G. *Addiction and Grace: Love and Spirituality in the Healing of Addictions.* Reissue ed. San Francisco: HarperOne, 2007.

McChesney, Robert W. "The Invisible Mugged Traveler: Encountering God as Hero or Casualty." *The Way* 64, no. 1 (January 2025).

McChesney, Robert W. "The Morally Injured Íñigo de Loyola: New Insights for Ignatian Spiritual and Pastoral Care." *The Way* 61, no. 4 (October 2022).

McChesney, Robert W. "Noticing *Hibakusha*: A Trauma-Informed Reading of the Incarnation Contemplation." *The Way* 62, no. 4 (October 2023).

McDonald, Joseph, ed. *Exploring Moral Injury in Sacred Texts.* Philadelphia: Jessica Kingsley, 2017.

McDonald, MaryCatherine, Marisa Brandt, and Robyn Bluhm. "From Shell-Shock to PTSD, a Century of Invisible War Trauma." *PBS News Hour.* November 11, 2018.

McFarland, Dennis. *Nostalgia.* New York: Pantheon Books, 2013.

McGough, Matt, Krutika Amin, Nirmita Panchal, and Cynthia Cox. "Child and Teen Firearm Mortality in the U.S. and Peer Countries." KFF. July 18, 2023. https://www.kff.org/global-health-policy/issue-brief/child-and-teen-firearm-mortality-in-the-u-s-and-peer-countries/. Accessed June 11, 2024.

McKenzie, J. L. *Dictionary of the Bible.* London: Geoffrey Chapman, 1965.

Meagher, Robert Emmett, and Douglas A. Pryer, eds. *War and Moral Injury: A Reader.* Eugene, OR: Wipf and Stock, 2018.

Meissner, W. W. *Ignatius of Loyola: The Psychology of a Saint.* New Haven, CT: Yale University Press, 1992.

Meninger, Karl. *Whatever Became of Sin?* Portland, OR: Hawthorn Press, 1973.

Mescher, Marcus. *The Ethics of Encounter: Christian Neighbor Love as a Practice of Solidarity.* Maryknoll, NY: Orbis, 2020.

Miller, Laurence. *Practical Police Psychology: Stress Management and Crisis Intervention for Law Enforcement.* Springfield, IL: Charles C. Thomas, 2006.

Miller, William R., and Harold D. Delaney, eds. *Judeo-Christian Perspectives on Psychology: Human Nature, Motivation, and Change.* Washington, DC: American Psychological Association, 2005.

Mills, Katherine L., Maree Teesson, Joanne Ross, and Lorna Peters. "Trauma, PTSD, and Substance Use Disorders: Findings from the Australian National Survey of Mental Health and Well-Being." *American Journal of Psychiatry* 163, no. 4 (April 2006).

Moon, Zachary. "Moral Injury and the Role of Chaplains." In *Moral Injury: A Guidebook for Understanding and Engagement,* edited by Brad E. Kelle. Lanham, MD: Rowman and Littlefield, 2020.

Munitiz, Joseph A. "Preliminaries to a Conversion." *The Way* 61, no. 3 (July 2022).

Nadal, Jerónimo. "Sixth Exhortation." *The Conversational Word of God.* Translated by Thomas H. Clancy. St. Louis: Institute of Jesuit Sources, 1978.

Nash, William P. "Commentary on the Special Issue on Moral Injury: Unpacking Two Models for Understanding Moral Injury." *Journal of Traumatic Stress* (June 2019).

Nash, William P. *Religion and Recovery from PTSD.* Philadelphia: Jessica Kingsley Publishers, 2020.

Nash, William P. "A 'Stain on the Soul': Why Moral Injury Requires a Different Treatment Plan than PTSD." *Mastering the Treatment of Trauma.* National Institute for the Clinical Application of Behavioral Medicine, Module Four. https://www.nicabm.com/confirm/mastering-the-treatment-of-trauma-cwzsb/.

Newberg, Andrew. "Neurotheology: This Is Your Brain on Religion." National Public Radio author interview, December 15, 2010. https://www.npr.org/2010/12/15/132078267/neurotheology-where-religion-and-science-collide.

Newberg, Andrew, and Mark Robert Waldman. *How God Changes Your Brain: Breakthrough Findings from a Leading Neuroscientist.* New York: Ballantine Books, 2009.

Nieuwsma, Jason, Melissa A. Smigelsky, Jennifer H. Wortmann, Kerry Haynes, and Keith G. Meader. "Collaboration with Chaplaincy and Ministry Professionals in Addressing Moral Injury." In *Addressing Moral Injury in Clinical Practice,* edited by Joseph M. Currier, Kent D. Drescher, and Jason Nieuwsma. Washington, DC: American Psychological Association, 2021.

Norman, Sonia B., and Shira Maguen. "Moral Injury." *PTSD: National Center for PTSD.* https://www.ptsd.va.gov/professional/treat/cooccurring/moral_injury .asp. Accessed June 21, 2024.

O'Brien, Kevin. "How Can We Adapt the Spiritual Exercises in Our Times?" Interview with Sean Salai. *America.* July 20, 2016.

O'Collins, Gerald. "Memory in the Spiritual Exercises and John 21." *The Way* 59, no. 3 (July 2020).

Orbey, Eren. "A Trailblazer of Trauma Studies Asks What Victims Really Want." *New Yorker.* May 2, 2023.

Palmeri, Frank. "In Praise of Speculative History." *Chronicle of Higher Education.* July 10, 2016.

Park, Crystal L., Joseph M. Currier, J. Irene Harris, and Jeanne M. Slattery. *Trauma, Meaning, and Spirituality: Translating Research into Clinical Practice.* Washington, DC: American Psychological Association, 2017.

Park, Crystal L., and Donald Edmondson. "Religion as a Source of Meaning." In *Meaning, Mortality, and Choice: The Social Psychology of Existential Concerns*, edited by Phillip R. Shaver and Mario Mikulincer. Washington, DC: American Psychological Association, 2012.

Patton, Kimberley Christine, and John Stratton Hawley, eds. *Holy Tears: Weeping in the Religious Imagination.* Princeton, NJ: Princeton University Press, 2005.

Paxman, Gail. "When His Eyes Were Opened a Little: The Role of Noticing in the Spiritual Exercises." *The Way* 61, no. 2 (April 2022).

Pearce, M., K. Haynes, J. Currier, K. O'Gara, and H. G. Koenig. *Spiritually Integrated Cognitive Processing Therapy (SICPT) Veteran/Military Version: Therapist Manual.* Durham, NC: Duke University Center for Spirituality, Theology and Health, 2017.

Pearce, M., K. Haynes, N. R. Rivera, and H. G. Koenig. "Spiritually Integrated Cognitive Processing Therapy: A New Treatment for Post-traumatic Stress Disorder That Targets Moral Injury." *Global Advances in Health and Medicine* 7 (February 20, 2018).

Percy, Jennifer. "What People Misunderstand about Rape." *New York Times Magazine.* August 22, 2023.

Percy, Jennifer. "How Does the Human Soul Survive Atrocity?" *New York Times Magazine.* November 3, 2019.

"Perspective Taking." *APA Dictionary of Psychology.* https://dictionary.apa.org /perspective-taking. Accessed June 18, 2024.

Pfister, Oskar. "The Illusion of a Future: A Friendly Disagreement with Prof. Sigmund Freud." *International Journal for Psychoanalysis* 74, no. 557 (1993).

Piwowarczyk, Linda, Kathleen Flinton, and Fernando Ona. "Refugee Resilience and Spirituality: Harnessing Social and Cultural Coping Strategies." In *Refugees and Asylum Seekers: Interdisciplinary and Comparative Perspectives*, edited by S. Megan Berthold and Kathryn R. Libal. Santa Barbara, CA: Praeger, 2019.

Plante, Thomas. Editor of *Spirituality in Clinical Practice*, online interview. https://www.apa.org/pubs/highlights/editor-spotlight/scp-plante.

Pollard, C. Alec. "What Is OCD & Scrupulosity?" International OCD Foundation. https://iocdf.org/faith-ocd/what-is-ocd-scrupulosity/.

Pope Francis. *Evangelii Gaudium* (The Joy of the Gospel). Vatican. November 24, 2013.

Pope Francis. *Fratelli Tutti* [All Brothers]. Vatican. October 3, 2020.

Purcell, Mary. *St. Ignatius Loyola: The First Jesuit.* Chicago: Loyola University Press, 1981.

Quinn, Philip L. "Sin." *Routledge Encyclopedia of Philosophy*. London: Taylor and Francis, 1998.

Rambo, Shelly. "How Christian Theology and Practice Are Being Shaped by Trauma Studies." *Christian Century*. November 1, 2019.

Richardson, Natalie M., and Angela L. Lamson. "Understanding Moral Injury: Military-Related Injuries of the Mind, Body, and Soul." *Spirituality in Clinical Practice* 9, no. 3 (September 2022).

Rieff, Philip. *The Triumph of the Therapeutic: Uses of Faith after Freud*. Wilmington, DE: Intercollegiate Studies Institute, 2006.

Rizzuto, Anna-Maria. "Psychoanalytic Considerations about Spiritually Oriented Psychotherapy." In *Spiritually Oriented Psychotherapy*, edited by Len Sperry and Edward P. Shafranske. Washington, DC: American Psychological Association, 2004.

Rolheiser, Ronald. *The Holy Longing: The Search for a Christian Spirituality.* New York: Doubleday, 1999.

Rosenbaum, S. I. "The Age of Trauma." *Harvard Public Health Magazine*. September 30, 2021.

Rosmarin, David H. "Psychiatry Needs to Get Right with God." *Scientific American*. June 15, 2021.

Saritoprak, S. N., J. J. Exline, and H. Abu-Raiya. "Spiritual Jihad as an Emerging Psychological Concept: Connections with Religious/Spiritual Struggles, Virtues, and Perceived Growth." *Journal of Muslim Mental Health* 14, no. 2 (2020).

Schore, Allan N. *Affect Regulation and the Origin of the Self: The Neurobiology of Emotional Development.* New York: Routledge, 2015.

Schwartz, Jeffrey M. "Neuroplasticity and Spiritual Formation." Biola University Center for Christian Thought. April 18, 2019. https://cct.biola.edu/neuroplasticity-and-spiritual-formation/.

Scott, Bernard Brandon. *Hear Then the Parable: A Commentary on the Parables of Jesus.* Minneapolis: Augsburg Fortress Press, 1989.

Scott, Bernard Brandon. *Reimagine the World: An Introduction to the Parables of Jesus*. Santa Clara, CA: Polebridge Press, 2001.

Shay, Jonathan. *Odysseus in America: Combat Trauma and the Trials of Homecoming*. Repr. New York: Scribner, 2003.

Sherman, Nancy. *AFTERWAR: Healing the Moral Wounds of Our Soldiers*. New York: Oxford University Press, 2015.

Simon, Paul. "I Am a Rock." *The Paul Simon Songbook*. Accessed July 27, 2024. https://www.paulsimon.com/track/i-am-a-rock-2/.

Southwell, Robert. *The Complete Works of R. Southwell: With Life and Death*. New York: Andesite Press, 2017 [1876].

Spadaro, Antonio. "A Big Heart Open to God: An Interview with Pope Francis." *America*. September 13, 2013.

Spence, Joanne. *Trauma-Informed Yoga: A Toolbox for Therapists*. Eau Claire, WI: PESI Publishing, 2021.

St. George, Donna. "Teen Girls 'Engulfed' in Violence and Trauma, CDC Finds." *Washington Post*. February 14, 2023.

St. John of the Cross. *The Ascent of Mount Carmel*. Translated and edited by E. Allison Peers. Mineola, NY: Dover Publications, 2008.

Stillman, Sarah. "Hiroshima and the Inheritance of Trauma." *New Yorker*. August 12, 2014.

"Suicide Statistics." American Foundation for Suicide Prevention. https://afsp.org/suicide-statistics/. Accessed June 11, 2024.

Sutterlin, Nicole A. "History of Trauma Theory." In *The Routledge Companion to Literature and Trauma*, edited by Colin Davis and Hanna Meretoja. New York: Routledge, 2020.

Tellechea Idígoras, José Ignacio. *Ignatius of Loyola: The Pilgrim Saint*. Translated by Cornelius Michael Buckley. Chicago: Loyola University Press, 1994.

"Understanding Child Trauma." Substance Abuse and Mental Health Services Administration. https://www.samhsa.gov/child-trauma/understanding-child-trauma. Accessed June 17, 2024.

Van der Kolk, Bessel. *The Body Keeps the Score: Brain, Mind, and Body in the Healing of Trauma*. New York: Viking, 2014.

Vieten, Cassandra, Ron Pilato, Kenneth I. Pargament, Shelley Scammell, Ingrid Ammondson, and David Lukoff. "Spiritual and Religious Competencies for Psychologists." *Psychology of Religion and Spirituality* 5, no. 3 (2013).

Wang, P. S., P. A. Berglund, and R. C. Kessler. "Patterns and Correlates of Contacting Clergy for Mental Disorders in the United States." *Health Services Research* 38, no. 2 (April 2003).

Werdel, Mary Beth, and Robert J. Wicks. *Primer on Posttraumatic Growth: An Introduction and Guide*. Hoboken, NJ: John Wiley and Sons, 2012.

Wicks, Robert. *Bounce: Living the Resilient Life*. New York: Oxford University Press, 2010.

Wilde, Oscar. *A Woman of No Importance*. London: Methuen, 1894.

Winnell, Marlene. "Religious Trauma Syndrome" (series of three articles). *Cognitive Behavioural Therapy Today* 39, no. 2 (May 2011); 39, no. 3 (September 2011); 39, no. 4 (November 2011).

Wood, David, and John Montorio. "Moral Injury." *Resources for Moral Injury*. Dart Center for Journalism and Trauma, Columbia University Graduate School of Journalism. April 9, 2015. https://dartcenter.org/content/moral-injury.

Wortmann, J. H., E. Eisen, C. Hundert, A. H. Jordan, M. W. Smith, W. P. Nash, and B. T. Litz. "Spiritual Features of War-Related Moral Injury: A Primer for Clinicians." *Spirituality in Clinical Practice* 4, no. 4 (2017).

Yandell, Michael. "Do Not Torment Me: The Morally Injured Gerasene Demoniac." In *Moral Injury: A Guidebook for Understanding and Engagement*, edited by Brad E. Kelle. Lanham, MD: Rowman and Littlefield, 2020.